PEOPLE IN
HIGH PLACES

PEOPLE IN HIGH PLACES

Approaches to Tibet

AUDREY SALKELD

JONATHAN CAPE
LONDON

First published 1991
© Audrey Salkeld 1991
Jonathan Cape, 20 Vauxhall Bridge Road, London SW1V 2SA

Audrey Salkeld has asserted her right under the Copyright,
Designs and Patents Act 1988 to be identified as the author of this work

A CIP catalogue record for this book
is available from the British Library

ISBN 0-224-02883-9

Typeset by Computape (Pickering) Ltd, North Yorkshire
Printed in Great Britain by
Butler & Tanner Ltd, Frome and London

Contents

Illustrations

for Peter

TO SEE THE
HIMALAYA

The Siren Call

As the dew is dried up by the morning sun, so are the sins
of men dried up by the sight of the Himalaya, where Shiva
lived and where the Ganga falls from the foot of Vishnu
like the slender thread of a lotus flower.

Skanda Purana

THERE ARE MOUNTAINS and there are the Himalaya. Newer, greater
than any other range on earth, they are king among mountains; 'A
hundred divine epochs would not suffice to describe all the marvels of
the Himalaya,' warns the Sanskrit proverb. Yet the sage Nagasena
attempts it in a single sentence: 'Five thousand leagues around, with its
ranges of eight and forty thousand peaks, the source of five hundred
rivers, the dwelling place of multitudes of mighty creatures, the producer of manifold perfumes, enriched with hundreds of magical drugs,
the Himalaya rise aloft, like a cloud, from the centre of the earth.'

Granted his first leave after two years in India, a young subaltern,
not yet twenty-two, determined to 'plunge right in'. Forty years
afterwards, he could remember as freshly as ever the strange exhilar-
ation that seized him when he stepped out into the clear Himalayan
dawn on that first morning. Two glorious months of discovery lay
ahead. 'I kept squeezing my fist together, and saying emphatically to
myself and to the universe at large: "Oh, *yes!*, Oh, *yes!* This really *is*.
How splendid! How splendid!"' And from that moment, he lived for
the high snows and passes, and the lands beyond the ranges.

The young soldier with the thirst for adventure was Francis Edward
Younghusband. Within three years of those tentative approaches he
had made a remarkable 4,000-mile trans-Himalayan journey from
Peking to Kashmir, crossing the Gobi Desert, the Aghil mountains and
the mighty Karakoram. He rediscovered the old Muztagh Pass into

Baltistan, enduring so hazardous a descent of it with his ill-shod and frightened little party that all were lucky to survive. The year was 1887. His success brought him the Gold Medal of the Royal Geographical Society and a diplomatic commission to explore all the high passes between the Karakoram Pass and the Pamirs.

Twenty-five years after Younghusband's great journey a middle-aged French woman came tramping through the lush forests of Sikkim with their dripping waterfalls and wild orchids. She had been packed off East by her husband in the hope that it would clear her head once and for all of the Oriental nonsense that had obsessed her for so long. Perhaps then, she could settle down to a life more fitting the wife of an important railway executive in Tunisia.

Instead, when Alexandra David-Neel topped the last pass and saw spread before her the immense tableland of Tibet, 'with its distant horizon of peaks bathed in strange mauve and orange hues, and carrying queerly shaped caps of snow upon their mighty heads', she knew these were the solitudes she had yearned for since childhood. They sang a song she instinctively recognized. Life till then had been merely a 'tiring, cheerless pilgrimage'. Now, at the age of forty-four, she had come home. She never returned to her husband's house.

'The Himalaya are my drug,' a French explorer-friend once told me. All his adult life Eric Valli has wandered the high empty spaces of Asia, returning over and again to the same isolated villages until he became a familiar and welcome visitor. He is happy to share the seasonal round of his Himalayan friends, their work and worship and moments of fun. He loves nothing better than to travel with the yak caravans that filter up and down the high valleys of Nepal and into Tibet, maintaining a highly specialized trade which sustains delicate economies on both sides of the border. When, in Tibet, a measure of grain can be bartered for two of salt and, down in the Nepalese midlands, two measures of Tibetan salt may fetch as many as eight of mixed grain, the enterprising trader can increase a meagre harvest up to seven-fold, sufficient to sustain his family throughout the year. But sanctions and changing transport patterns threaten the centuries-old supply line. Eric Valli has the terrible feeling – 'a pinching of the heart', he calls it – that within ten years the high, mountain-locked valleys like Dolpo and Mustang will be deserted. Without the life blood of this trans-Himalayan trade, nobody will be able to stay in these harsh regions any more.

★

The area of Tibetan influence and religion extends beyond the political limits of that vast country. 'Ethnographic Tibet' spills into Sinkiang (Chinese Turkestan) and the western provinces of China, the Himalayan kingdoms of Sikkim and Bhutan, the high valleys of Nepal, and as far as Ladakh, the mountainous crossroads of Asia to the west, now part of the Indian state of Jammu and Kashmir. Yet for all its extent, Tibet through the centuries remained a mystery to all but its immediate neighbours. Barriers of mountains and wind-ravaged steppes, abetted after 1792 by a positive policy of excluding foreigners, served to maintain its isolation and cultural integrity, so that by the beginning of the twentieth century the Roof of the World was the least-known portion of the habited globe, and one of the least changed by time or outside influence. Despite determined effort, only a handful of European missionaries and trade agents had ever set eyes on Lhasa, Tibet's capital city – and none since 1846.

It is hardly to be wondered that this little-known, lofty outland tantalized explorers and romantic travellers. Surveyors were eager to get to grips with its features and rugged contours, even if trained native 'pundits' of the Indian Survey had from the middle years of the nineteenth century made a remarkable job of illicit intelligence gathering. Naturalists and geologists dreamed of skins and samples, mountaineers of being allowed a crack at the world's highest summit, which straddled the border between Tibet and Nepal, forbidden of access on both sides. Philosophers wanted to tap into ancient wisdom and spiritual powers for which Buddhist and Bon scholars were known, and to understand the mysteries of death and reincarnation.

But to the imperial powers of Britain, Russia and China, Tibet represented an unsettling vacuum on the board of the Great Game. To ambitious players of the game – diplomats and soldiers alike – Tibet was seen as an opportunity for personal advancement. And therein lay the seeds of its ultimate tragedy.

After a chance meeting with the explorer Ney Elias on a train to Simla in April 1889, Younghusband dreamed up a ruse for travelling to Lhasa in disguise, and even won grudging approval for it from the British Foreign Secretary. How galling then to have his hopes dashed by the peremptory veto of his own commanding officer. The years passed, Younghusband continuing to reap glory for his solitary explorations and intelligence-work and becoming ever more deeply committed to playing the Game. By 1902, Lord Curzon – recently appointed as Indian Viceroy – became convinced that a secret deal had been struck between Russia and Tibet which threatened to allow Tsarist forces to the very border with British India. Younghusband shared these fears, and agreed to act as Commissioner for what was originally intended as a pacific expedition into Tibet the following year to discuss frontier and trade matters. When all attempts at diplomacy failed and letters to the Dalai Lama were returned unopened, Younghusband extended his mission onwards to Lhasa. Several thousand brave but virtually defenceless Tibetans were killed attempting to resist the advance. There were few British casualties.

To Younghusband, then, was granted his long-desired view of the 'Dwelling place of the Gods' (as the city's name translates from the Sanskrit). With barely suppressed excitement, he wrote in his journal:

> There it was at last, the lightwaves of mirage dissolving the far outline of the golden roofs and dimly-seen white terraces, the great palace of the God-King – the Potala. Tomorrow, an epoch in the world's history will have been marked. There will be no more forbidden cities. Tomorrow, 4th August 1904, when we enter Lhasa, we will have unveiled the last mystery of the East.

Despite the sorry slaughter, Younghusband's men had shown a measure of restraint and no wholesale brutality or looting followed their occupation of Lhasa. Once the required Tibetan signature was secured on the Lhasa Convention, the Mission withdrew. Younghusband was subsequently reprimanded for exceeding British government instructions and found his career summarily blocked, but he had – strangely enough – won the respect of the Tibetans for his gentlemanly handling of the affair. When their country was invaded by Chinese Manchus 1910, it was to the honourable British that the Tibetans looked for support. As so often in their history, in an hour of need the Dalai Lama's people found themselves alone.

That occupation was short lived. Revolution in China prompted Chinese forces in Lhasa to mutiny against their own officers, and Tibetans were able to use the ensuing chaos to drive the interlopers from their borders. Next time the oppressors arrived, in 1950, they were not to be dislodged, and a brutal programme was initiated to purge the ancient Tibetan way of life. The country was restructured as an 'autonomous' region of Communist China, its borders once more sealed against the outside world.

Until the middle of this century Nepal maintained its mediaeval lifestyle in even greater seclusion than Tibet. Then suddenly the doors

14

opened and, with no preparation at all, the Nepalese welcomed in a raucous modernity. Explorers and scholars scrambled to be first to the unvisited hills – though, of course, it was white-man's arrogance to consider the Nepalese Himalaya 'unknown' simply because Westerners had not been there. Maps existed and a network of tracks linked villages and sites of pilgrimage. It was all very well known.

★

Scholars, scientists, mountaineers, pilgrims . . . the siren call of the Himalaya promises something different to each, yet in answering that call, each finds far more than he seeks, so that in the end it becomes hard to tell one from the other, man of action from philosopher. The indefinable mystery contained in the bright mountains and within the tiny fortresses of civilization, perched in such delicate balance between life and death, touches them all.

I asked the mountaineer Doug Scott what the Himalaya meant to him. He joked: 'Hard work and heartache, that's what!' Then he laughed. 'The funny thing is that when you're there, among them, you know all the answers, everything you ever wanted to know. You can see exactly what life's all about. But it evaporates as soon as you come away. Perhaps that's why you have to keep going back!'

Younghusband recognized a kinship between mountains and man for, as he said, were they not both made of the same original earth? His zest for mountain adventure found expression in later years when, as President of the Royal Geographical Society, he steered the early imperial ventures to Mount Everest. He had undergone a mystical revelation towards the end of his Tibet mission, a crisis of ecstasy which left him overflowing with a sense of love and brotherhood; thereafter he dedicated himself to the promotion of international understanding, founding the World Congress of Faiths. The Himalaya had granted him a glimpse of heaven.

★

For myself I cannot pretend to anything more spiritual in my longing to go to the Himalaya than the desire to see them with my own eyes. I had made no special study of Tibetan or other Himalayan culture, had little understanding of the depths and meaning of the various religious teachings. All I knew was what could readily be picked up from books of travel and mountaineering. Of those I had read plenty for, in our house, books spill over from every corner, spawn under beds, and my

15

mountain books outnumber them all, threatening one day to over-whelm us in an avalanche as they build to a tottering range of their own.

To see the Abode of Snow had been a long-held, if hazy dream from childhood, though with the passing of time I found the imperative increased. Since the early 70s, when I first started writing my regular 'People' column for *Mountain* magazine, you might say I had been almost mesmerized by the stories I heard from Himalayan climbers – some astonishing stories – of life in the high peaks. I would be approached from time to time by other writers and film-makers for historical information, finding myself regarded, often by complete strangers, as a repository of Himalayan knowledge. The situation seemed ridiculous – why be content with secondhand magic?

One person who fed the longing more than any other was the famous Everest climber Sherpa Tenzing, a man whose home was the Himalaya. I met him once when he came to London and found a warm, quiet-spoken man, almost exactly as I imagined, with smoky sad eyes but that sudden dazzling smile which had become so familiar in the early summer of 1953, when he and Hillary grinned from every newspaper.

This was his seventh Everest expedition and a year earlier he had come within a whisker of success with the Swiss alpinist Raymond Lambert. He used to joke afterwards that if they'd had a cup of tea then, they could have made it, but for twenty-four hours the two had nothing to eat or drink, and their oxygen apparatus had frozen solid.

'Everyone happy even we climb so high,' Tenzing recalled fondly. 'No flowers up there, so sahibs they make us garlands with sausages!'

From the small village in the Solu Khumbu, where he grew up, Tenzing used to take his father's yaks to the highest pastures on the southern flanks of the Himalaya. He was never happier than when wandering free among the mountains. 'Everest place my home,' he explained, adding proudly, 'people say I must got third lung because I take yaks so high!'

Everest was not the name by which he knew the great peak in those days. In his village, Thami, it was simply 'Mountain So High No Bird Can Fly Over It': Chomolungma. Close by was the Nangpa La pass leading to Tibet, and often the young Tenzing would clamber up a ridge above there to gain a better view of the So-High mountain. The monks used to say Buddha lived on top, so it seemed a kind of pil-grimage to get up there. This sense of mountains as sacred places never left him, but he also came to recognize his enjoyment of climbing for what it was, in very much the same way as a westerner might.

'I was ten – eleven maybe – when I first hear about Everest expeditions,' he told me. 'Many Sherpas go Darjeeling, get work. They say mans come from far away just for make climbing this mountain. Sherpas from our villages, they climb with them. Some die. One year sahibs die too, Mallory, Irvine, but still I want go there. More than anything I want climb this Mount Everest.'

One night in 1933, when he was just nineteen, Tenzing ran away to Darjeeling. Word was around that the British were coming back for another go at the world's highest summit, and he was bitterly disappointed to be passed over by the expedition's selectors. But two years later there was no mistake. With Eric Shipton – whom Tenzing recalled mistily as his 'very, very friend' – he took part in a remarkable whirlwind reconnaissance that climbed 26 peaks and surveyed a wide stretch of countryside to the north of Everest. From then on, Tenzing accompanied all British and Swiss attempts on the mountain until the first ascent, including the freakish lone attempt by the Canadian, Earl Denman, in 1947.

'Twenty year nearly I go expeditions.' There was pride in the old man's face. 'No just Everest. Tirich Mir, Bandar Punch, Satopanth, Kadarnath, Nanda Devi . . . Everest no easy, but Nanda Devi – me that the very dangerous! Nowhere hold, and ice so slippy.

'Big, little, I climb. Very little time home, but I have family – no climb, no eat! No house, no land, very small money those days!'

It was a different story after Everest. Overnight Tenzing became a world celebrity – a demigod, almost. '*Zindabad!*' the cry went up. 'Long life to you!' He was showered with medals and decorations. Pandit Nehru made him the Director of Field Training at a brand new Institute for Himalayan mountaineering in Darjeeling, instructing him to train a thousand Tenzings. By the time he retired, just before I met him, he could take pride that India's mountaineers were firmly on the map, and he had travelled the world as an unofficial ambassador for Sherpa people. Nowhere did he need any introduction, and in all that time he had lost none of his natural curiosity and unaffected charm.

'You must come in Darjeeling,' he told me as I said goodbye. 'Or if you go to Solu Khumbu, tell me. I find someone who look after you if I not there.'

I didn't go to Darjeeling. I didn't go to the Solu Khumbu. But nine years later I caught my first giddy sight of Everest from the Rongbuk Valley in Tibet, where Tenzing's own early attempts were made. The great Sherpa had passed away in Darjeeling a few months before.

SKETCH MAP OF MOUNT EVEREST AND THE RONGBUK GLACIERS
From surveys by Major Wheeler, with route and camps
of the 1922 expedition added by Colonel Strutt

18

TO WALK ON
MOUNT EVEREST

In Search of
Mallory and Irvine

Bound for the top, I'm ever on my way,
Bound for the top, climbing day by day,
Bound for the top, and though the trail grows steeper,
I'm bound for the top, and still climbing!

(Pre-War campfire ditty)

ONE SUNDAY MORNING in June 1924 two Englishmen set out to climb the final slopes of Mount Everest. They were spotted shortly after midday high on the north-east ridge and 'going strong for the top'. Then, clouds rolled in and they were never seen again. To this day nobody knows whether George Leigh Mallory and Andrew Irvine set foot on their glistening summit, nor what disaster befell them. Four expeditions to the mountain during the 1930s discovered no trace beyond an ice-axe lying on slabs just above Camp VI at 27,500 feet, and this was widely held to mark the scene of an accident.

With the passage of time, most people came reluctantly to believe that the pair's gallant bid to climb to the world's highest point must have failed. The official first ascent of Everest had to wait until 1953, when Hillary and Tenzing reached the top by the southern Nepalese approach. Hillary had looked for but did not find – as afterwards he put it – 'any sign of Mallory's passing'. So, while Hillary and Tenzing found their place in the history books, Mallory and Irvine remained secure in the realms of national myth. For a while, at least. Perhaps it was inevitable that the matter would not be left unquestioned.

In 1971 an article appeared in *Mountain* magazine suggesting that it was perfectly possible, indeed more than probable, that George Mallory reached the summit of Everest before he disappeared in 1924.

19

The argument rested essentially on the amount of bottled oxygen believed to be available to the two climbers on the fateful day.

It was not the theory of an experienced mountaineer, still less of an Englishman, but was elaborately, if flamboyantly argued by an American businessman, Tom Holzel, who shortly afterwards repeated his case for a successful ascent nearly thirty years before that of Hillary and Tenzing in the London *Sunday Times*.

Although Holzel's evidence was much the same as that which, in the 1920s and 1930s, led to the generally held view that Mallory and Irvine had almost certainly failed, his new interpretation drew an immediate and outraged response. Who was this outsider to think he could wade in and supply motivations and decisions that pared away layers of British sensibility? Holzel's version of events was unthinkable to any English gentleman who believed the expedition embodied all that was admirable in public school team spirit and good form. It would never have occurred to Mallory, so the furious counter-argument went, to send down the flagging and inexperienced Irvine on his own so that he, the fitter man, could take their oxygen supplies and, with a solo dash for the top, snatch the prize for himself.

Mallory deserved the summit. No one disputed that. By 1924 he was the most experienced Himalayan mountaineer of his generation and this was his third attempt on Everest. There were few who did not harbour the secret fantasy that, against all the odds, he and Irvine were the first to tread those distant snows. So why all the fuss? Holzel persuaded himself that these perverse Brits preferred the public face of heroic failure – another Captain Scott – to any search for the truth.

He had made no totally implausible leaps in the logic of his argument, by modern reasoning at least, and he could not comprehend why a serious re-examination of events should be so smothered in a blanket of moral indignation, why people should not want to know. A similar disregard for reason accompanied dismissal of a Chinese claim to have reached the summit in 1960 on the grounds that they could produce no photographs to back it up, though that was hardly surprising since they arrived at the top in the middle of the night. The pictures the Chinese took lower down failed to convince a climbing establishment unwilling to accept that relative novices to the high altitude game could succeed where several strong British attempts had failed. In this case, it was convenient to forget that many of the British pioneers – Geoffrey Bruce and Sandy Irvine among them – reached untrodden heights with no previous experience whatever.

As a mountaineering archivist and historian, I had long thought there must be more to discover in the Everest story. I could not, I found, align myself completely with Tom Holzel. My own Britishness rebelled at the idea of parting the two men, as his scenario required, but I felt sure that, with investigation, the clues could be made to support a different interpretation. Already I had spent several months browsing through the 'Everest archive' at the Royal Geographical Society, a collection of fifty-six dusty boxes stuffed with correspondence and memorabilia relating to the early expeditions. It would be necessary to re-weigh every scrap of information, however small, and to look beyond the record to satisfy myself that no excessive historical 'editing' was colouring the picture. I sought out the two remaining survivors of the 1924 expedition, Captain John Noel and Noel Odell (the last person to see Mallory alive), whose memories at their advanced age were to some extent set by constant repetition, though they helped me to come to grips with a period and social structure that was not my own. Hindsight is a valuable tool, but you have nothing but your imagination with which to recreate the exact awareness of the day, for common knowledge is one thing not written down at the time, simply because everyone is assumed to be in possession of it.

It was soon clear, when I began to correspond with him in the mid-seventies, that Holzel was not a man to abandon a quest when faced with stiff opposition. Indeed he relished controversy, and was soon demanding to know climbing speeds, capacities of oxygen cylinders and their flow rates, and much else that could only be verified on the British side of the Atlantic. He became convinced that if Mallory and Irvine were carrying cameras, then any film they contained could even now reveal whether or not they got to the top. More than anything, Holzel was resolved to go to Everest himself, to conduct a thorough search – for clues . . . for cameras . . . for bodies . . .

So determined was he that he went so far as to invent a closed-circuit oxygen apparatus designed to deliver an indefinite supply of breathable air that would facilitate long sallies into the Death Zone. He plotted a secret (but eventually stillborn) expedition to the forbidden north side of Everest, at the same time pursuing the proper channels in case the political climate changed. He even solicited the help of a sympathetic United States Liaison Officer in Peking – one George Bush.

When the Chinese allowed a Japanese reconnaissance team to travel through Tibet to Everest in 1979, Holzel's optimism soared. The barriers appeared to be lifting at last. Other nationalities clamoured to be let in too. The next year Japanese mountaineers were back, and the first Europeans arrived. Yasuo Kato followed Mallory's route to the summit; Reinhold Messner, during the monsoon period, scaled the mountain alone, adopting the Great Couloir route favoured by Colonel Norton in 1924; and an American lawyer, Andy Harvard, came up the Kangshung glacier to photograph Everest's steep eastern face which Mallory had decided in 1921 was not a viable way up.

Soon the Chinese themselves were once more on the mountain and rumour spread of their discovery of a body on a terrace at 26,575 feet on the north side, below and in direct line with where the old ice-axe had been found in 1933. In other words, at exactly the spot a body, or bodies, might be found if the axe indeed marked the scene of an accident. The Chinese later denied it, but if it were true, then those desiccated remains could belong to none other than Mallory or Irvine. Holzel was convinced it was the younger man, Irvine.

There was no mention of a camera.

Holzel was not going to be satisfied until he had been to see for himself. His request for a permit, although still on the table, remained unprocessed by the authorities in Peking. He published a feature supporting the Chinese claim to have climbed the mountain in 1960, which in any case they had successfully repeated in 1975. He fired off intricate instructions to every team fortunate enough to gain access to the north side of Everest on how best to handle fragile exposed film. Sooner or later, he was sure, somebody would happen upon a camera, and he did not want the precious evidence it could reveal to be thoughtlessly destroyed.

Although Holzel's approach still offended many mountaineers, there were others coming round to his way of thinking. Whether or not Mallory and Irvine had split up, team after team were now demonstrating that the summit could be reached without using oxygen, thereby removing the idea that Mallory or Irvine would automatically perish if their cylinders ran out.

We had corresponded for ten years before we met in 1984, when Holzel was visiting London on business for his Boston-based computer engineering company. I had arranged to introduce him to Captain John Noel, then in his nineties, at his home in Kent. The two men hit it off at once. They shared the same entrepreneurial resourcefulness and highly individual approach to exploration. As a young subaltern before the First World War, Noel had succeeded in slipping into forbidden Tibet, not as other travellers bound for Lhasa but with the idea of trying to reach Everest. When he was captured by the men of a local warlord, he was only forty miles from his goal. To secure his release, he spun some story about being a tea planter in pursuit of a robber, and returned to his regiment, where his colonel demanded to know why he had overstayed his leave. Claiming that his calendar had been washed away in a flash flood, Noel escaped with a curt but restrained reprimand and an order to 'take two next time'.

Holzel's plan for an expedition to search for Mallory and Irvine seized the imagination of Captain Noel who at once set himself to thinking up ways in which public interest could be aroused. For the life of him, he could not understand why no one had launched such a quest years ago. There was something else he and Tom had in common, and that was a special association with the star Arcturus. As a prisoner of war in France, Noel had made his escape behind enemy lines by taking bearings from Arcturus, and later on the North Col of Everest he again contemplated the bright, orange star when wondering how the universe was formed. When founding his computer business, Holzel had named it after Arcturus, the 'Guardian of the Bear'.

It must have been at this time that I drew an enthusiastic response from a publisher to the idea of a book reassessing the Everest story as it appeared from the documentary evidence. Surely that would arouse interest in a search on the ground. Before the year was out Tom and I had secured a joint contract for a book which we called *The Mystery of Mallory and Irvine*, and his venture had taken a great leap forward.

Upon returning home Tom Holzel had been surprised to receive a visit from two New York Chinese waiters, offering to ease his permit request through the necessary formalities in Peking. Who on earth were these men? How could they know the details of his application? Were they spies? He had no way of checking their credentials, and only one of finding out whether they could be trusted with the considerable advance payment requested. Good as their word, in a few months Holzel heard officially that he could go to Everest in the autumn of 1986. Springtime would have been better, before the monsoon, when conditions in the Himalaya would be warmer, with less wind and snow, but at least he had secured the route he wanted: the North Col. This would give him access to both the Upper North-east Ridge – Mallory's route – and the North Face, where any body, or bodies, were presumed to lie. Now he could begin putting his team together.

Soon after receiving his go-ahead, Holzel was approached by a small production company keen to make a documentary film of his search.

By an astonishing coincidence this partnership of three climbing friends – Andrew Harvard, David Breashears and George Bell jr – called itself Arcturus Motion Pictures. It was nothing if not a good omen, especially as Andy Harvard was the man whom years before Tom had wanted as Climbing Leader for his abortive secret attempt. Since then, the tough young lawyer had led the successful American expedition to Everest's Kangshung face.

A deal was struck. Harvard was once more invited to become Holzel's deputy and given a free hand in selecting the team. Later, for administrative convenience, Tom stepped down as leader in his favour, becoming instead the Expedition's Chairman. David Breashears was made climbing leader and put in overall charge of the film-making. A high-altitude cameraman with two Emmy awards to his credit, he had already been twice to the top of Mount Everest and was now des-patched to Nepal to secure a strong Sherpa support team. My task was to find a British co-producer for the project.

One of the first approaches I made was to Alistair Macdonald, a television producer and presenter working at that time for BBC Northwest. He and I had come to know each other through work with the British Mountaineering Council.

'Fancy a trip to Everest?' I teased him with the blunt unexpected question over the phone.

Of course, once he had the full picture, I knew the opportunity to have his own crack at the 'Big E' would be irresistible, as it would for any climber. The BBC was less sanguine about committing a large budget to what was seen as essentially an American enterprise. A few months later it was a different story: Mallory and Irvine were not only national heroes, but both from the north-west county of Cheshire. When the BBC in London and Bristol began showing serious interest, Alistair got his budget and a commission from BBC Manchester to travel to Tibet with the climbers.

'I really think we'll go!' he said with a grin, flinging his arms round me as we left the first planning meeting with the men from Arcturus. But we were not home and dry yet.

Large expeditions to the Himalayas are costly, and if we were to do the job properly, more finance would be needed. A British team, hoping to attempt the still unclimbed Pinnacles of Everest's North-east Ridge at the same time as we would be on the North Face, was in serious difficulties. Andy made contact with the leader, Brummie Stokes, to see what facilities could be shared to bring down costs for both of us. Stores, oxygen and transport were possibilities. At last, it was agreed that our expedition could call on the services of their two doctors in exchange for allowing them, in an emergency, to descend the mountain by our easier North Col route.

It was not enough. We would have to broaden the scope of our expedition if we were to go to Tibet.

★

By the beginning of 1986 the summit of Mount Everest was known to have been reached 209 times by 187 climbers. This figure included five women, among whom were no Americans. There was nothing sinister about this: American expeditions in recent years had frequently incorporated women climbers who were as good as any in the world. It was just a matter of chance that none of them had so far made it all the way to the top. Yet newspapers were happy to enlarge the issue into a cause for national concern, especially after a Canadian, Sharon Wood, snatched the title of 'First North American Woman up Everest'. However artificial the concept, 'putting' the first American girl on the summit of the world's highest mountain became a cause for which sponsorship was not difficult to find.

That settled it. By introducing three of the best women climbers from the United States into our team, and agreeing to film their attempt for ABC Sports Television, the remaining finance for our expedition was secured.

Brummie's British team remained in suspense for longer, far short of their financial target. I spoke to the journalist Peter Gillman, and ten days before their official – but increasingly doubtful departure date, he got a feature about them into the *Observer* newspaper. In less than a week a firm of City brokers stepped in with the requisite cash, and the 'Seligmann Harris British Mount Chomolungma North-East Ridge '86 Expedition' was born. It was a name, as Mo Anthoine, one of the British climbers, observed, to fair trip off the tongue.

★

All of us wondered what Sir Edmund Hillary would make of our quest. For more than thirty years he had enjoyed celebrity as one of the heroic pair whom the world recognized as the first to climb Everest; might he be sensitive to our attempts to discover if Mallory had pipped him to the post? There was no apparent rancour when he agreed to let us film an interview with him at the Explorers Club in New York.

25

'Obviously it would make some difference to Tenzing and me,' he said, 'if they got to the top. I guess we would be downgraded a little bit . . . to being the first two men who got safely down again!'

But wasn't that was the point? If you die on the descent, even after climbing a mountain for the first time, can it really count as a first ascent? Mischievously, he declared, 'I'm rather inclined to think that maybe it's quite important, the getting down.'

So he had no intention of being ousted, whatever was discovered! All the same, Hillary allowed, Mallory had been an inspirational figure and it would have been a fitting reward for all his efforts if on that final day he *had* set foot on the mountain summit.

★

Tom Holzel succeeded in raising even more hackles when publicizing the expedition. 'Why am I doing it? Because Mallory's there,' he would announce, shamelessly.

Just as he had been taken unawares by the vehement response to his 'separation theory', so now he underestimated the strength of popular feeling among climbers, especially those of an older generation, that his was a morbid pursuit after matters of death that could yield no certain answers and only leave a trail of doubt and disillusion. Let the heroes rest in peace was the plea, and it was one that clearly Hillary shared. What would happen, Hillary wondered, if a frozen corpse were to be found? Would it be filmed or photographed and the grisly images exhibited? Would its possessions, such as camera or clothing, be removed? Would teeth or other organic samples be taken for autopsy? And afterwards what would happen to the remains? Would they be brought home for decent Christian burial, or left naked in the snow for other climbers to find and film?

My friend Doctor Charles Warren, who had been to Everest three times in the 1930s, wrote a letter to *The Times* expressing his deepfelt hope that no relics would be found, and quoted an epitaph from a climber's grave in Grindelwald at the foot of the Eiger:

> Here let us leave him; for his shroud the snow,
> For funeral lamps he has the planets seven,
> For a great sign the icy stair shall go
> Between the heights to heaven.

The Editor saw fit to publish only one response, but it was a surprising and particularly heartening one to us. It came from a nephew of

Andrew Irvine, wishing the expedition every success. 'I am sure that Sandy, with his inquiring mind, would be happy that there is still interest and speculation over their achievement, and would not think of the proposed search as desecration.'

The families of both Mallory and Irvine were generously supportive. For more than six decades they have wondered what became of their loved ones and wanted to know. A younger brother of Irvine's told me that if Sandy's body were found, he expected to come out to the Himalaya to identify it. Not one among Mallory's sisters' families gave us anything but helpful encouragement, as did his son and daughter. There never was any question of disturbing remains, of course, and no way of bringing a body down the mountain – for identification or for any other purpose.

Each of us on the expedition had private feelings in the matter. The riddle is, after all, a powerful and emotive one. I, for one, would prefer not to know beyond the last vestige of doubt that they had failed, though that is hardly a proper response for an historian. The enigma remains vividly alive, the spirit of the dead climbers free and undaunted: would it, could it, still be so when entombed in the bleak certainty of a pile of bones?

No-one expresses concern that the body of the solo-mountaineer Maurice Wilson is churned periodically from the East Rongbuk Glacier in ever-deteriorating condition. Photographs of his bones have appeared on peak-time television with no attendant outcry. But then Wilson was nobody's hero; rather a quixotic, hopeless figure. Nor is it recorded that anyone shouted 'Ghoul!' when an expedition went in search of the remains of Captain Robert Falcon Scott. Why should that be different? Is it the passage of time between death and search that alone alters the emphasis? What Tom Holzel and the rest of us were learning was that whoever dares to tamper with myths is moving in a realm beyond the reach of reason.

In a long letter to Tom, one interested correspondent attempted to grade the emotional responses to the investigation. To ensure immortality for the two climbers – the best of all possibilities, he considered – it was essential for no bodies to be found while gaining some evidence (photographic presumably, or some object from the summit) that indicated the two men had made it to the top. The same evidence coupled with the discovery of bodies was next best, but it put paid to the myth: Mallory (and Irvine too, although he is always a more shadowy figure in people's consciousness) would then be deflated into a statistic – hero for a day, but ultimately just another dead climber.

Keeping the *status quo* rated third in this man's scale: it preserved hope and the mystery, retained Mallory as the beckoning spirit, ahead of his time; it allowed, in other words, anything to be possible.

The unsettling limbo of finding bodies with no answer to the mystery raised only images of pain and pointlessness. Finally, he considered what difference positive proof of failure would make. Such knowledge coupled with no bodies reduced the episode to one of defeat – no superhuman powers; just rest in a 'proper element'.

The very worst scenario of all for this writer he called the Icarus Syndrome: to find the dead climbers and to know that they failed. This reduced their efforts to a vain attempt. They had foolishly bitten off more than they could chew and were doomed from the start. The two were sadly only human after all.

Until the women's attempt on the summit was incorporated, ours had been a climbing expedition whose stated objective was the eccentric one of *not* climbing to the top – or at least, not primarily.

Perhaps this never was possible. Climbers, after all, climb. As high as they can go, the summit ever beckoning them on. Their spirit, their training, their individualism, whatever makes them good at what they do, demands it. They may suppress personal ambition in the interests of getting someone from the team up, but it would take a very unusual constellation of climbers to turn their backs on the summit altogether. When that summit is Everest, for which permits are so hard to come by, it would surely be asking too much of anyone to conduct the kind of search Tom Holzel had in mind – particularly when, to reach the area he required examined, the searcher would first have to battle almost to the top of the mountain. Any climber would know he was unlikely to be in so good a striking position ever again.

Though interested in the Mallory and Irvine story, the mountaineers recruited on to our expedition were all acutely sensitive to the adverse criticism the whole idea of a search had been getting in some quarters. No matter that this was largely based on misconception, they sought to distance themselves from any accusation of intrusiveness or bad taste. There was noticeably less talk now of finding cameras, and none at all (by anyone but Tom) of employing metal detectors in the search.

As the day of departure approached, the emphasis swung from a detective search to that of pure climbing. The ultimate aim in most minds was to see an American girl make it to the summit of Everest. Nothing would be found, nothing achieved by remaining at home.

Fixity of Purpose

IT HAS ALWAYS interested me how little people change, how little we ever seem to learn from experience. It is almost as if we cannot escape from ourselves: we make a mistake, rue it deeply, yet, faced with the build-up towards a similar situation, seem unable to react any differently.

The 1922 expedition launched two assaults on the mountain before the monsoon rolled in. The consensus was to call it a day. But Mallory decided to make one last attempt – against all odds and despite his own intuitive sense that it was mere foolishness now that the snow had come. 'It seemed to me too early to turn back, and too easy – we should not be satisfied afterwards,' he said in justification. His resolution resulted in the deaths of seven porters, and he was grief-stricken with remorse. Yet in 1924, when again the party had made two creditable attempts on the summit and were ready to withdraw, Mallory appeared to have put the incident from his mind. Once more he took the fatal decision to launch a last-ditch effort, this time with young Irvine.

Why?

He must have thought there was an outside chance of their pulling it off. Maybe, the pair did reach the top, as many hope and believe, though there could never have been more than the slimmest chance that they would make it safely down again. For himself, Mallory had long since accepted the risk that he might die mountaineering, but assuming that he felt (besides any affection) a responsibility for his young companion in view of the latter's inexperience, Mallory would not knowingly have consigned Irvine to death. He must have believed the situation was retrievable anywhere along the line. Were the deaths, then, bad luck, or bad judgment?

A Bristol psychologist, Glin Bennet, has identified a factor in the build-up towards accidents that he calls 'perseveration'. When an individual is faced with the chance of redressing in some measure an earlier miscalculation, all too often he only compounds the damage by a seeming inability to take up that chance. Dr Mike Ward recognizes something similar in mountaineering: a 'fixity of purpose' is how he describes it. Some degree of fixity of purpose is clearly necessary if one is ever to scale a mountain or sail an ocean. I was curious to learn at what stage that becomes unhealthy and affects legitimate caution?

I decided to put the question to Dr Bennet. Could he, I wondered, discover in the Everest literature any clues to Mallory's state of mind in 1924? And should we consider anyone who goes repeatedly on expeditions as obsessive – or dedicated? There is some evidence that Mallory was reluctant to go to Everest that third time, telling close friends that it would be more like war than mountaineering, that he didn't expect to come back. In the light of what happened, the temptation is to see that as self-fulfilling prophecy; and it is disturbing that his eventual decision to go might have been made more out of a sense of duty than any real desire to return to the mountain. How often it is that 'one last time' which proves so disastrous. It is as if the promise of ending the commitment after an enterprise seeps into the enterprise itself; it affects the fragile balance of mind and mountain, so necessary for the constant re-assessment of risk.

When I visited him, Dr Bennet was interested to hear of our expedition, and of Tom's fifteen-year involvement with the Mallory and Irvine story. We discussed the character of Mallory only in the most superficial terms, however, and as I made to leave, the doctor said, 'I don't think I can help you with anything useful about Mallory's state of mind. But I am concerned by what you tell me of Tom Holzel. His interest does strike me as obsessive, and my advice to you is to be very wary!'

★

As far as I was concerned, Tom's invitation to continue the hunt in the field seemed a preposterous idea. I went through all the motions to make it happen without ever believing that it could. From time to time I would say to Peter, my husband, and to my three sons, 'Of course, I can't really go!' and be amazed when, instead of agreeing with me, they always replied, 'You'd be crazy not to!' Accounts of earlier Everest expeditions did nothing to buttress my resolve. They merely bore home a painful awareness of what could happen to middle-aged mountaineers. Dr Kellas died on the way in to the mountain in 1921, and Harold Raeburn broke down so severely that he, too, was dead within a few years. In 1924, General Bruce's heart played him tricks on the Tibetan plateau. All were men in their fifties who had been active throughout their lives. I was still smarting from my fiftieth birthday, and took hardly any exercise at all.

On the other hand, Chris Bonington had recently climbed Everest at the age of fifty, and on the same expedition David Breashears had shepherded to the summit an American millionaire who, at fifty-five, became the oldest person to have reached it. At least I wasn't set on going to the top. I would be very happy if I made it to the basin beneath the North Col at 21,000 feet, where the old Camp III used to be sited, but going to altitude is always an unpredictable business. Often it is the young, the strong and fit ones who experience difficulty. No one can say with any certainty who will cope or who collapse.

The only reliable way to combat severe mountain sickness is to move down to a lower altitude quickly, but once on the Tibetan plateau, was there anywhere lower you could go? I remembered a girl I had worked with who died suddenly on a Himalayan trek; I doubted if she had reached the height at which we were intending to place our Base Camp. Everest physicians Charles Warren and Michael Ward wrote me friendly, cautionary letters; they clearly had misgivings about my going, and my brother, a London Consultant, wanted to be sure the expedition was taking a good doctor.

'Well, we haven't got one,' I told him. 'But two are coming with the Brits.'

'Army doctors?'

I supposed they might be, since the British expedition had begun as a military one, but I couldn't see what difference that would make. All he would say was that at least they should be good at bullet wounds.

One by one all reasons for hesitating evaporated. The days running up to departure were spent trying to get the Mallory book finished; it was to be published on our return in November. My brain was in a fever of urgency and all my preparations seemed hasty and ill-complete as time ran out. Peter and I were able to snatch one last day to ourselves in Brighton, for a mooch round the Lanes and a winey lunch. I bought two expensive books on Tibet, a pith helmet and a herd of ebony elephants. Peter cooed at a stuffed bear, but reined himself in: it would only scare the dog. His grasp on reality was by then far firmer than my own.

Before I knew it, I was taking a last look at the house and garden, the cat and the dog, and was – unbelievably – kissing the family goodbye.

★

The expedition had been assigned a liaison officer by the Chinese authorities in Peking – or Beijing, as we now learned to call it. Mr Song had been to Everest before and would stay with us until the trip was over. By another of those quirks of coincidence, he was one of the mountaineers with the Chinese expedition of 1975, when the body of the 'Dead English' was said to have been found. We also gathered a young interpreter, Mr Jhao, a timid young language student with no interest in mountains at all, so far as we could discover, and who had never before been far out of Beijing. From the start 'Boy Jhao' was overawed by our expedition leader, which was not altogether surprising. With his sharp attorney manner and his thick bushy black beard, Andy Harvard could intimidate far more practised men of the world. Throughout the protracted protocol negotiations with the Chinese Mountaineering Association, Andy would clap a firm hand on Jhao's shoulder and urge him to fight our corner more forcefully. Whenever possible Jhao preferred to sidle up to one of us with his queries, rather than confront the beard, but always the answer was the same.

'Sorry, Jhao. You'll have to ask Andy that.'

Jhao would nod miserably. 'Mister Haa-vaad, aahh!' You could see him wishing he had found other employment for his summer vacation.

★

The ABC-film we were to shoot of the women's struggle on Everest was for a series, 'Spirit of Adventure', sponsored by Mutual of Omaha. Without this assignment the expedition would have been stillborn.

Sue Giller, rising forty, was the oldest of our three women climbers, and the only one with previous Himalayan experience. She had made two earlier attempts on Everest, both by hard routes, and this was her fifth big expedition in six years. Small and spare, Sue was deceptively strong and fiercely independent. It was nothing to see her shifting loads of more than a hundred pounds on her own. By her code, you said what you meant, did what you said, and pulled your weight without complaining. Except that in Sue's case you pulled rather more than your weight. If she ever felt weakness or fatigue, it never showed. She made it her business to know how everything worked, and throughout the trip performed running repairs to hard- and software. Andy put her in charge of high-altitude stores and equipment, and with some inexplicable flash of inspiration billeted her with me. It turned out to be a felicitous pairing.

Years ago Sue had been an analytical chemist. To gain the freedom to spend more time on mountains, she worked in climbing stores, instructed outdoor sports, and now, from home, programmed computers. It was a question of getting priorities right. You ignored the fripperies: climbing was what it was all about.

In many ways, Mary Kay Brewster was Sue's counterpart: a tall, languid beauty who took her femininity so seriously as to include a little black dress and a gossamer shift in her Base Camp wardrobe. Her altitude ensemble was perfectly coordinated in lilacs and sugar pink. Alistair Macdonald, with his preference for blondes, was bedazzled, and could only blink when he met her in Beijing. 'A remarkable woman,' he kept saying. Yet no one should be seduced into thinking her a helpless damsel.

All her life Mary Kay had been irrepressible, refusing to be left behind when her brother went off camping and climbing. She moved west from Ohio to be in the mountains, spent summers in the Grand Tetons and Wind Rivers, and winters in Boulder, Colorado, climbing and skiing. To enhance her fitness, she had taken up long-distance cycling, running and swimming, and for four years competed on the triathlon circuit, which included the notoriously rugged Hawaii Ironman event. At twenty-eight, Mary Kay was about to make a fresh start as a medical student, but she wanted that elusive first-American-woman-up-Everest riband tucked under her belt first.

The third girl with eyes for the summit was Cathy Cullinane, a last-minute addition to the team, just weeks before we left, when another climber found herself pregnant. Brought up in California, Cathy used to go back-packing and camping with her family, and took up climbing at the age of sixteen. Nowadays, she lived most of the year in Jackson, Wyoming, working for the Exum Mountain Guides service or, in lean times, as a nurse. She was perennially good-natured, a warm, brown, downy presence, everyone's girl-next-door. She consoled and comforted, patched up broken skin and bruised egos.

All three knew that even if we were in a position to get one of them to the top of the mountain, in all probability it would be just that: one only. Worrying which of them would be selected injected a tension between them, a repressed competitiveness, but this was probably no different nor more significant than that experienced by any male team-member towards his comrades. The concept that from the start the girls were being 'nurtured' for the summit was artificial. They had been brought along for that very reason: to be conducted to the top, and to be filmed getting there. Sue found this galling. She would have preferred everyone to arrive at the base of the mountain on an equal footing, and for the climb to be directed on the far more sensible basis of ability and performance. In her opinion, since expeditions had become trapped on this 'first-woman' treadwheel, quality mountaineering had gone headlong out of the window.

★

The flight to Tibet took us first over green mountains, then yellow and brown ones, and finally over vast ranges of snow-covered giants. The plane dipped low into valleys between moulded peaks the colour of corn, with braided jade rivers in their wide bottoms, touching down at last at Lhasa Airport in blazing sunshine.

All day long I had been worrying that, once out of the pressurised cabin, I would keel over in the thin air. Lhasa, after all, stands at 12,000 feet. Consciously, I steadied my breathing before walking slowly down the aircraft steps. Nothing. I didn't need to gulp in air. I was fine. It felt as normal as at sea level. No, it felt marvellous! The colours were brilliant, the air like wine. This was the Roof of the World, and it was wonderful!

Andy cuffed a huge bear-like arm round my shoulder. 'What's it like, Audrey? The Himalaya after all this time?'

I beamed. We seemed in the grip of a kind of communal hysteria. Our spirits simply would not stop soaring. We jabbered and joked through the hour-long drive into the city, and stopping to photograph a huge carved and painted buddha in the hillside, we spilled from the bus like children.

Then, ahead, over a long bridge, rose the fabled Potala Palace. This most potent symbol of Tibet was every bit as wondrous as legend had described, but there was little of cheer in all the bleak utilitarian new building that had sprung up around it. We pulled into the front yard of the raw white block on the outskirts of town, the Lhasa Hotel. A Holiday Inn, no less. At least from the balcony at the end of my bedroom corridor, through a gap beside the cinema and above the tangle of electric wires, I could glimpse the Palace of the Gods on its red hill, traditional winter home of the Dalai Lamas and the junction between earth and heaven.

The hotel was crowded, it being the only place in Lhasa where foreign tourists are encouraged to stay. It cannot be said that it is exactly like a large hotel anywhere in the world, even if that is the intention. Oxygen is provided in all the rooms, bubbling through a flimsy apparatus of glass and tubing between the beds. Burgers in the burger-bar are made of yak. Canned drinks explode as they are opened because of the reduced air pressure. Someone once must have told the chef that Westerners like a full cooked breakfast; now he stays up half the night frying eggs. The centrepiece of the serve-yourself buffet each morning is an enormous ziggurat of congealed, cold, rubbery eggs – just like the ones you can buy in joke shops at home.

On the evening of our arrival I was impatient to see what lay outside this air-conditioned world. With Alistair and Mary Kay Brewster, I dashed down a dusty tree-lined boulevard to meet our first Tibetans.

★

In 1986 I was shamelessly ignorant of the extent of the Tibetans' ordeal since the Chinese invasion of 1950. Of course I knew that their culture had all but been wiped out; that of more than 6,000 monasteries and temples at the time of the invasion, probably less than a dozen remained, and even those were now museums. It was common knowledge that the Dalai Lama and over a hundred thousand Tibetans lived in permanent exile in India and Nepal. But the human tragedy behind these facts eluded me. To go to Tibet is to become involved, to love it and grieve for it. That much I had learned from the old Everesters; fifty or more years may have passed since they last saw this dry land, but it and its people still held them in thrall; its sadness haunted them. Since my visit, I too have sought to know more, and my one regret is that there must have been clues and nuances I missed at the time simply because I was not sensitive enough to detect them.

Under duress, a Tibetan delegation to China in May 1951 was made to sign what has become known as the Seventeen Point Agreement. This denied Tibet its status as an independent nation, and decreed that 'step by step' Tibetan troops should be absorbed into the Chinese People's Liberation Army. The relentless programme of colonization and collectivization which followed met stiff resistance in almost every village. Prominent members of local society were rounded up, and if after beatings and public humiliation they failed to repent their 'crimes against the people', they were executed.

As a method it was singularly effective, although in Eastern Tibet the Khampas and their neighbours the Amdos proved impossible to subdue. Ghenghiz Khan had been unable to bring these proud warriors to heel, and they were not about to surrender now. Fiercely, they harried the occupying forces, opposing all reform. Chinese garrisons, particularly those in remote areas, were attacked and wiped out. But the rebels paid heavily for such militancy. Nowhere in Tibet were the atrocities more hideous than in Kham and Amdo. In one village 24 leading members of the council were burned alive at the stake. In another, two dozen parents were put to death by having nails driven into their eyes for refusing to see the virtue of sending their children to Chinese schools. After an uprising in Lithang in 1956 a long siege was brought to an end by bombing the town's monastery in which several thousand villagers were sheltering.

The Khampas organized themselves into a cohesive guerrilla force and in 1959, led by the eighteen-year-old Chime Youngdong of Benchen Monastery, marched into Lhasa to beg the young Dalai Lama to lead a revolt against the Chinese.

The 'God King' was in an impossible position. As a devout Buddhist he could not condone bloodshed, even when the blood was that of his country's ruthless oppressors. Yet he had no wish either to be China's puppet. Torn with anguish, he made his secret flight into India, where he set up a government in exile and dedicated himself to apprising the world of the plight of his benighted countrymen. Before leaving Tibetan soil for the last time he renounced the Seventeen Point Agreement.

Even as he fled, fierce fighting broke out in Lhasa, which the Chinese swiftly crushed with tanks and heavy mortar. Nowhere is it recorded how many thousands died in the two days of battle, but ten thousand Lhasa Tibetans are known to have disappeared, either killed or sent into forced labour.

This was not the end of the struggle for freedom. Guerrilla activity continued over the next fifteen years, waged latterly from bases across the Nepalese border in Mustang and Dolpo. Tibetans continued to die in hundreds of thousands as their old way of life was brutally purged and disastrous famines followed the Chinese imposition of new farming patterns. Children were sent away for indoctrination and all religious observance was forbidden. Ancient Chinese tortures were revived: scalding, slow burning, flaying, disembowelling, crucifixion. In the collective madness that was the Cultural Revolution, denunciatory *Thamzing* sessions whipped up further violence; and monasteries and shrines throughout the land that were not already flattened were shot to bits.

This did not merely represent the annihilation of religion and its practise throughout Tibet, but an incalculable loss to history and scholarship. The few books that existed in the country were all in the monasteries – some of them manuscripts a thousand years old, copied from Indian originals that had long since been lost. In his fine book *Hidden Tibet*, Roger Hicks has suggested that it is not unrealistic to compare the Chinese destruction of centres of learning in Tibet with the destruction of the library of Alexandria in AD 640. By comparison, the book-burning of the Inquisition or of the Nazis was the work of uncoordinated amateurs, he says.

The Dalai Lama's lonely plea for assistance in freeing his people from Chinese rule fell on deaf ears. For years the United Nations declined even to discuss the matter.

By the end of the 1970s Han Chinese outnumbered Tibetans in most cities, and the country was bankrupt and starving. Following the repeated failure of winter wheat – the preferred staple of the Chinese – Tibetans were at last allowed to return to growing barley, the only crop that prospered in their harsh land. In desperation the Chinese looked to tourism as a way out of the crisis. The Potala and Jokhang in Lhasa were hastily patched and painted, as were a few monasteries along the proposed tourist routes. State hotels were built.

At first, only select parties were allowed in, which included mountaineers who were easy enough to contain and single-minded enough not to ask too many questions. Their peak fees were a useful bonus. In 1985 Lhasa was declared a 'second-category open city', which meant there were few restraints on foreign visitors provided their visas were in order.

We could still, then, consider ourselves earlybirds in all this, such new-found freedoms being only a year old. Lightheartedly, we shot footage in the Barkhor market and inside the Potala without fear of retribution. Amid the gilded ornament on the Potala roof, Mary Kay and Cathy joined a team of Tibetan women who were tamping down a new mud-plaster floor. As so often here, the dreariness of repetitive labour was eliminated by ritualizing the task: the women swayed and sang as they jabbed their tamping sticks up and down in unison.

The sight of Westerners getting wrong-footed in the dance was occasion – if such were needed – for the Tibetans to dissolve into delighted giggles.

Walking round the city, the Chinese presence could not be ignored. Belching factories, straight streets, grey blocks, red brick, the tin roofs of the Communists – had all but swamped what was left of Tibetan Lhasa. Looking down from the Potala roof, we saw only a small island of higgledy streets in the relentless grid. The green uniform of China's guardian army was visible everywhere and miniature versions were on sale in the Barkhor market for children to play soldiers. But the market – for so long closed – was functioning again, and between the carpet and prayerwheel stalls, travel-worn pilgrims once more measured their length in the dirt as they made a triple circum-prostration of the sacred Jokhang temple. They no longer needed to fear a bullet in the back for doing so. Unchallenged, Khampas swaggered in arrogant groups, fingers in the belts of their flares, long hair bound in coils of scarlet yarn. They wore high boots and daggers, and changed tourist money for local Renminbi, the 'people's currency', on the black market.

Inside the Jokhang, the holiest temple in all Tibet, which had been shelled in the Lhasa Uprising and vandalized by the Red Guards, the courtyard was full of giant timbers which craftsmen were planing for its refurbishment. Paint was bright and fresh; the extravagantly gilded roof gleamed, and a long crocodile of pilgrims inched patiently forward, past the battery of butterlamps in the entrance, to revere the jewel-studded statues.

It is impossible to know which figures are exaggerated and which underestimated when assessing the dreadful toll of the Chinese years. Maybe as many as 1,200,000 have died in the Tibetan 'killing fields', as suggested by film-maker and author Vanya Kewley. More than a million, certainly – that was the claim of a 1988 Parliamentary Human Rights Group report, and it supports the Dalai Lama's own appraisal. In any case, it seemed a long way from the Lhasa we were seeing. Official readiness to admit that serious mistakes had been made – particularly after the upheavals of 1959 – surely gave cause for hope?

We couldn't know that the year we were there was to prove the calmest period in Tibet's troubled modern times and that the following autumn the deep undercurrent of resentment would break surface once more. Then the world learned a new word: 'splittists', those led astray by the Dalai Lama, so the Chinese claimed, were attempting to draw Tibet back to the 'feudalist serf system and hysterical retrogression.' Monks were shot dead after firing on a police station where demonstrators were being held, and six months later thirty militant monks were clubbed to death after tear gas had been used to flush them from the Jokhang. Police shot blindly into a crowd, killing demonstrators; and in December 1988 tourists were among those wounded in another police attack. It was rare for outsiders to witness such outbreaks of violence, as by a freak of the Tibetan calendar, days of social importance when demonstrations could be expected fell mainly outside the tourist season. At the first whisper of trouble martial law is invariably declared and all borders sealed. A lorry driver told *Observer* journalist Jonathan Mirsky, 'The Chinese are trying to compress us like buttered barley into a smaller and smaller ball.'

An exiled Chinese journalist Tang Daxian, produced – again for the *Observer* – filmed evidence of a stage-managed massacre that took place in Lhasa in early March 1990, in which as many as 450 monks, nuns and civilians were killed. Nobody knows how many were taken into custody. You could call it a warm-up for Tiananmen Square later that spring.

Venturing to the Interior

WHILE MAKING OUR last phonecalls home we learned of the deaths of Al Rouse and Julie Tullis on K2. In all, thirteen victims were claimed that summer by the world's second highest mountain in an unprecedented series of disasters. Both Al and Julie had reached the summit before perishing in a high camp where several mountaineers were pinned down by bad weather. What made the tragedy more shocking was that Al had still been alive when his companions made their bid to escape. His mind wandering, and pleading desperately for water, he was too weak to accompany them. Julie had died in her sleep a few days before.

Of the seven people caught in that lethal trap, only the Austrian mountaineer Kurt Diemberger and his compatriot Willi Bauer made it back down the mountain alive. The details were not available to us then, and indeed only trickled out over months and years as various accounts were published, and then analysed and pronounced upon. I was badly shaken by the news. Julie had been a friend for more than twenty-five years, from when I first went climbing on the sandstone outcrops of Kent. She was shy in those days, and very pretty, with an air of fragility about her. Already married to Terry Tullis, it was touching to see how he encouraged and protected her. As time went on they both showed great flair for encouragement, spending their lives introducing people to climbing and enjoying particular success with handicapped youngsters.

In the four years before her death Julie had taken part in no fewer than six expeditions to the world's 'eight-thousanders' – the fourteen mountains over 8,000 metres (26,250 feet) high. She always climbed with the film-maker Kurt Diemberger, working as his sound-recordist. Together they went to the top of Broad Peak in 1984, and above the magic 8,000 metre-line on the north side of K2 and on Nanga Parbat.

There was an element of churlishness towards her achievements on the part of British mountaineers. She was seen as being in love with the idea of climbing, as an appendage of Kurt's, coasting on his experience. But Julie was able to introduce the mental discipline she had discovered in martial arts into her climbing, and she brought a strength of her own to the partnership, acting as a steadying foil to Kurt's volatility. Though neither was in the first flush of youth, they complemented each other perfectly for the style of mountaineering they preferred.

I cannot but believe that more generosity would have been shown had her record been that of a male mountaineer. So many expeditions would not then have been as lightly dismissed, nor the motivations questioned. A lifetime's dedication to the sport would have spoken for itself. It will be a long time yet before women find their way on to British expeditions in anything like the numbers they do on those of other countries. There were none among Brummie's Brits on the North-east Ridge in 1986.

★

The bus bumped and rattled along dirt roads on exhausted shock absorbers. Fumes belched into the body of the vehicle. Windows that would not shut let in a fine, talcumy dust that soon settled over everything. Out came the face-masks and scarves, and for Alistair, whose last BBC-assignment had been a Sahara crossing, his *shemagh*, a voluminous black Arab head-dress. The first pass out of Lhasa offered tantalizing glimpses of alpine flowers. Gentians or blue poppies? We were not close enough to see. The road followed the shoreline of a beautiful cobalt blue lake, Yamdrok Tso, before climbing an even higher pass beyond. Labouring to its crest, about 16,500 feet, the bus spluttered feebly and died.

With patient resignation the Chinese driver pulled out his bag of tools. We were miles from anywhere.

As a child, I was known as a 'bad traveller', quickly greening whenever I ventured into buses and cars. Tube trains were even worse: my family used to have to interrupt a journey at every station and rush me to the surface for air. It took us hours to get anywhere. Happily those days were well behind me – or so I had believed until I clambered aboard this contraption. For me, the enforced stop was more than welcome and I staggered queazily outside to gulp down the meagre air. I was just beginning to take an interest in the stunted plantlife of the bleak pass when I heard Andy negotiating with a passing group of German film-makers who had stopped to see if we needed any help.

'Can you take one of our party down to lower altitude?'

I wondered who was feeling the height. Everyone looked fine to me. Then, with a stab of horror I realized I was the one Andy was seeking to dispatch. This was terrible! There was no way I wanted to become separated from the rest of the party. How could I be sure I would ever meet up with them again? No, no! I would refuse to go. Although I was the oldest team-member, it still came as a harsh shock whenever I encountered this over-protective concern for my welfare. Did they think I was going to peg out – or what?

The bus suddenly spat into life, and I was spared any humiliating evacuation. We continued through Gyantse to Shigatse, where we arrived late in the evening, to find our film crew which had travelled ahead in the expedition 'jeep' waiting anxiously on the steps of the town's one hotel. They'd had the good sense to make sure that supper was kept for us.

Once the decision was taken to allow tourists inside Tibet, the Chinese hastily erected a handful of hotels to what they considered approved western standards. With little to go on, architects must have looked in wonder at imported brochures and done their best to produce visual facsimiles. There was little understanding of the intricacies of what they were installing. The Shigatse Hotel appeared very grand with its wide marble foyer, but upon eventually finding our rooms – not easy for the room-numbers were replicated on each floor – we discovered the opulence to be an illusion. My room-mate, Sue, made a dive for the bed by the window, and let out a loud shriek when it offered no resistance to her bounce. I peeled back the bedclothes. A thin horsehair mattress was laid immediately on top of raw tree-trunks, pine logs split in half lengthways, curved sides uppermost and with the bark still in place. There were en-suite facilities – a shower and a loo – but if we wished to make use of the shower, then it would have been necessary to sit on the loo to do so, positioned as it was directly beneath the sprinkler. There was no drain-away, nor any lip to the cubicle. The room next door was already under two inches of water, presumably because the previous occupants had seized their chance just before leaving.

It should have come as a surprise to find any water at all. Few of the other government hotels we stayed in were able to produce even a dribble from taps or flushes. And the crazy thing was that all of us would have preferred to stay in typical Tibetan accommodation rather than this ersatz luxury. That was something the authorities were not relaxed enough to allow. To have only a few hotels makes it easier for them to keep tourists under control; and by insisting that groups travel on expensive government-arranged vehicle and accommodation packages ensures that a significant revenue from tourism goes into party coffers.

When the Lhasa Hotel opened its first 250 rooms in 1985, the intention was that it should become a showpiece hotel for the China International Travel Service (CITS). Spacious and well-equipped with bars and several restaurants, it was looking to attract wealthy visitors on the Round-the-World circuit. All its disastrous first season proved was that the expertise did not exist in Tibet to provide the multi-star service such travellers have come to expect. The concession for running the hotel passed to the Holiday Inn chain, and when we arrived a new manager had been installed for only a few days.

She was surprised to discover that a large number of the rooms in one wing were mysteriously locked. Nobody could put their hands on the keys: all the original locks appeared to have been changed. When, finally, she had the rooms broken into, Tibetan families were discovered in occupation. The first workers had moved in their dependents and, having no use for fancy tiles and fittings, had rolled back the carpets and built traditional cooking hearths in the middle of the floor!

★

Stopping by the roadside the day we left Shigatse we opened the paper bags given to us by the hotel as we left. Lunch: hard-boiled eggs (hundred-year-old ones by the look of it), doughballs and some sickly sweet candies. Immediately ragged children clustered close and word went around among the birds.

'What kind are they?' I asked Andy, as much to make conversation as out of any curiosity.

'Don't ask me. There are raptors, and there are little brown things. That's all I know about birds.'

Same as people, really, I thought, and handed my bag to the nearest urchin.

★

Although twelve of us had come in to Tibet through Beijing and across China, as expedition protocol dictated, we were also the first group to be allowed to bring in Sherpas and additional supplies over the border with Nepal. Five American climbers and our sixteen Nepalese team-members travelled by open lorry from Kathmandu through the Himalaya and across the Tibetan plateau to join us in Xegar. They arrived covered from head to foot in green dust. The hugs and back-slapping greetings of old and new friends sent clouds of dust billowing into the air. At last we were all together, and only one day's drive from the mountain. There was partying that night and a lot of bad cases of 'malaria' the following morning.

Before the Chinese invasion of Tibet in 1950, Xegar was known as Shekar Dzong, the Shining Glass Fort, on account of its complex of gleaming white monastery buildings and hermit cells that clung like honeycombs to the side of the hill dominating the village. Four hundred monks lived here in those days. On the hilltop was a medieval fortress. All is rubble now. Monasteries and forts have been reduced, not by honourable decay, but in the frightening fervour of the Cultural Revolution.

To the early Everesters Shekar Dzong seemed enchanted, a setting for a fairy story. It is still a magic spot, despite its heartbreaking ruins and the insensitive straggle of concrete blocks that now constitute the main street. Set in a broad valley flanked by raked hillsides, the town clusters around the base of this steep, rocky outcrop which rises like an island from a patchwork of emerald barley fields. An enlarged St Michael's Mount, those first visitors called it. If the great conical hill, a thousand feet high, is no longer 'studded with diamonds glistening in the sunshine', no desecration can rob it of its natural majesty.

This was the first place where our route coincided with that of the pioneer expeditions. In those pre-war days climbers were obliged to approach Everest in a great semicircular loop from Darjeeling, travelling on pony and on foot. The trip took them several weeks, whereas we of the China contingent had been deposited here in two days from Lhasa, two days of hard driving in our ramshackle bus and the expedition jeep.

In 1924 Mallory and his party rested in Shekar for two days, camping in a little walled garden surrounded by willow trees as guests of the Dzongpen, or head man. Here they unpacked their oxygen equipment, which had become badly damaged in transit, and young Andrew Irvine set up a workshop in his tent. Before long, crowds of curious villagers, anxious to see what the young 'Yellow-head' was doing, pressed so tightly round him as almost to block out the light.

With the exuberance of youth (he was only twenty-two), Irvine chased them off with a loudly hissing cylinder of oxygen.

'I've never seen men run so fast,' he laughed afterwards. 'They must have thought it was a devil coming out!' The genie of the flask.

Irvine snipped and soldered, tapped and tightened, eliminating leaks and sweating-in recalcitrant pressure gauges, to come up with what he called his 'Mark V' apparatus. This saved four or five pounds on the issued version, but at nearly 30 lbs in weight the contraption was still an awkward load for a climber to carry. He and Mallory with two of the others spent an hour and a half on their second evening in Shekar testing it out on the steep slopes of the Dzong.

Of their oxygen cylinders, 38 were found to have leaked, despite having been checked and topped up where necessary in Calcutta. With so depleted a supply, and only four or five sets safe enough to use, their ability to take advantage of oxygen on the expedition was already in doubt. Two of the half-empty cylinders were polished up and presented to the Chief Lama in the monastery, for use as gongs of different tones. He, too, was told that each contained a devil so powerful its breath would kindle a spark. To demonstrate the fact, Irvine let out a little of the gas on to some smouldering incense, which immediately burst into flames.

We were staying in what appeared to be an old military compound, a collection of single-storey functional blockhouses that now comprised the Ding Ri County Hotel – or New Tingri Guesthouse (the town these days often being referred to as New Tingri). To ensure that we all knew how to behave, the house rules were posted on a wall by the gate. They concluded: 'Forbid drunken, quarrel, rude action etc. Taken to the police station if anyone did'. We were making a fine collection of these tourist injunctions: the Lhasa Hotel had warned those who did not follow its rules, 'You will be fined 20 yuan and thrown out into the elements', and Chengdu Hotel charged us:

Be polite and graceful. Liproars are not allowed. The guest shouldn't walk out of the room with his upper part naked. It is not allowed to drink wildly in the room. Gambling as well as other dirty games are not allowed. Guns and bullets should be sent to the local arsenal or police station for keeping.

Clearly, no one had high hopes of foreign devils conducting themselves with any propriety.

45

I notice that my diary entries for the five days we spent in Xegar concentrate largely on food. First night: 'Dinner was awful. Haute cuisine obviously not a Tibetan feature, but there are hoopoes nesting under the eaves of the dining block.' Next day: 'Breakfast was dough-balls and rice porridge. Hard to raise much enthusiasm . . . dinner almost identical to last night.' Fifth day (by which time our sherpas and stores were with us): 'Sue and Pemba secure a stove and pan and we fry yak cheese sandwiches and spam for lunch. Bliss after the food we have been getting!'

★

Much of our stay was spent filming, and several times we visited the old Dzong. On the first afternoon, feeling breathless at the altitude of 14,200 feet, I stopped at a ruined red tower halfway up the hill and let the others go ahead. Within a few minutes two small boys appeared, asking for pictures of the Dalai Lama. This is a perennial cry: how I wished I had brought with me bundles of pictures of his Holiness, although I have since learned that only one per person is allowed into the country. The young urchins began clearing rocks to give themselves a flattish surface, then to my surprise began performing traditional songs and dances. They kept good time with each other, and only occasionally would they pause and argue which way a certain movement should be done. The elder of the two, a lad of about six with no front teeth, had a very strong voice and would obviously be a useful member of any folk group in town. All afternoon they danced on, stopping only to share a tube of peppermints I found in the bottom of my bag. It was fine entertainment – all the more special for being impromptu, and just for me. When I was rejoined by Tom Holzel and David Swanson, who had come down the hill ahead of the others, the smallest boy, who I doubt was more than four years old, gravely took me by the hand and guided me back down the steep track.

An easier path to the Dzong avoided the old monastery by following first a dry gully to one side, then traversing around to the back of the hill. Usually you can see Everest from the top, but on the two days I clambered up, the distant views were obscured by sullen cloud. None the less it was a bewitching place, not just because it is so obviously treasured as holy by the local people, who have festooned it with bundles of sticks and prayer flags, but for the beautiful flowers growing near the top: blue and white wild delphiniums and, best of all, the Virgin blue of Himalayan poppies. Lammergeiers circled lazily. Choughs and ravens squealed and croaked.

On the col, just before the scramble to the final fortress, I found an old musket shot, the size of a child's marble, embedded in soft sand. The position was just where you would imagine the limit of range to be for something fired from the top. I wished I could tell precisely how old it was. Ancient firearms would have been used in Tibet until quite recently, and this mediaeval fortress must have defended many a siege before falling to the gunpowder of the Red Guard. I popped the little ball into my pocket, an unusual souvenir. Now, whenever I take it up and roll it in the cup of my hand, I am whisked at once back to that dry Tibetan hillside.

I was suddenly aware of the soft tinkling of many bells as a shepherd with a mixed flock of sheep and goats materialized from the stony scrub. The animals spilled around me and over the edges of the col. They must have been approaching for some time along the crest of the ridge, but were so finely camouflaged among the speckled rocks that I had not noticed them until that moment.

The first travellers allowed into Tibet in the early 1980s after the years of Chinese occupation spoke of packs of wild dogs that roamed the countryside, menacing every village. In deference to tourists, some effort was made to control their numbers, but still almost all Tibetan families own at least one dog, and there are countless more that belong to nobody. Ken Bailey, the youngest member of our team and one of those to come in with the Kathmandu group, covered some of the distance here on a mountain bike. He told us that coming into a strange village was simply terrifying. Dogs would appear from everywhere, barking, snarling and lunging at his feet. He devised a system of peddling very quickly when he saw a settlement coming up, so that he could streak through and raise his legs up out of harm's reach, should it prove necessary.

A motley gang of curs patrolled the Guesthouse compound, led by a huge yellow mastiff with torn ears. They pestered for scraps during the day and kept up an unearthly racket at night, but as long as you kept in with the big fellow, the others were no real trouble. He saw to it that they kept their distance. One trekker we met, driven mad by the nocturnal howling and barking, hit on the idea of tranquillizing the lead dog with a sleeping pill. Certainly, there wasn't so much noise the night he slipped it its mickey finn, but in the morning one of the other dogs was found savaged to death. Without the dominant dog to ward off trouble, scavenging outsiders were able to get into the compound and cause havoc.

★

From Xegar to Everest the trails were too rugged for our bus, and the rest of the journey would be made in old army lorries. Andy took off with the majority of the China contingent on the fourth day, suggesting that Tom and I might like to hang on another night, acclimatizing with those who had arrived from Kathmandu.

'I'll send back a truck for you all tomorrow,' he said.

Nothing came.

I was beginning to despair of ever reaching, or even seeing, this illusory mountain. Towards evening, a passing driver brought in a sack of ice screws he had found on the road. They must have tumbled unnoticed from one of our lorries on its way in. We spent another day in the sun. At least it was never dull here: everyone stops – tour groups, climbing parties. A Danish mother and her teenage daughter were hitch-hiking through China and Tibet, but the girl was suffering badly from altitude sickness. She had been taken into the local hospital for the night and kept on oxygen. The Chinese doctor there is something of a miracle-worker. He came from Shanghai as a postgraduate eleven years ago, never intending to make it more than a short visit, but he has been in Xegar ever since, running the hospital single-handed, treating about sixty patients a day and doing his rounds of scattered homesteads on horseback. He promised to show us round the hospital, but at the last minute decided to run the Danish couple to a police post out of town so that they could be put on a vehicle to Kathmandu. The girl's condition had worsened alarmingly and it was essential she be taken down to a lower level quickly.

In the late afternoon three of us visited the small gompa (temple) recently built among the hillside ruins. A few monks had returned to live there and were supporting a couple of craftsmen working to replace some of the monastery's treasure, all lost in the Cultural Revolution. The gompa's only decorations were some pictures cut from magazines. A silversmith squatted in the dust, putting finishing touches to a large decorated plate. For many years the training of new monks had been forbidden in Tibet, and I was surprised to see a few young boys in the traditional maroon robes of monks scampering about in play. Perhaps at last controls were relaxing.

Despite their hardships, the Tibetans have somehow managed to

keep their religion and their memories alight, but I wondered what
youngsters in places like this knew of the country's former glory?
General Bruce once remarked that 'Forbidden' Tibet ran the risk of
becoming the most documented nation on earth. That was back in the
twenties when Western explorers were vying to reach Lhasa and, with
books and magazines in mind, photographed every street and festival
they encountered on the way. The Everest trips alone brought back
enough Tibetan pictures to fill several filing cabinets in the Royal
Geographical Society. Still there, they are a priceless record of a
vanished way of life – but have Tibetans ever seen them? What testa-
ment do they have to their lost heritage? How I wished I had thought
to put together photo-albums of Old Shekar and the Rongbuk
Monastery to bring as gifts for the people who live there now.

27 August Today, finally, we leave, although not as early as we
hoped. Always on Beijing time, it is dark here for the first two hours
after we get up. There are ridiculous rules about when electricity can
or can't be switched on, so to start with you have to grope around
with torches. Through a doorway, I see one poor lady tourist trying
to apply her false eyelashes by flashlight. She doesn't have enough
hands for the job.

In vain we urged our driver to stop for lunch. With no interpreter
on board, this involved some vigorous sign language. Catch his reluctant attention, rub tummies and roll our eyes, pretend to pop food into
our mouths and lift hands imploringly. If he understood any of this
pantomime, he showed no sign of it. Several times the lorry had
overheated on the steep track coming over the Pang La (the grassy col)
and our man was obviously trying to make up for lost time. We batted
down the hairpins on the other side like a flying pinball. Now he was
flinging the vehicle along the rutted valley bottom towards Chodzong,
bouncing us all from our seats.

When we reached the entrance to the valley leading up to Everest,
the reason for this urgency became clear. He wanted to put the rough
river crossing behind us before stopping. There was no bridge, and the
later we left it, the more meltwater would be unlocked into the
torrent's flow.

The expedition's jeep had come down from Base Camp to meet us.
Its Tibetan driver Kee-Chak sat passively on the far bank, where he
had probably been waiting several hours already, shrewdly reading the
waters so that he could talk us across by the safest passage. Our truck

nosed into the silt-heavy flood. Boulders rumbled under the wheels. Dove grey, icy cold water, four feet deep in places, washed over the running boards. Shouted instructions were almost lost in the tumult of water. At last, safely on the other side, we stopped for lunch. Dough-balls, for once, tasted absolutely delicious – eaten with yak cheese and tinned mandarin oranges.

I jumped into the jeep with Kee-Chak for the last leg of the ride up to Base Camp. Claggy cloud pressed down from the mountaintops on either side of the valley, and by the time we had reached the Rongbuk Monastery, fine drizzle had settled in. We did not linger. There would be time enough to return and explore here later. Early expeditions used to stop close to the monastery but our base was to be four miles further on, right under the snout of the Rongbuk Glacier. Two lines of stones guided vehicles through the rubble of the moraine.

The first view of base, as you rise over the last brow of the approach, is one of utter desolation, a bleached-out moonscape of broken rock and boulders, made the more miserable by this chill mist. Yet it was not inhospitable. Already a small colony of tents had erupted among the stones by the river. Ours clustered in the shelter of an elliptical hill of loose debris, while those of Brummie Stokes and the British expedition stood a short way beyond. A scattering of other tents outside 'city limits' attested to the presence of trekkers and smaller climbing groups.

Chair of Chomolungma

MONSOON CLOUDS HUNG thick and leaden as the jeep slewed into Base Camp. Even as close as this, there was no hint of the mountain, as there had been none from Shekar Dzong on the way in, nor from the top of the Pang La, nor yet from the Rongbuk Monastery. Everest, this 'excrescence from the jaw of the world' – as George Mallory once called it – was playing the coquette.

Friends leapt from their tents in welcome, and we greeted one another extravagantly as if we had been apart for months, not just two days.

David Breashears yelled, 'Audrey, we've got a surprise for you. Shut your eyes and wait here.'

I stood obediently as he dashed behind one of the larger tents. There was a scuffling on the stones, then, 'Okay, you can open them now!' Arms spread – 'Da-daa!' – he proudly displayed a wooden rocking chair. 'Look! We've even remembered the front porch!'

The chair rocked gently on its own small square of flat wood. 'Go on!' he urged. 'Try it!'

Regally, I sat, leaned luxuriously against its high back, curled fingers over the ends of its polished armrests, rocked tentatively back and forward . . . 'It's beautiful,' I whispered. Now I knew what I was expected to do all day: I should have brought my bonnet and parasol.

It was not until late in the evening that the drizzle let up and the clouds split to reveal fragments of gleaming white. Gradually the jigsaw pieces united and there it was – Everest – huge, heavy with snow, blocking the head of the valley.

This valley – home, as it now was – is some two hundred yards wide. Its sides are bounded by terraced banks of lateral moraine, which rise about a thousand feet to buttress steep mountainsides. Dotted round the valley floor are a number of small, more or less conical moraine hills (the one we were camped against more elongated than the rest) and, dividing us from the end of the Main Rongbuk Glacier, a huge transverse moraine cut across the valley like a high wall. The river presents a serious obstacle to further progress on one side for it cannot be crossed easily except when partially frozen over, as it often is early in the morning. The way to the mountain follows the lefthand edge of the glacier (the geographer's 'true' right bank), before bearing left into the East Rongbuk Valley.

Six members of a Chilean student expedition had sought refuge in our Anglo-American Tent City. Their attempt on 'our' route during the monsoon had been abruptly cut short a week before we arrived when their youngest climber, Victor Hugo Trujillo, was killed on the North Col. He stepped into a crevasse not far below the lip. Friends threw him a rope, but as he sought a way out he triggered a massive avalanche that swept him away. With him went the painstakingly laid line of fixed ropes.

The slopes of the col then, as now, were smothered under tons of loose powder snow, poised to collapse at the slightest disturbance. It is the most treacherous spot on the whole mountain, no place for any-one to be, but there is no other practical way to gain the North Col. In 1922 seven porters were lost here when Mallory led them up after a heavy fall of snow. Here, too, in October 1979 three Chinese climbers perished under an avalanche. (They included Wang Hong-bao, the man who had earlier found the body of the 'Dead English' on a high terrace.) The young Chilean's shocked team-mates were still trying to come to terms with their tragedy. Two of the party had gone ahead to relay the news home. The rest were packing up to follow in a few days' time.

★

We had been urged to drink up to six litres of liquid a day, but a day isn't long enough to boil that amount of water for thirty people. We did the best we could, and with many of us taking Diamox for acclimatization, which also has diuretic properties, it kept us on the hop. Four or five times a night we would need to leave the tent.

In the Himalaya, the skies are clearer and the stars brighter than ever I would have believed; the Milky Way slashes a shiny path from one horizon to the other, and the summits shimmer in starlight. When the moon comes up, it really 'doth shine as bright as day', and with a whole campful of expeditioners nipping in and out of tents like players in a Whitehall farce, it became difficult, if not impossible, on such an open site, to find shadows in which to duck out of view.

False decorum is the first thing to disappear on an expedition. Unzipping the tent door in the morning, eyes inevitably light on someone having a slash; or on Tom, determined to keep up standards even here, stripped naked and sousing himself like a herring in a barrel. With no shred of embarrassment, people earnestly discuss the state of their bowels at every meal, and humour quickly sacrifices subtlety to crudity.

★

It took several days at Base Camp before I felt up to much. I went down almost immediately with a chest cough and lost my voice, although not, I think, in response to the altitude. The two British doctors pronounced heart and lungs clean as a whistle: it was far more likely my own bugs having a field day, they said. Still, we were at 17,000 feet and some effects could be directly attributed to the sparsity of oxygen. Every movement was an effort. Lying sleepless and uncomfortable in bed at night, I would think hard before turning over, as it left me panting for so long afterwards. This must be what it's like to have a heart condition.

Sue Duff felt no such lethargy. She was a lone trekker who had hitched a lift in with us and was spending a few days cooking for the halt and maim of Brummie's team. All their fit members, including the chef, were up the mountain toting loads as they had no Sherpa porters. By filling their stoves with washing up fluid, she had got off to a bad start and it was as well she knew how to bake bread. How I envied her energy. Every afternoon she would stride off on sightseeing hikes and come back with wonderful tales of snowcocks and gazelles. Why couldn't I do that?

'Just give it time,' she sympathized. 'Come on, let's go up the moraine bank? That's not far and you get a terrific view of the glacier from there.'

It was less than a hundred yards and still out of my league. It was as much as I could do to drag myself over the little hill to where Tom and Alistair had constructed a magnificent thunderbox. Even visits there had to be rationed. Instead, I read and rested, and set up an 'office' in one of the frame tents. I had brought my portable typewriter, and the expedition had been loaned no less than three computers: two battery-operated laptops and a full-size *pc* which needed a generator to provide it with electricity. I pegged out all my maps and stacked boxes for bookshelves to house the Everest library. A tin trunk doubled as a desk. So like home (when I'd finished), I hardly needed to have travelled halfway round the world for it. At least it provided a refuge for Ronnie Faux, the reporter on Brummie Stokes' expedition, who would come across to write his communiqués for *The Times*.

Gradually I grew fitter, though the cough lingered. Soon I was strolling off by myself for an hour or two each day. My favourite haunt lay up a steep, narrow defile not far from camp, which gave access to the high terraces on the eastern side of the valley. From there you were rewarded with fine views of the tossed seracs of the Rongbuk glaciers and the ragged satellites of Everest. Pride forbad me from showing what a struggle I found it to scramble up there, so I would walk lightly out of camp till I was well hidden from view by the tumbled boulders of the gully, and only then allow myself to double over and strain after painful breath. Why, oh why, hadn't I got myself out to the Himalaya before it was almost too late?

Mornings were mostly warm and sunny, though it would cloud over in the afternoons with perhaps a little sleet or hail, and always a stiff, cold wind. Once the sun dipped low, the temperature plummeted, imprisoning will and limbs. In the five minutes of *Alpenglühen* each evening, when Everest's summit glowed a beautiful apricot against an indigo sky, we would dash outside with cameras, only to scuttle back moments later, all aesthetic sense shrivelled by the fierce cold.

★

Ronnie stood at the door of the office tent. 'The Swiss pair are down,' he said. 'Thought you might like to meet them – do an interview for your column, or something.'

Well, I would! A pity this was the day my voice had disappeared utterly. I smiled and nodded at them like an idiot, Ronnie making a stab at reading my lips and translating what he thought I was trying to say. A congratulatory thimbleful of wine brought back a husky whisper, but as a dialogue it was still embarrassingly inadequate.

Jean Troillet and Erhard Loretan had come to Everest two months before with a small band of friends. Troillet's heart was set on soloing the unclimbed pillar between the Hornbein and the Great Couloirs in the centre of the North Face; Loretan with the Frenchman Pierre Béghin wanted to repeat, more or less, a route climbed in 1980 by

Japanese mountaineers in the Hornbein itself. They placed a camp at the head of the main Rongbuk Glacier, within two hours of the foot of the face, then went off and scaled all the smaller peaks in the area by way of acclimatization.

They had no porters, no oxygen bottles and were not intending to place any high camps; the idea was to climb the mountain in the modern idiom, ultra-lightweight style and moving quickly. For that, they needed to be at peak fitness and conditions on the mountain had to be exactly right.

Plans faltered at the beginning of August when Loretan smashed himself up in a bad landing with his *parapente*. There was a lot of gore and it looked as if his ankle was broken, but some do-it-yourself stitching and a couple of weeks of hopping around on one leg saw him fit once more. The weather was not so accommodating. Messner, who made his astonishing solo climb of Everest at this time of year, declares that there comes a time during the monsoon when the winds from the east and those from the west cancel each other out to give a settled period long enough to climb up and down the mountain. Where was this magic window? It remained changeable almost all that month. Finally, on August 29, two days after I arrived in Base Camp, conditions were bright and clear. The three decided to concentrate on a single route, that of the Japanese in the Hornbein Couloir. They left their Advanced Base on skis in the evening and before midnight were on the face, carrying only a light sleeping bag, stove and some food apiece. All through that night and the following morning they climbed. At 25,600 feet, in deep stable snow, they at last hollowed out a cave and rested up for the afternoon.

Before it grew dark, they were off once more. Béghin found himself too sleepy to carry on and turned back towards the cave where he had left his sleeping bag, but was unable to find it. He slept in the open snow. Fortunately there was no wind that night and he escaped frostbite. The other two continued up the couloir. At Base Camp we had put together a telescope by rigging up a camera on a tripod, and with a very long lens were able to follow their progress. The tiny dots moved perceptibly up the narrow gully all morning. It looked frighteningly steep, head-on like this. The lower part of the face, we knew, had an inclination in places of some sixty degrees; up there, it was probably not quite as much, but steep none the less. None of us could concentrate for long on anything else. We hung round the camera all day.

Soon after lunch, at about 2.30 in the afternoon, we spotted Troillet and Loretan on the summit. Fantastic! We whooped with joy at their success. Incredibly, they had made the climb in less than forty hours.

Wisps of afternoon cloud began blowing over the face, hiding them from view, and two or three hours went by before it cleared once more. Eagerly, we raked the camera up and down the couloir, but they were nowhere to be seen. They should have been well on their way down by now. We looked again.

Nothing. Where on earth could they be?

Oh my God, what were those strange runnel-marks in the couloir? Had they fallen? Had it avalanched? Nagging more and more insistently at the back of our minds was the awful possibility that they had met with an accident.

And then, just before supper, we heard that they were down! Safe. They had glissaded from the top of the mountain back to their advanced base in less than four hours. Snow conditions in the couloir had allowed them to slide on their backs and their bottoms all the way down, using their ice-axes as rudders to control their speed.

Nothing like this had been heard of before. They were not two days away from their base. They had put all the climbing behind them while their impetus was high. It was not a 'prepared' climb; they'd had to break trail all the way up.

Béghin made another attempt that night but was unable to repeat their success. Tired and dehydrated, he kept losing his balance, and wisely withdrew from the face the next morning.

Minutes later, the whole couloir was scoured clean by a massive powder avalanche.

★

Andy had wasted no time in getting our expedition established on the mountain. David Swanson was dispatched up the East Rongbuk Glacier with four sherpas and a train of yaks to set up Advanced Base at 21,000 feet.

Almost inexplicably, Mallory had missed this approach when he first came here in 1921. He failed to appreciate that the fairly insignificant stream which tumbles into the main Rongbuk valley from a narrow gap between the end of Changtse (North Peak) and the high moraine bank on the eastern side of the valley-head was the outlet for one of Everest's huge glaciers. Instead, to get to the eastern side of the North Col he made an enormous detour of forty miles or more to the north and east of Everest, coming up the Kharta Valley and over the Lhakpa La. It was left to the surveyor, Wheeler, towards the end of that expedition, to discover that the little watercourse led to the East Rongbuk Glacier and provided a far more direct way to the North Col. After that it became the regular route to the foot of the mountain, a journey of about twelve or thirteen miles.

For some reason, in the early days, no one believed you could coax yaks above Base Camp, and so the massive movement of stores was undertaken by largely unacclimatized porters – with disastrous results, it has to be said, in 1924. From a base slightly lower than ours, the pioneers required two interim camps before Advanced Base was reached. One is more usual these days; and we placed ours next to that of the British on a windy bend of the glacier below Kellas's Rock Peak. We called it Yak Camp.

When Swanson arrived at the head of the glacier, within sight of the North Col, Brummie's team already occupied the central hollow. He erected our first tents close by, on sloping ground in the shadow of a rocky outcrop, where they should be safe from avalanche. A second yak train followed a few days later. The long process of ferrying up our 6,000 pounds of food and equipment had begun.

On sunny days, this snowy basin was like a furnace. Whether humping loads across to the North-east Ridge, as were the British, or to the foot of the North Col, like ourselves, it was sweltering labour. To David Breashears, Mike Weis and Sherpa Nima Temba fell the task of climbing the Col and investigating a site up there for our Camp III, all the while uncomfortably aware of what had happened to the Chileans in the same spot barely two weeks before. As the best line of ascent on the unstable slope still appeared to be the one they had followed, our three kicked their way upwards, trading leads, and trying to free what was left of the old ropes still buried under feet of snow and ice.

Exertion magnified the effect of the heat, and all attempts at conversation disintegrated into ragged breathing. Before long, the dazzle off the snow and the repetitious movement forced them into shells of their own discomfort, operating individually and on only marginal awareness. Only when they reached the spot where the avalanche had sheared away were they snatched back to reality. A huge white scar defined the fracture line.

'God! Look at that! What a monster! The poor sod never stood a chance.'

'Should we try another way? Can't say I care much for this.'

'There isn't a better way. This will be safe enough if we fix it again. Look, we're almost up, anyway!'

It was true. They were not far below the lip, and now at least a breeze was blowing, making the climbing easier. They decided to press on, replacing the torn Chilean ropes with fresh ones.

By 5 September, forty yak loads had been delivered to Advanced Base Camp and five members had been up to the new Camp III on the North Col, but before Sherpas can be coaxed on to a mountain in earnest, they like to hold a *puja* to get them off on the right foot with the gods. According to their calendar, the first propitious day for this was two days hence, and everyone began trickling back to Base Camp for the grand ceremony of blessing.

*

My role as 'expedition historian' was not clearly defined. I doubt if there had ever been such a creature. All mountains – and none more so than Everest – wear their history in their reputation and their routes, so you could say that in a sense every mountaineer is an historian. In choosing the way he will approach the mountain, he is acknowledging history, at the same time as adding to it.

Mallory, with Guy Bullock, first set foot on Everest in 1921. Since then, several thousand people had climbed on the mountain in the course of 110 expeditions. By 1986 the summit had been reached 209 times; 78 people had died on the mountain's icy slopes. More than 300 books and innumerable articles had been written about climbing the peak, and several films made. How much did I need at my fingertips? I put together a skeleton library that I didn't feel I could manage without – my Linus blanket – paying special regard to George Mallory. I brought copies of many of his letters and other writings, as well as the books that had been written about him. I wanted to see the mountain through his eyes and words. It wasn't much as libraries go, but a great deal in terms of excess baggage – an expedition luxury.

Everest is a constantly renewing time capsule. As time progresses, articles left on the mountain assume the nature of historical artifacts. We deplored the detritus of recent expeditions – the tins and packages that would never rot, and as many as we could we collected and burned or buried – but we danced a jig whenever we came upon pre-war bits and pieces. The first time David and Mike Weis came down from Advanced Base Camp, they rushed eagerly into camp with two barely rusted oxygen cylinders, skinny and rounded at the ends like a couple of salamis.

'Look, hey look!' they called. 'These must be ancient, mustn't they?'

I recognized immediately the distinctive shape of the bottles used by George Finch in 1922, the first time oxygen was seriously employed in high altitude mountaineering. In white paint on the side was stencilled '3 lbs 10 oz' – their weight when charged. Any leakage would have been ascertained merely by weighing.

I could be less certain about a primitive crampon that was brought in later by Mike Yager. It looked old without a doubt, in fact was identical with one in the Alpine Museum in Zermatt said to have been used by Edward Whymper in 1865. But crampons changed very little in Europe over sixty or seventy years and this one could well have been a relic of the 1920s, though very few were brought here then. I didn't know what had been available to the Chinese. Even coming much later to Everest, they may well have only had very old climbing accounts to go on when they began manufacturing mountaineering equipment.

Appreciating an expedition historian as a novelty, people worked hard at keeping me supplied with things to identify. The British, not surprisingly, found the whole business a great joke. Paddy Freaney shot me a line about finding an old pair of Finch's skis at Advanced Base, and Joe Brown sent over a rude potsherd he claimed was Mallory's teapot spout. One obvious source of investigation would be to try to locate remnants of the carved tablets from the memorial cairn put up in 1924 to all those who had died attempting to climb Mount Everest.

It was a substantial monument, 15-foot high, built by Howard Somervell and Bentley Beetham on one of the conical hills near their base camp. The intention was that it should stand for many years 'to greet the next Expedition and tell of the dangers of the mountain', yet when climbers did return after a nine-year gap, it had all but disappeared. Whether pious Tibetans had destroyed it as an erection to false gods, or the stones were pillaged for the construction of herdsmen's shelters, it is impossible to say. It would not have fallen down.

Various expedition books remark upon the discovery of broken pieces of carved stone. The year before we were there Basque mountaineers found one bearing the inscription '1921 KEL'. Dr Kellas had died on the way across Tibet in 1921. In 1982, after diligent searching,

Charlie Clarke turned up the broken headstone which had originally read 'IN MEMORY OF THREE EVEREST EXPEDITIONS', as well as a number of smaller fragments, including one 'MA', part presumably of the plaque to Mallory and Irvine. We had also picked up a rumour that a large part of the Mallory and Irvine tablet now adorned the living room of a Dutch mountaineer. If other pieces had gone home as souvenirs, I was going to be very lucky to find anything at all.

The original Base Camp was easily located from Captain Noel's photographs – a flat, grassy patch among distinctive moraine heaps. Perhaps not the 'meadow' Somervell described, and by no means always green – more often the tussocks are blond and wispy like old hair – it is the most naturally hospitable spot in the upper reaches of the valley, and as such still a popular camping site. Unfortunately this has resulted in it becoming little more than a lofty rubbish heap. I started turning over all the flattish stones on what I took to be the hill of the memorial. All I found was toilet paper – and worse. (Leave never a turd unstoned.) An hour or so of this was more than enough, and I was about to give up when one cracked flagstone did reveal an inscription. Eagerly I dusted it off and traced the letters with my finger.

It bore the name of a climber from a 1984 American expedition – one, moreover, I knew for a fact was not dead. Was this cruel wishful thinking on the part of others of his team?

*

For the puja a small altar was improvised out of packing-crates on one of the moraine mounds in the centre of camp, and an archway of prayer flags strung across the path towards Everest. Juniper wood had been brought in for the fire, and offerings of tsampa, candies, beer and rum were laid out for the gods. Our sirdar, Nawang Yongden, officiated, chanting the requisite prayers as one by one we knelt before him to be blessed, and knotting strands of red silk around our necks for protection.

The formalities completed, we tossed tsampa over each other for luck, and – the gods by now having taken what they wanted – were allowed to consume the ceremonial drink and goodies. Then we linked arms with Sherpas and yakmen to form a huge circle and danced an undulating measure for an hour or more until we dropped. For the occasion, Mary Kay had dressed in her sugar-pink shift and black stockings, offering a vision so startling that it proved altogether too much for the earthy curiosity and wandering hands of our Tibetan friends.

'Asks for all she gets,' our menfolk said with singular lack of sympathy, but let out enraged yelps when the yakmen groped them with the same good-natured randiness. Sauce for the goose was okay, but no goose for the gander . . . that was far too saucy!

★

Brummie Stokes's expedition was to have been an exclusively SAS affair, and as such would have had, I'm sure, more of an element of cloak and dagger about it. A change in Commanding Officer during the planning stage resulted not only in SAS support being withdrawn, but in Brummie's precipitate resignation from the Regiment. He found himself right by his principles though high and dry as an ex-sergeant-major with a pile of expedition kit, a protocol in his pocket, and no team beyond the three who had made the stand with him. For help he turned to one of the few civilian climbers he knew, the Scottish mountain guide Paul Moores, whom he made his deputy. Together they produced a list of names, mostly made up of the climbing heroes of Brummie's youth: Joe Brown, Mo Anthoine, Paul Nunn, Bill Barker, Sam Roberts, Wal Thompson, Clive Rowlands . . . Invitations were issued until there were assembled seventeen well-seasoned members with four hundred years of hard climbing experience between them. The magazines were unkind enough to dub this the Golden Oldies expedition.

Its objective was the long North-east Ridge of Everest, which runs from the Raphiu La to the North-east Shoulder, where it joins the 'Mallory Route' coming up from the North Col. Immediately before this junction is a contorted and extremely exposed section that has come to be known as the Pinnacles. Here, in 1982, two highly respected British climbers − Joe Tasker and Pete Boardman − disappeared while attempting the first crossing. Another British team on the same ridge three years later failed to gain the Pinnacles, but did manage to see a ghost: three members attested to a red windsuited-figure climbing high above them when all in their team were accounted for.

The full ridge extends for more than three miles, with a vertical gain of eight thousand feet, some of this in very steep steps. It is the longest of Everest's formidable ridges and unreasonably treacherous after new snow. Even in those passages where the ridge rises at a relatively gentle angle, the ground underfoot falls away steeply towards the East Rongbuk; on the other side, large fluted cornices overhang the abrupt east face of the mountain. A fine and delicate path must be trodden between them.

To the early climbers this route was known as Finch's Folly. George Ingle Finch and, before him, Harold Raeburn were the only climbers to consider it offered a feasible way to the summit – both, incidentally, supremely fine climbers on ice. Mallory took a hard look and concluded that the 'last section of the (North) East arête should go; but rocks up to the shoulder are uninviting', and in a letter to an alpine friend described this part of the route as 'a very nasty corner', saying he had 'little hopes of it'. It is no less daunting to today's climbers, for supposing you were to successfully negotiate these tricky Pinnacles (three of them) and reach the Shoulder, there would still be a mile ahead of you, and a height-gain of 1,500 feet to make along a ridge already notorious for its difficult 'First' and 'Second' steps.

Advanced Base had to be situated well clear of the avalanches that thunder down from the North-east Ridge and the North Col. It meant that the British team had a mile-long trek across crevassed glacier to get to the start of their ridge, even though they cut two sides off a triangle by gaining the ridge via a previously unclimbed rock spur. This became known as Bill's Buttress when Bill Barker, in 1986, did most of the leading on it. The task fell to him as the only one of a four-man forward party sent to establish Interim and Advanced Base Camps to arrive with full climbing gear. A hiccup in logistics not only robbed the rest of axes and altitude boots, but saw to it that for a week they had no cooking pots, no cutlery beyond a dessert spoon Joe Brown found in his rucksack pocket and, worst of all, no teabags. None the less they could boast two umbrellas and 190 packets of pear drops.

After three weeks on the mountain, most of the British climbers came down for a rest and a beano. For a couple of nights there were alarming sights of inert bodies being dragged across stones and stuffed into tents, but once the 'low-altitude headaches' had cleared, members all trooped back up the hill, refreshed.

From a distance, it was always possible to tell an American from a Britisher on the path ahead of you. The Americans – men and women – had a curious habit of wearing their shorts over coloured tights, like Batman, whereas Brummie's gang were dressed identically in baggy navy babygrows. And of course there weren't any women with them

— apart, that is, from Rongbuk Rosie. Naked as the day she left the plastics factory, this grotesque inflatable had been brought along to chivvy drooping aspirations. Ronnie Faux has already committed her unique qualities to history:

> Her blonde curls had the texture of valve springs, heavily made-up eyes opened and shut in contrived ecstasy, scarlet lips were permanently agape. Parts of her were meticulously fashioned, other bits more carelessly shaped – hands and feet, for example, had the clumsy look of third degree frostbite before the black sets in. When the sun shone Rosie expanded to the size of some hideous Bavarian bierkeller wench with Falstaffian arms and legs and a straining mainsail of a bosom. On frosty nights she became anorexic; pink, plastic flesh sagging emptily, with wrinkles appearing where no human wrinkle ever ventured . . .

The Sherpas had never seen anything like it, and sought to outbid each other to buy her when the expedition was over.

Women – of the uninflatable kind – were part of the world traditional British climbers left at home, expeditions for them being in a sense an elaborate form of escapism, a going out to play. Our climbing women were regarded by our neighbours with curiosity and a degree of reserve that Mary Kay worked hard to dispel.

'Hey!' she would hail cheerily, falling into step beside a Golden Oldie puffing his way to Advanced Base. 'You look tired. Here, let me carry your pack for you.'

'We'll stop letting you come with us unless you make it look harder,' Mo had scolded her once.

'No, no!' she replied quickly. 'I was dying – really, I was dying!'

★

At the beginning of September, to augment our diet, we had bought a yak for slaughter. Its grisly, butchered head still lolled around Base Camp wearing an affronted expression. The first day we had liver for lunch; and the next day liver for lunch; and by the third day couldn't help wondering how much liver a bloody yak had. Then it was time to start on other bits. It was very bad timing, therefore, soon after we had at last eaten our way through it, to have a young animal in our baggage train fall into a crevasse just outside Advanced Camp.

Slabs of rock had been laid across a slight snow-lined dip in the

63

moraine to enable the yaks to negotiate it more easily, but for some reason one animal took it in his head to ignore this path and, instead, make a beeline across the unblemished snow of the hollow. Looking at the hole he left, it was hard to believe it had been big enough to swallow a yak, even a small one – and indeed, looking at the meagre patch of snow, surrounded as it was by rocks, impossible to imagine that a hole so deep could have been lurking anywhere under there at all.

The unfortunate beast wedged in a slot, suspended by its load. With a rope thrown round its horns it could probably have been dragged clear, but the yakmen – worried for the load – decided to cut that free first, and in so doing committed the yak to the deep. It fell another twenty-five feet before coming to rest again, and there it jammed solid. It must by then surely have been dead, which was some comfort, for it would have been impossible to extricate in one piece.

We were, of course, obliged to reimburse the yak-herder for his loss, and for the saddle and saddle bags and blankets that also went down the hole – so he said – with the poor creature. Altogether it proved a very expensive unbudgeted item, and after some days, the profligacy of leaving so much valuable meat untouched down there really preyed on us. Folk were kicking their heels, waiting for the latest blizzard-snow to consolidate before they could go high again; what better way to fill in time than to launch a salvage mission? A joint effort was arranged between British and American climbers, and the booty would be shared.

Some initial butchering would be necessary inside the hole, that much was clear, even though the crevasse was only two feet wide and there was scant room for manoeuvre down there. Moreover, the yak wasn't at the bottom: the chasm continued beyond it, nobody knew how far. It would be a tricky operation, no doubt about that.

A metal belay stake was hammered into the ice beside the hole and Joe Brown lowered tentatively inside.

'How good is that belay?' Mary Kay wanted to know.

'Wouldn't trust it myself,' said Mo, 'but it's good enough for Joe.'

'What was that?' came a muffled shout from the hole.

'Nothing, Joe. I've got you.' Mo smiled evilly, 'Nearly.'

The yak was upside down. It must have plunged in head-first. Joe struggled for an hour, getting colder and colder, and coming up eventually with little to show for his pains but the naughty bit, which he brandished aloft triumphantly.

Lhasa's Potala Palace, built by the Fifth Dalai Lama in the seventeenth century, seen through the prayer flags on Chokpori Hill in August 1986

The meat market in Lhasa

Impromptu Tibetan dance at the old Dzong, Shekar

View of Xegar (Shekar) from the ruins of the hilltop fort

The classic North Face view of Everest from the Rongbuk Valley at sunset

Puja ceremony. Mary Kay Brewster excites Tibetan curiosity (left), Sue
Giller receiving blessing (right), and all the team throwing tsampa for luck

Life at Everest Base
Camp. Seated among
the moraines – Ken
Bailey, Audrey
Salkeld and Roger
Vernon; Catherine
Cullinane trying out
the rocking chair; and
Catherine Freer being
interviewed for the
film by Donna de
Varona

Mike Yager had a go. He scrabbled away at the walls before hitting on the idea of puncturing the yak to let out some of the accumulated gas. That enabled him to fiddle a rope round the cadaver in the tight squeeze.

After four hours the mutilated carcass was dragged clear of the hole. Now it was the turn of the British cook, Pat Green, to butcher it with no more tools than a bread knife and a snow saw. Two more hours and it was reduced to manageable chunks of meat which were distributed between the two teams. Joe claims he ate six fillet steaks that night. I grimaced at the thought of more yak curry and reckoned to go vegetarian for a bit.

It is said that the air in Tibet is so dry and cold that meat will keep without going rotten for over three years, and grain for five hundred – maybe even five thousand, if anyone was to put it to the test.

Two 'support treks' had been organized to help raise funds for our expedition, and the first group arrived in camp with Jed Williamson, a close friend of Andy's. He was quickly persuaded to 'abandon' his charges and stay on with us. We needed all the climbers we could get. Al Read could deliver the trekkers back to Kathmandu when he went out to buy stores and escort our sick kitchen boy to hospital. Every night since we first arrived Arjun, a Tamang, had been running an alarming fever. It failed to respond to any antibiotic or febrifuge in the British medical arsenal. 'A clear case of demonic possession, that's why,' declared Mike Yager, who'd lived a long time in Nepal, but conventional wisdom in Kathmandu, backed up by laboratory tests, later plumped for typhoid.

The senior of the two doctors with the British team was Philip Horniblow, who also doubled as Base Camp Manager. He was a radiologist, although his fame in climbing circles rested upon a successful, if messy, operation, performed some years before at 23,000 feet on Everest, on a Gurkha soldier with a bad case of haemorrhoids. His colleague, John English, a young London dermatologist, was able to make a medical name for himself after this expedition by describing a previously unknown species of high altitude wart.

★

My diary records September 19 as a day of heavy traffic. At midday George Bell and Donna de Varona arrived to work on the film about our women climbers, closely followed into camp by the lorries of the Air-Over-Everest Expedition – fourteen climbers, hang-glider pilots and film crew, with eleven Sherpas. They settled in across the moraine to work on the West Ridge. Unfortunately for their plans, the authorities refused to allow their three aircraft on train or plane from Beijing, insisting they follow by truck. Now, who knew how far behind they were?

Hitching a ride in with the Air-team were Dave Cheesmond and Catherine Freer, fresh from an American expedition to the north side of K2, where they had safely weathered the storms which caused the deaths of Al Rouse, Julie Tullis and the others. 'Cheese' was immediately welcomed on to our expedition and, fully acclimatized, went straight up to assist David Breashears with high-level filming. Catherine, who also hoped to join us, was told to wait: the matter needed careful consideration.

In a sense, this was odd, for at the time most people agreed that Freer was America's best female Himalayan climber. She had a reputation for great toughness and also came perfectly acclimatized. If it was really important to 'put' a woman on top of Everest, there could have been no likelier candidate. Not that the concept was one with which she herself felt comfortable. If there was any 'putting' to be done, Freer was emphatic: she would rather be one of the putters than the put.

For days the issue was discussed in secret huddles. Sensing that the difficulty arose because she was so good, was seen perhaps as a threat by the other women, Freer said, 'Look you guys, I don't want to be in the film. I won't interfere with anything you've planned. Let me be part of the camera team. You can edit me out of all the footage.'

It was not clear to me how much the threat argument held good; Giller and Freer were the best of friends, and would have liked nothing better than to have been on an expedition together from the outset. Still, there was prickliness over the whole women issue due to the artificial nature in which it was being played, and in the end, the opportunity slipped by. Freer joined the Air-Over-Everest West Ridge team, but she shared most of her Base Camp time with us.

★

Donna de Varona is an American sports TV-presenter, an ex-Olympic swimmer, who had been engaged as 'on-camera host' to introduce the ABC-film. She and George Bell were to spend a couple of weeks with us. They brought in little luxuries they thought we might be missing – the latest magazines, chocolate peanut butter cups and a supply of toothpicks. George carried mail, too, from the States, but nothing, sadly, for me. Life has its compensations, however. A few nights before, when we were sitting in the mess tent over supper, a grubby hand had been thrust through the door-flaps bearing a picture post-card. It was addressed: *Audrey Salkeld, Base Camp, Rongbuk, Tibet* and was from my student son, Adam, who was touring Southern India. I had no idea where the nearest post office was, nor who in this part of Tibet could read English, but a yak herder had volunteered to bring the card for the last part of its journey up the long Rongbuk Valley. Delivered right into my hands – that was some service!

Other unexpected visitors wandered in and out of camp. The American Ambassador to Nepal had his photograph taken sitting in my rocking chair, with Everest behind, for the ambassadorial Christmas card. One afternoon I recognized among a group of trekkers coming up the valley a British climbing doctor, Peter Steele, who now lives in Canada.

'I've heard *all* about your expedition,' he told me primly when I hailed him. 'Where are the British? Which are their tents?'

He clearly believed all the stories that were bandied around about us and did not want to be seen fraternizing with body-snatchers! Let him get his cup of tea from the others then – if he could find anyone at home. Sue Duff had now left and almost all Brummie's climbers were up the mountain.

Hospitality had begun to wear a little thin in all the camps, except when it came to visiting between ourselves. So many of the 'trekkies' who came up here expected us to be on display, like some sort of heritage museum. They poked around the tents and equipment without invitation to see for themselves how we lived. We could as well have been dressed dummies. 'Hey, take a look in this one,' they would sing, unzipping my office tent. 'There's a woman in here typing!' And then they expected refreshments to end their tour. Two came up with hepatitis but received little sympathy from the British doctors; the last thing they needed up here was an epidemic. Still, there were exceptions to everything. One beautiful female cyclist, by name Veronique, having biked in from Chengdu with two companions, was a welcome guest for several days, causing absolute havoc among our menfolk. So much washing and shaving suddenly!

To our dismay, there were a number of thefts from tents. Even a tent went missing. Solo-climber, Roger Marshall, who was camped close by, had a large amount of money stolen when he was up the mountain, and one day two Danish travellers, who were taking a closer look at Everest, came back to find their tent, too, had vanished. John Roskelly, who was leading the second of our supporting treks, had seen a couple of people taking it down earlier. Just as it got dark, he, David and Al Read formed a posse and went down the valley with Kee-Chak, the jeep driver, 'to get those guys'.

They swaggered back into camp an hour or so later, David with his right fist all taped up, boasting that they had overpowered the culprits after a fierce scuffle.

'We've got them tied up in the Rongbuk Monastery,' David said, 'waiting to be accompanied back to Shekar later this evening by the Chinese liaison officer. Kee-Chak was marvellous, he pinned them down for us with a flying tackle.'

Not only did we swallow this implausible story, but we rewarded 'our heroes' with one of the precious bottles of wine we had been saving for special occasions – and the rogues had the gall to polish off the lot by themselves! Alistair rushed outside to congratulate Kee-Chak.

'Jolly good job you did there,' he told the astonished man, thumping him on the back and, ignoring the blank expressions all round, pushing him and the Sherpas into the cook tent. 'See this guy gets well rewarded for his night's work,' he said. The conspirators could bear our gullibility no longer.

'Nothing was stolen,' they hooted. 'It was all a big misunderstanding. The people who removed the tent were friends of the Danes. They'd left a note to say what they were doing, only it blew away.'

'But your hand, David?'

'Camera tape! Did you really believe all that malarkey? We never thought we'd take you in!'

Very droll. Never mind, our reprisal came later. The next time David was high on the mountain, we radioed up that Veronique had returned unexpectedly, and was asking for him. He was all set to come hurtling down – all climbing forgotten – before he rumbled us. Still, the fact remained, someone on this moraine had eyes wide open enough to take things when no-one was looking. Yak herders were known for their deep pockets, but usually they only went for articles left outside tents for which they could see an immediate use, like water-bottles (they went for mine) or old boots. I think probably my woolly muffler shared the same fate. One of the Chinese drivers was caught with a stash of expedition gear in the back of his van when he was driving out to Lhasa. With all the interpreters, liaison officers and drivers to the various expeditions, we had a sizeable Chinese community at Base Camp, and now, sadly, all were viewed with a certain suspicion.

★

Ed Webster came to Everest as photographer to the solo mountaineer Roger Marshall. He'd had to guarantee that he would make no attempt of his own on Everest. He could have a crack at whatever else took his fancy, Roger said, so long as he didn't go and get himself killed. He was needed to take the triumphal pictures if Roger's own climb was successful.

While Roger was resting down at base during a short weather clearance in August, Ed decided to tackle the East Face of Changtse, Everest's satellite North Peak. He was turned back by steep loose ground thirty feet below the final ridge, but the next day tried again. This time, taking a more direct line before traversing on to the ridge, he made it, and after eleven hours of climbing stood alone on the 24,780-foot summit, watching the sun rise over the Himalaya. From his feet, the slender elegant ridge swept down to the North Col, then up again, linking him with the North and Northeast Ridges of Everest. Earth's highest pinnacle was caught in the first splash of sunlight. All around in the icy stillness rose other mountain giants – Cho Oyu, Kangchenjunga, Jannu, Nuptse, Pumori. 'It was the greatest day of my life,' Ed said afterwards. 'Like going to heaven and visiting with the angels for a day.'

His climb, a first ascent, brought no congratulations from Roger Marshall when, weary after sixteen energetic hours, Ed finally clattered into Base Camp. Roger was angry with himself for having passed up one of the rare weather lulls. As the season progressed, and Roger's ambitions were repeatedly frustrated, he grew noticeably morose and more withdrawn. In an attempt to follow the same line as the Swiss in the Hornbein Couloir, he strayed off route and was forced to give up, exhausted. Coming down then to find his money stolen was the final, bitter blow. With nothing to show for more than eighty days on the mountain, glumly he packed for home.

★

One night, when Sue was up the mountain and I alone in our Base Camp tent, I woke to hear a strange wailing coming – it seemed – from high up the gully of bullseye rock behind the Air-Over-Everest camp. I call it a wailing, but that doesn't quite fit. Certainly it wasn't a roar, or a bellow, but a sound somewhere between those and a howling – a banshee noise. The idea of a dog or a wolf flashed through my mind to be quickly dismissed. This was a cry I had never heard before.

Of course it couldn't be a yeti. I told myself that sternly, though I had to admit it would be poetic justice if it were. Only a few months before I had been unwise enough to cast doubt on the validity of what is perhaps the firmest of all 'evidence' that exists in favour of the Abominable Snowman – Shipton's famous footprint photograph. A spoof, I said. Shipton was always something of a joker, I said. Well, I couldn't dismiss this sound so easily. What on earth was it? Would a snow leopard make a noise like that? Alistair claimed to have seen large pug marks in the sand by the river one night, and we had all laughed, thinking it was Mao-tei, the Chinese firewater talking. But . . . perhaps he was right? Of course this couldn't be a yeti. Could it?

'Record it,' I told myself, and fumbled for the switch on my tape recorder.

There was little to hear above the crackle when I played it back next morning. I hadn't been brave enough to step outside the tent to make the recording, or even to open the flap!

When Mallory climbed the Lhakpa La in 1921, he and his party were astonished to see giant footprints in the snow. His porters immediately identified them as those of *metoh-kangmi*, the Abominable Snowman. The Lhakpa La was not ten miles from Base Camp as the crow flies, but the creature has been reported even closer than that. In 1935 when the young Tenzing was here on his first Everest expedition, his father trekked over from Nepal to see him, across the Nangpa La. He had to spend a night alone at Camp 1 as Tenzing was up the mountain, and in the morning, when it was just starting to get light, he was wakened by a whistling sound outside the tent. Raising the flap a fraction, he was able to make out a creature coming down the glacier towards him. He knew it for a yeti, for he had encountered one before on the Barun Glacier. He'd been so close to it that time he'd been ill for a year afterwards and lucky not to die. He didn't want the same to happen again and he hardly dared breathe until the creature passed on down the glacier out of sight. In 1959, when a Russian scientific expedition was vainly hunting yetis in the Pamirs, a report broke in the newspapers suggesting they could be looking in the wrong place. According to Tibetan porters, a Russian mountaineer had been killed

70

and devoured by a yeti on Mount Everest that spring. The porters heard the man calling for help, as well as cries of the yeti, but were so terrified they ran away. It is a well-known fact throughout the Himalaya that small yetis (or *meh-teh*) feed on men, in contrast to their bigger cousins (*dsu-teh*) who prefer a diet of yaks.

★

Two hang-gliders in their long travelling cigar tubes were finally delivered to our friends across the valley, the third having fallen off the back of the lorry. Luckily Tibetans have yet to discover a use for such contraptions and it was still lying at the side of the road when the driver went back a few days later. Steve McKinney, the Air-Over-Everest leader, could not wait to get a test-flight off the ground.

The kites were hauled to the top terrace of the moraine bank behind camp and erected. Poised, two pilots and their cameraman shivered away up there all morning as the wind, which had blown so assiduously ever since we had been here, began playing frivolous games. At last, in the middle of the afternoon, with the windsock pointing firmly down-valley – McKinney jumped.

Immediately the sock collapsed again limply.

He fell like a stone, recovered slightly, then, coming in to land, lost the last whisper of breeze and smashed nose-first into the ground. His forward impetus meant the crash juddered on, smashing plane and McKinney repeatedly into the boulders before grinding to a crumpled halt.

'He's *beaked*!' they shouted, those who knew the jargon.

There was a long and ominous pause before the fallen Icarus showed sign of movement, by which time we had our cameras rolling and were dashing across to interview the poor sucker.

McKinney was no stranger to spectacular smashes. As the world's fastest man on skis, the father of speed skiing, he made something of a hobby of them. Fortunately for him, he had been wearing his customized, wind-piercing ski helmet this time. It lay misshapenly beside the wreckage, but McKinney himself had come away with only superficial bruises and cuts. He would need better luck if he was to launch himself from the West Ridge later in the trip. There had been a lot of talk of finding a thermal to lift him right over the summit of Everest, but as he sat there, dazed, among the stones, all interest in such a scheme had for the moment waned.

★

Before I came on this expedition, I used to try to picture how I would fill my days when the others were up the mountain. I fancied I might persuade our interpreter to give me Chinese lessons, if he was stranded in Base Camp, too. Fat chance of that! We rarely caught sight of any of our Chinese friends, for – good or bad weather – they squirrelled themselves away the whole time inside one of their tents. 'Don't ask me what they get up to in there!' Philip would snort with affected disgust as the zip snapped shut behind them.

I need not have worried, anyway: there was no shortage of jobs to be done, even if the Sherpas took care of all the cooking. I scarcely completed any of the crosswords I had snipped from *The Times* in case days hung heavily. And throughout the whole trip, there was only one afternoon when all the climbers were out of camp together. That left just me and Base Camp Manager Al Read sitting outside Andy's tent like Darby and Joan in our camp chairs, muffled against the sharp wind. In an hour and a half we had exhausted all we could think of to say, and were glad to see Ken Bailey stumbling back across the glacier waste to join us. More often, there were at least half a dozen of us down there, and Philip Horniblow, the doctor from 'next door', who used to join us for supper each evening, suitably attired in tweed jacket and cravat. Mary Kay had secured for the expedition a selection of gourmet meals and fine Californian wine. Sipping smooth malt whisky after one of these feasts, I would reflect fondly on the delights of the open air life.

For the benefit of Donna and the support trekkers, a 'shower' was rigged up in one of the tents, though there was always a queue to use it. Tom continued to favour his barrel, and Mary Kay would disappear down-river to a pool that she knew. If you wandered that way you would see her perched like a Lorelei on a sunny rock, combing out her golden tresses.

Above a Fortified Wall

I woke one day in the third week of September to see an enormous streamer of snow blowing from the top of the mountain. The jet-streams were dipping lower. Spirits soared. Surely this heralded the end of the monsoon. At last the weather pattern should settle and winds clear away much of the hampering snow. Already a few rockbands were appearing where previously all had been white. Steve Shea and two Sherpas spent a night on the North Col, ready to climb higher the next day and, as they hoped, to establish Camp V at 25,500 feet. We could expect to see real progress over the coming weeks.

It was a false dawn: another bad storm hit us on the night of the 28th, pinning Sue and Jed on the North Col, unable to move up or down, and every few hours having to shovel their tent clear of the fast-building snow. Almost everyone else – from all the expeditions – retreated down to base once more, where a belated party was being held in the British camp to mark Joe Brown's fifty-sixth birthday.

We tripped across the moraine with cake and candles, balloons and good wishes to share a night of whisky and crude humour. It put the Americans in touch with their sourdough past. Just like an old mining camp, they rhapsodized still full of it next morning, and spent the rest of the day trying to remember words to all the songs they'd heard. Halfway through supper, Al Read grabbed me excitedly and burst out, 'Twinkle, twinkle little rectum. Great things happen when you least expectum.' Try as he might, the other verses eluded him.

On the first day of October we rose early to wave goodbye to George and Donna. With them went 'Boy Jhao' and our head cook, Nima Tenzing, down to Khasa on the Nepalese border to buy supplies. It left all base camps without the emergency vehicles upon which Chinese authorities place so much insistence (and so great a fee). The British jeep, with the team's liaison officer and interpreter aboard, had taken off for a joy ride in the middle of the night two weeks before and not been seen since. It went to Lhasa for the moon festival and ran off the road on the way back. One Chinese eventually returned, heavily bandaged; the other still languished in hospital. It was said that they spent three days in a roadside ditch before any Tibetans could be persuaded to come to their aid. The Air-Over-Everesters had never had a jeep of their own, and were now at peak vulnerability, with members poised to jump with their hang-gliders from the West Ridge. There would be little any of us could do to help in an emergency. They were even between doctors since one, injured in an avalanche a short while before, had hitched a lift out on our jeep, and it was a week or more before his replacement could be expected in.

Once people started up the mountain again, I began to get fidgety, worried lest I should never be allowed to go higher. George Bell had kept me occupied most afternoons that he was here writing bulletins for the *Los Angeles Times*, so that I hadn't even been able to keep up my training walks. For several days I had not been out of Base Camp at all. Some weeks earlier, in anticipation of going up one day, I had put my altitude boots on a yak train, only to have Jed take them off again.

'No chance of you needing those,' he'd said. (Damn his officiousness!) When Donna set off towards Advanced Base for some filming, that seemed an ideal opportunity for me to go at least part of the way up with her. Andy would not hear of it.

'There'd be nobody to bring you down if there was any trouble,' he said. Same old story. He still thought I was going to snuff it at the slightest opportunity.

Weeks were slipping away. The little plants in the rocks and crevices were beginning to turn yellow and red. Summer was almost over and soon we could expect it to get very much colder. From the position of having days stretching ahead indefinitely, for the first time I began to wonder if this expedition would achieve anything at all. Our high camps were a long way from being properly stocked, and we couldn't blame it all on the weather: we had been so busy seeing to it that our 'support trekkers' went up the glacier if they wanted to, and with our filming – always a tediously protracted and time-wasting business. It was clear that we now needed to crank into much higher gear, but still the weather would not respond. Storm after storm rolled in, dumping new snow on the mountain. Each morning at Base Camp we woke to a sharp frost or ephemeral sprinkling of snow.

★

74

One afternoon Tom and I walked down to Rongbuk. He had the idea that monks in the old days might have kept some sort of 'monastery log', or daybook, which, if it still existed, could perhaps contain mention of the round-eyed foreigners who marched up the valley to climb the Goddess Mother in the Wood Mouse Year. The old Lama of Rongbuk was a great favourite of all the pre-war expeditions; they used to come to be blessed, and he clearly enjoyed these encounters as much as they. If the day-to-day business were recorded somewhere, how fascinating it would be to find out what Tibetans made of the deaths of Mallory and Irvine and the others. Of course it was a long shot, we knew that, but we had seen a library of old manuscripts in the 'chapel' and were curious to know what they were. We took Nima Tenzing and the Tibetan kitchen boy, Tsintin, as interpreters, but luck was against us. The incumbent lama was away and nobody at the monastery knew anything at all about old papers. That was an end to it.

Tom wandered off to photograph among the ruins and the rest of us were invited to take tea and tsampa with an old Tibetan nun. She led us into a low, cramped hovel, lit only by a six-inch-square, glassless window and a small smokehole in the roof. In the gloom, I was able to make out a cubicle no larger than five foot by seven. Beyond a single shelf on the wall, it was entirely plain: no furniture. We knelt on the beaten earth floor, and 'tea', when it came, was gritty and sooty, with a buttery scum on top, unlike anything I'd had before. The dry ground barley, too – proffered in a little leather draw-string pouch – had a taste you would need to acquire. I fixed a smile and swallowed it down, trying not to choke. All the same, I wanted to shout with joy and excitement. This was the first time I had been inside a Tibetan house, and the first time I had stepped outside the bubble of familiarity we, as tourists, carry along with us, even here. I had never thought to experience the privilege of real contact with local people – maybe this too was indirect, but it was in part real. And I might as well have stepped into a mediaeval world. Once, all the cottagers of England would have lived like this.

The old woman was pleased to have outsiders to talk to, so few people lived at Rongbuk now. Poor ruined Rongbuk, which was once one of the most important religious establishments in the land, a jewel among jewels. The nun and young Tsintin exchanged gossip nineteen to the dozen. After a while she brought out a dried leg of goat, hoping to persuade Nima to buy it. From the look of it, she'd had it hanging up for years. Selfishly, I was glad when I realized he had Sherpa rations in mind and not ours. Good-natured bargaining went on for some time before a deal was struck and the gruesome relic stuffed into Nima's canvas bag just as Tom burst in through the doorway.

'Come on!' he commanded in that brisk, mood-shattering way he has. 'Time to go!'

The Sherpas knew a high-level route back up-valley, which took us through the old village. Normally, keeping to the valley floor, you gain no impression that there were once so many buildings here. Several hundred houses lay in ruins. Little more than their outlines remained on either side of the track, and acres of strewn rubble. Rumour has it that the Red Guards were able to enflame young Tibetans to do much of their destructive work, filling them with a demonic passion to erase old Tibet. It is hard to believe now, when the young are at the forefront of a renewed will to expel Chinese occupiers from their country.

You can see how idyllic it must have been, why for centuries Rongbuk was renowned as conducive to the highest transcendental enlightenment. More than four hundred monks used to come here for religious teaching and spiritual refreshment. Hermits and anchorites immured themselves in caves and stone shelters in the surrounding hills. Captain Noel has told of a reputed saint here in the 1920s who for fifteen years remained sealed in almost total darkness in a rock cell below Everest. Year after year, he squatted motionless, meditating. Fellow monks brought bread and water once a day, which they passed to him through a hole in the wall. One evening, while watching, Captain Noel saw a hand come out to take the meagre rations. It was muffled. Not even sunlight was allowed to touch the holy man's skin.

From here, the oblique view up the valley towards Everest was one of the finest I had seen, especially in late afternoon light, like this. It gave, for once, a vertical, rather than a horizontal picture of the great mountain at the end of its funnelled valley. I fired off half a film before Tom asked to borrow the camera to check his own exposures.

'I don't think you're winding on properly,' he said, opening it up to take a look. I always meant to go back and take the photographs again, but somehow never did.

We scrambled above the nunnery ruins to some abandoned buildings. Was this where Captain Noel's hermit lived, or were they herdsmen's shelters? Inside one we found a hearth and old pots and dishes, as if the occupants had left in a hurry. Higher up the cliff, we could make out more buildings and chortens, but already it was getting late – and cold. We strode back to camp in gathering darkness, a bitter wind pecking at our faces.

★

On one of my walks along the high medial moraine, I came upon a long wooden pole with wire stays attached to it. I took it for a survey marker, probably Chinese, since Chinese scientists have swarmed all over these hills in the course of climbing and exploratory expeditions.

The Chinese were late arrivals on the world mountaineering scene, probably inspired by the famous ascent of Everest from Nepal by Hillary and Tenzing in 1953. Already in occupation of Tibet, the People's Government was not slow to promote the policy of making, as they said, mountaineering serve economic construction, national defence and high-altitude scientific investigation. The Chinese Mountaineering Association was established and soon claimed ascents of Muztagh Ata and Kongur Tiube, which convinced the new mountaineers they were ready for their own attempt on Everest. Premier Chou En-lai gave his personal approval and instructed that a road be built to the base of Mount Everest in order to facilitate the approach. But Chou also let it be known that if they made the attempt, they were expected to succeed. Convoys of lorries began rolling in to Base Camp on 19 March, 1960, when the party was said to comprise:

> 214 men and women, one-third of them being of Tibetan nationality. Among these were workers, peasants, P.L.A. men, serfs who had just been freed from serfdom in Tibet, teachers, students, scientific researchers, medical workers and government functionaries from various parts of the country. In the expedition, there were seventeen Masters of Sports, eighteen First Grade Sportsmen and a greater number of Second Grade Sportsmen. The whole group averaged 24 years of age.

Prime-ministerial intervention, new roads, a team of 214? By any reckoning, that is great indulgence for a mountaineering venture – even one to the Roof of the World. National honour has a high price, but would all this effort have been put into an enterprise without a darker objective? It is worth remembering the strategic frontier position occupied by Mount Everest and the developing political scene.

The Dalai Lama's flight to India and the Lhasa Uprising took place in 1959, the year Chou gave his blessing to the mountaineers. China and Nepal were squabbling over the ownership of Everest's summit, and within Sikkim, Bhutan, Ladakh, and even parts of Nepal, apprehension was growing over which of them would be next in line for Chinese 'liberation'. Rumours told of massed troops at various points along the Himalayan borders.

After their defeat in Lhasa, Khampa rebels regrouped in Tsang, the province immediately to the north of Everest. They entrenched themselves in Tingri and Shekar, where their numbers were constantly augmented by Tibetans coming back over the Himalaya from India via Sikkim and Nepal. The area was the scene of intense fighting towards the end of 1959 and early in 1960, particularly during the midwinter months when small detachments of Khampas attacked Chinese garrisons. The Khampa advance was greeted by outbreaks of defiance in the monasteries, too, which were well aware they were under sentence of extinction. According to Michel Peissel in *Cavaliers of Kham*, Rongbuk, 'already the scene of considerable violence in August 1959, took up arms once more, while to the north a bloody battle took place between the Khampas and the Chinese at Tingri'. Although little was heard of this in the West, the ascent of Everest from the north by three men in May 1960 found its way on to front pages around the world. That one of them was Tibetan was remarked on as potent proof of cooperation between the Chinese and Tibetans.

Yet this was a time when refugees from Tibet were pouring into India in ever-increasing numbers. Hugh Richardson was first to speak to some who had trekked there from the villages between Shigatse and Mount Everest. They told him that teams of Chinese officials had begun arriving in their area in August or September 1959, and had immediately appointed councils from among people with no land of their own. The purpose of these was to arrest, denounce and assault the yeomen farmers, to imprison them and confiscate their land, livestock and jewellery. Lamas and senior monks were subjected to similar treatment, with gangs of professional bandits brought in by the Chinese to reinforce the accusers. In *Tibet and its History* Richardson remarked that a far greater number tried to escape than ever succeeded.

Intent on transforming Tibet into an impregnable fortress, the Chinese were said to have deployed half their occupying troops along the Himalayan border. It even became known to Tibetan fugitives as 'Mao's Underground Great Wall'. When resistance reached a new peak in the spring of 1965, Peissel reported bitter and prolonged fighting in the Tingri-Shekar region, where the Chinese were 'once again obliged to use their air force in massive bombing raids'. By August, the Khampas were claiming between fifty and eighty thousand men under arms inside Tibet.

The following year the country was swept by the undisciplined fervour of the Red Guard movement. Cultural revolutionaries openly attacked the Chinese Liberation Army, at the same time plundering temples and monasteries and committing fearful civilian atrocities. For two years chaos and terror reigned on two fronts, with the Khampas exploiting the situation. It might seem an odd time to launch a mountain expedition, but between 1966 and 1968, the peak years of the Cultural Revolution, the Chinese undertook the 'Mount Jolmo Lungma Scientific Expedition'.

An illustrated propaganda record issued afterwards showed team members cheerfully taking theodolite readings and letting off weather balloons. Chairman Mao held that 'China ought to have made a greater contribution to humanity', and such scientific research was considered to be in compliance with this. Heavy-handed play was made of camp harmony, and captions told how Tibetan and Han nationality expedition members would '. . . sing hilariously at a forward camp' and '. . . study Chairman Mao Tsetung's works together at 6,200 m. altitude'.

The expedition features somewhat differently in John Avedon's *In Exile from the Land of Snows*, one of the most comprehensive documents of the Chinese Occupation years. Avedon discloses that the command centre for the entire 638-mile Himalayan front was Shigatse, and that a key unit lay on the northern slope of Mount Everest, near the district headquarters of Tingri. Early in 1968, he says, a high-ranking team of miliary officers escorted six scientists to Everest and, after their return, a twenty-square mile zone was sealed off. Even Tibetan road workers in the area were replaced by Chinese soldiers. In May half the scientists returned in company with twenty-six PLA officers, followed by convoys of equipment. Avedon reported:

By September large caves in the surrounding hills, their outlets carefully camouflaged from aerial reconnaissance, were reported to be linked by tunnels wide enough for jeeps and trucks to pass one another. Their dimensions were such that whole regiments, according to refugees and Sherpas from Nepal, could be quartered within.

More camps were set up on the surface, and by 1970 high ridges in the area began sprouting radar dishes

Indian intelligence suggested that the sophisticated radar complex operating in western Tibet was capable of functioning as tracking stations for satellites and missiles. That Peking later relocated its major nuclear facility in the heart of Tibet (from where medium and inter-mediate range missiles could be trained on major Indian and Soviet targets) appeared to confirm this. That was at Nagchuka, north of Lhasa, and the Tingri 'tracking station' was clearly in place to support it, Avedon said.

I did not see his book until I was on my way home, and in the course of my walks had not spotted any evidence to suggest military silos around the Rongbuk Monastery. Yet there were side valleys none of us explored, and vast tracts of barren land between Everest and Tingri.

Chinese mountaineering has continued to be a pawn for greater politics. In 1969 Lin Biao and his cohorts declared 'athletics are useless', whereupon even Chou En-lai's support was not enough to preserve the national mountaineering team through to the end of the Cultural Revolution. But it was reinstated by Premier Deng Xiao-ping in 1975, when another large Sino-Tibetan team was allowed to come to Everest. Among its number was Wang Hong Bao who found the 'dead English'. Once more the summit was reached, this time by nine climbers who included the 'daughter of a serf', Phantog. This time, too, they took no chances on being believed, climbing to the top in broad daylight and taking plenty of film and photographs. On the summit they left an aluminium survey tripod.

★

October 5 – a big day: to Yak Camp at last! Tom, Ken Bailey and I left base at mid-morning and an hour later caught up with Ronnie Faux, who was also on his way up the East Rongbuk Valley. We lunched together on nuts and raisins, then crossed the river (above where Camp I used to stand in the pioneering days) to scramble over heaving moraine.

'Hurry up, no more stops for another hour!' Tom, out in front, was impatient for action. Luckily for me, Ken, close behind, set more store by gentle encouragement. 'Take all the time you need,' he said. 'Catch your breath.'

That was the big problem – catching sufficient breath. I walked with a ski pole for balance, and on steep uphill stretches could only manage twenty or thirty paces before doubling over the pole and gasping fit to burst. In places the track was no more than narrow footholds on crumbling scree, overhanging long drops to the river. We passed under loose boulder slopes threatened by melting cornices, marking the abrupt north end of Changtse. Bill Barker of the British team had a very narrow squeak here earlier in the season. He was crossing with Mo Anthoine and Joe Brown when a boulder, more than ten feet high, detached itself and came bounding down the slopes towards them. They all ran like crazy, Joe managing to leap across the river with Mo fast on his heels. Bill was still hurtling down the screes when the boulder caught up with him. By a freak of fortune it was then in mid-bounce and sailed clean over him with a couple of feet to spare. As Joe was quick to observe, it would have taken his head right off if he had stayed where he was.

On their first trip up here Tom and Alistair found this a delightful picnic spot, but usually people scuttled quickly clear of the ominous cornices. When I heard that one of Doug Scott's Tamang cooks had been killed in an avalanche above Base Camp the following year, I suspected it must have been in this narrow lower section of the East Rongbuk valley. Further up, a single tall ice pinnacle in a pool of water marked the snout of the glacier, the surface of which was mostly invisible under mounds of scree.

To get to interim camp could take anything from four to eight hours, and at my pace, I had expected to require the full eight, so it was with pleasant surprise we arrived there a little before four in the afternoon just as the late sun gilded the hillside. Six hours seemed to me a not discreditable performance.

Three tents stood on a moraine bank above the curve of the steep-sided valley, with stately ice ships sailing around the bend. It was a magnificent, if exposed, setting. The British occupied a rather more sheltered spot a hundred yards lower down, where their huddle of small, blue domes surrounded a luxurious, communal frame tent for cooking and sitting about in. Early in the trip, our team passing up and down the glacier had been welcomed to share the comfort of this mess tent, and now we took it for granted that we cadged meals there and only used our own tents for sleeping in. Ken, the freshest after our trudge, cooked the evening meal for us, and for Ronnie and Al Read, who had followed in our wake. The yakmen struggled in after dark to sleep in the hollow of a stone-walled *sangar*, covered with a tarpaulin.

For shelter, the yaks slumped close to the tents at night. The thin tent fabric screened them from view, but it couldn't keep out the smell or their noise. They are prodigious chewers and farters. I knew cows were supposed to have four stomachs, but yaks, if the gurgle of their internal plumbing is anything to go by, have twice that number. Yet this intimacy was not uncomforting; very quickly you learned to appreciate their foetid warmth.

I was woken next morning by the tent being suddenly zipped open. Framed in the circular hole was the shaggy head of one of our yak drivers. He stared at me unblinkingly for some minutes and then called his friend over. Two weatherworn faces pressed inquisitively into the tent, discussing what they saw. Clearly, they didn't know what to make of me. Was I man or woman? And if the latter, what on earth was I doing up here? Anyone with hair as bleached and white as mine had to be of venerable age in their eyes. Certainly, after two months of high altitude sun, my face was as wrinkled and burnt as any old Tibetan crone. It was a disconcerting scrutiny, but not threatening in any way, and after fingering a few of my bits and pieces in the tent, they closed the door again and retreated to what they saw as the infinitely more comfortable sanctuary of their *sangar*, from the chimney of which issued a kippery smell.

It had snowed to a depth of nine inches in the night, and there was very little visibility. In consequence all movement up the mountain had stopped once more, for us and for the British. The plan had been for Ken and I to go up to Advanced Base on the following day or the day after that, having satisfied everyone that we had acclimatized here at what was, I supposed, 19,000 feet. My worry now was that, if the bad weather continued, people would start coming down again and we would have to move out to make way for them. I didn't relish the thought of struggling up here again.

Sherpas are not keen on women joining expeditions. They say sex on mountains brings bad weather. Well, if the storms we'd been experiencing here were anything to go by, somebody on our side of the hill must have been having a lot more fun than I was privy to.

To Each His Dream

RONNIE FAUX SCRAMBLED to the top of a mound to make his morning radio link between Yak Camp and base. 'The Colonel's coming up today!' he announced as he stepped back into the shelter of the mess tent.

I had not met Brummie Stokes before – he was not down at base for Joe's party – and I wondered what to expect. Imagination was all too readily coloured by stereotype images of SAS-men – hooded, hard-nosed, trained to do terrible things with piano-wire. Certainly there could be no doubting Brummie's toughness: he'd had his knee shot off in a Gulf campaign, lost all his toes climbing to the top of Everest, and broken his neck when he went back to the mountain for a second go. Yet here he was, back for more. Not someone to tangle with, by the sound of it. Would he know of my part in Gillman's *Observer* article, which, though it had brought in funds for this Everest trip, at the same time implied that an earlier SAS-venture retreated from the mountain in disarray? I'd been told that Brummie's patron and hero, David Stirling, founder of the regiment, was not amused by that remark, and Brummie, I felt sure, would be of equal mind.

I decided to get things a bit shipshape and bustled about washing up mugs, stowing smelly socks out of sight, and even giving the cooker a desultory wipe round. It began to snow and the wind got up, tugging and worrying at the tent, making it crack like a mainsail. Brummie blew in with the worst of the blizzard and called at once for a bowl of hot water. The old frostbite injuries were playing up and he needed to dunk what was left of his feet. He was rampantly bearded, wild-haired, wild-eyed as the Ancient Mariner. His small frame, crouching over the steaming bowl, suggested barely suppressed power. He couldn't sit still for long. The stores were plundered for bully beef tins and potato powder, and soon Brummie had set about making rissoles enough to feed a batallion, humming tunelessly to the Chieftans on his walkman.

The tin plate was piled high when, towards dusk, several refugees from ABC straggled out of the murk in desperate need of fortification. They had encountered such thick snow in the Corridor-section that it had cost them six hours of waist-deep wading to get here. They were done in. Roger Vernon, our second cameraman, was exhibiting early signs of pulmonary oedema. He looked grey and alarmingly frail. The last fifty feet from the glacier to the mess tent is a shocking pull at the end of the day, and I raced out to help him for he looked as if he wouldn't make it on his own.

'You mustn't frighten us like this,' I scolded, hauling him into the warm. He ought really to have gone all the way down to base, but it was out of the question that night. We packed him at once into bed on oxygen. At first light he was escorted on further.

Ken, Tom and I sat it out while others passed through on their way down, and the Sherpas struggled back up to Advanced Base with Brummie. In the afternoon Ronnie, too, went down, relieved here as Brit-in-Residence by Loel Guinness, Brummie's 'Administration Officer'. Dave Cheesmond brought a sick Sherpa down – and so it went on, comings and goings, for several days. The ever-changing faces prevented us from getting bored, or too much on each other's nerves. I read Saul Bellow's *The Dean's December* and swopped it with Loel for Günter Grass's *Dog Years*. In a week we told all the stories we knew and played every card game.

A pot of water was kept on the boil for passing climbers and, following Brummie's example, we made sure there was always food ready that could be warmed up quickly. We sampled all the delicacies in the Britons' amply supplied store cupboard: tins of fruit and fruit cake, plum puddings, rice puddings, syrup puddings. There were sacks of powdered egg and milk, Horlicks and Bovril, and candy bars, nuts, condensed milk, cream cheeses and crackers. It was like Christmas, though however much we stuffed our faces, weight kept melting off us at this altitude. I couldn't recognise the gaunt sticks that were my limbs, and when I looked into a tin-mirror, the raddled face that stared back at me was that of a stranger. I stopped combing my hair when it came away in tufts. Thinking back, I wonder if that could have been an early indication of scurvy, for although I popped the occasional vitamin pill, we'd had no fresh milk and scarcely any fresh fruit or vegetables for weeks – no barrel of limes, like the old sailors.

The yakman's dog opted to stay with us. He'd had enough of traipsing up and down with the animal trains, getting nothing but sore feet for his pains. He settled down, fur fluffed, on the pebble-strewn ice outside the mess tent, confident that someone would see him right. The first morning I spotted him there, I took out the breakfast scraps, telling him, 'You'll be all right today, old fellow,' then a few minutes later I noticed Joe Brown sidle outside with a candy bar. Mo was next with a tasty slice of Dundee cake, and Brummie slipped the brute some bully beef. That dog stuffed the equivalent of a whole year's rations in the few days of its summer holiday on Everest mountain.

Once the weather permitted activity to be resumed at Advanced Base, Tom trekked up there with a yak train. Days were suddenly much quieter without his adversarial arguing. 'Do I detect an acid edge in your relationship with Tom?' Ronnie had asked me, and certainly I was growing weary of constantly having to defend my corner. One day Al Read had taken Tom out for several hours, ostensibly to break trail in the Corridor, but in reality to burn off some of his inexhaustible energy. Now only Ken and I were left, forbidden to advance further. Labelled as doubtful acclimatizers, we were obliged to wait for an oxygen regulator to be taken up before climbing higher.

It was the second week of October. The trucks to take us home had been ordered for 1 November, and those for the British team a week earlier. We were thus in the odd position of pushing ahead with the climb at the same time as taking steps to clear the mountain. Time was running out, and without cooperation with the weather, it might not be possible to make any further progress. While we waited, Ken and I went for short strolls along the spine of the medial moraine. Giant seracs – some of them a hundred feet in height – flowed past in serried ranks on either side. Where steep little icefalls came down to join the main glacier, there was such an eruption of pinnacles that they looked like those crystal gardens you can grow in waterglass at the bottom of jamjars. Through our glacier-glasses, the ice was the palest translucent Renoir blue, though dazzlingly bright if we took them off. Nourished for so long on pictures of this glacier, it was hard to believe I was here at last. In the sun it was a crystal, glistening world, but already we knew how quickly bad weather could transform this weird thoroughfare into the *via dolorosa* of the early expeditions. In 1922 Bruce had written:

You never saw such a change as the South wind made . . . your great trough down the glacier between II and III became a roaring torrent and the funny outcropping seracs were all tumbling about, and the whole of the hillsides were in a dangerous and moving condition in two days.

A yak train dropped off my plastic altitude boots. They seemed awfully heavy, and when I looked, I saw why. Still stuffed inside were the batteries Peter put in there to save space when he was helping me pack my kit at home. When the time finally came for Ken and I to move on I left these double boots behind. Just sitting around in them had stopped all the circulation in my feet: it would be crazy to wear them in snow. It meant abandoning my Yeti-gaiters as well, since they did not fit anything else. Instead, for the big day, it was back to my trusty suede walking boots. I worried about insulation and vapour barriers, and decided to make my own with polythene bags between sock and Brasher-boot. It worked perfectly. My feet stayed snug and dry all day, though we were constantly plodding through deep snow.

'Get a rhythm going,' advised Sue, as she and David strode out with us. She demonstrated a slow step with a hesitation in the middle, something like a death march. I tried it and was able to keep it going for several hours as we trudged up the medial moraine, and up and down all its little undulations. But it was too slow for the others, and they took it in turns to stay back and keep me company. I could have used the trick of the God Chenrezi, who legend tells us was raised to the top of Everest on a sunbeam.

All round us bristled brilliant sharks' teeth of ice, the moraine driving like a highway between them. Early Everest films showed Chaplinesque figures strutting jerkily through this chaos of sculpted seracs, snapping off icicles to use as walking sticks; and in the thirties, when Raymond Greene saw it for the first time, he felt he had strayed into a land of art nouveau glass. Designed by a megalomaniac Lalique, he said.

We met Brummie on his way down, hurtling along at top speed to get help and oxygen for one of his cameramen. A short while later we passed this man too, looking very seedy and sorry for himself. A three-man crew had joined the British expedition in Base Camp at the last minute – much to the surprise of Tony Riley who till then had thought himself the sole cine-photographer on the trip. He was immediately promoted to altitude cameraman and the newcomers, none of whom had set foot on a mountain before, worked stolidly away at Advanced Base for two months. This poor fellow was suffering the effects of his stoicism.

Around two o'clock we reached the start of the section we called the Corridor, and the Brits always referred to as the Tubes. It was a chasm near the edge of the glacier, where it skirts the eastern walls of Changtse, a steep, rising channel banked by blue ice cliffs. Mary Kay and Mike Yager were sitting on a rock at the entrance, having come down to meet us. We made this our lunch stop.

'Still time to go back, Aud,' David said.

Go back? Why on earth should I want to do that? 'I'm not going back!'

'Well, we're only half way, yet. Do you think you'll be able to make it right up to ABC?'

Make it or bust, I thought. I'd waited a long time for this. I wasn't about to give in now.

'Best get on, then. What have you got in that bag?'

They tipped out my rucksack and shared the items between them so that I could travel lightly.

It was deep snow in the Corridor and hard to find a rhythm again as I planted my feet in secondhand post-holes. Most of the others forged ahead, leaving Mary Kay and Yager to watch out for me. Just as it was getting dark, we met Steve Shea, guarding the bridge over a wide, deep, water-filled crevasse, which they had been obliged to strengthen recently with extra bits of sectioned ladder.

'Here, have a swig!' He handed me a thermos of warm sweet tea. 'Only another hour now.'

God, I thought we were there. Thought it was just round the next corner. Another whole hour – hell's bells!

Everything looked pitch black through my prescription glacier glasses, but whoever had opted to carry my normal spectacles was now long over the horizon. I'd have to go on seeing through a glass darkly, or not see at all.

As we came out of the confines of the Corridor, it started to snow and a sharp wind smacked us in the face. But with all this effort, I didn't feel cold – didn't even want the constriction of zipping up my down jacket. I'd been bundled in far too many clothes all day and felt like a dancing bear. They must have slowed me down as much as anything. Still, I was on automatic now, a walking zombie.

'Watch yourself here,' David said. 'It's where the yak went down. Put your feet where I do.' The path of stones had long since been buried under snow. I wondered what other crevasses lay hidden underneath.

We must be getting closer now, surely? David had me by one arm, someone else steered the other. More and more people came clustering, pulling, encouraging . . . friends everywhere. Mary Kay had nipped up to camp for a hot water bottle.

'Tuck this inside your coat!' she breezed. 'Can't have you getting cold.'

There was more chance of heat stroke! My goggles fogged. It didn't matter too much, others were propelling me on. I didn't need to see.

Then, suddenly, we were there. I was hugged and thumped and congratulated and pushed into the mess tent in a blur of shiny smiling faces.

'You've made it! Well done! We've waited supper.'

A bowl of soup was all I could manage. What I really wanted was to curl up and sleep. It had taken eight and a half hours to get here, with an awful lot of help from my friends. I was immensely touched that they should seem as delighted as I was to have made it. Here at last! At the foot of the North Col. I could scarcely believe it.

I'd have a good look round in the morning. Too dark now.

'Come on,' said Sue. 'Let's show you which one's home.'

We tucked into one of the little blue and grey dome tents, our boots and belongings stuffed in tightly around us. Andy came to check that all was well.

'There's a bottle of oxygen outside,' he hissed to Sue. 'Just in case.'

But I didn't need it. I slept like a top and woke next morning to a beautiful blue day.

★

The sepia fold-out panoramas which illustrated early accounts of exploration in the East Rongbuk Glacier convey an exaggerated spaciousness. Perspectives are distorted in the seamless juxtaposition of component photographs. What surprised me most as I stuck my head out of our tent door on that first morning at Advanced Base Camp was the sense of enclosure: where was the vast sweep the pictures had suggested? Changste and the North Col rose to our backs, with the long North-east Ridge of Everest wrapping round almost to enfold us on one side. Looking down across the glacier, the view was sealed by a barrier of lesser peaks and the high pass of Lhakpa La. This was the way Mallory had approached in 1921 when he missed the entrance to the East Rongbuk. Everything was under deep snow, and it was hard to imagine that when the Chileans had arrived here a few months earlier, they were able to walk as far as this in trainers. I would be wise to remember that these innocuous-looking snowfields concealed crevasses and to be careful to wander only trodden trails. Tom, who was having great fun with a sledge and teaching the Sherpas to ski, was likewise directed to keep to proven slopes.

The rocky outcrop against which we were camped must have been Captain Noel's 'Eagle's Nest', the viewpoint from which he filmed all activity on the mountain with his telescopic lens. Close by here, also, would be the spot where the 1935 exploring party had come upon the body of Maurice Wilson. Charles Warren made that gruesome discovery when he climbed ahead of his companions. He had been sitting on a rock waiting for them to catch up when he noticed a boot sticking out of the snow, together with what he took to be the remains of a tent.

'I say, there's a perfectly good pair of Lawrie-boots and a tent up here!' he shouted back to Eric Shipton and the others, thinking he had stumbled upon an old dump. Only when he approached more closely did he realize with a shock that this was a man lying huddled in the snow. He knew it at once for Maurice Wilson, the Walter-Mitty Yorkshireman who had disappeared while trying to climb Mount Everest on his own the previous year.

Wilson believed firmly that God would not let him die. Had he not, as a young man, been delivered from the bloody trenches of Ypres, and survived terrible machine-gun injuries? Later, when critically ill with TB and close to mental breakdown, wasn't he restored to rude health by the magical powers of fasting and prayer? He was clearly being saved for a purpose, and believed there was nothing this forceful combination of faith and fasting could not achieve. Certainly it would get him to the top of Everest, and without the need for additional oxygen or fancy equipment.

'People will have to listen to me, then,' Wilson had said. 'I shall be *some*body. I shall be allowed to do the tests I want on my experimental machine.' For Everest, it seemed, was only a stepping stone in his greater quest to explore the stratosphere.

In the sad event, the potency of prayer failed to hoist him up the ice chimney that barred the way to the North Col, and fasting went out of the window when he discovered a food dump of Fortnum and Mason potted quails and Carlsbad plums left by the 1933 expedition. He perished from cold, exhaustion and collapsed hopes in his tent sometime at the beginning of June 1934.

A fickle public, which had followed his earlier adventures with gusto, was only too ready now to dismiss him as a crank. His death – seen as an elaborate suicide – wiped out any achievement in having reached so far. Yet Wilson's story is not without a cussed touch of glory.

His first plan had been to fly himself to Everest, crash land on the Rongbuk glacier, and from there step it out nimbly to the summit. That he had never before piloted a plane gave him not a moment's pause. He bought a secondhand Gipsy Moth – which he re-christened *Ever Wrest* – and booked some flying lessons with the London Aero Club in Hendon. An inept pupil, it took him a long time to gain his licence, but he demonstrated enormous flair when it came to publicity. His picture appeared in all the papers, but in bureaucratic circles the gravest concern was being expressed over his vaunted flight. The Air Ministry forbad him to take off. Wilson tore up their telegram and left.

After a circuitous journey, necessary to outwit the long arm of officialdom, he landed at last in Darjeeling. There, upon being refused permission to overfly Tibet or Nepal, he sold his plane and engaged three Sherpa porters. In disguise and travelling much of the time by night, Wilson made his way out of Sikkim and across Tibet to Everest, where the porters accompanied him as far as Camp III. (That would have been at much the same spot as I was now.) Higher they could not be persuaded to go. Wilson went on, alone, to make a number of fruitless attempts at the Col. On the last occasion he told his helpers to wait for him for ten days, then, if he did not reappear, to return home without him. They claim to have waited three weeks and then retreated, starving, to Rongbuk, before eventually making their way back to Darjeeling.

Shipton, Warren and Edwin Kempson have all described the finding and interring of Maurice Wilson's body. Warren said:

> . . . it was decided to bury him in a crevasse; the moraine was changing too rapidly for a surface burial there. So we wrapped him in his tent, and after cutting away the lip of a suitable crevasse slid the body into the depths where it immediately disappeared from sight. We all raised our hats at the time and I think that everyone was rather upset over the business.

That evening they sat together under an overhanging rock in the snow, while Kempson read aloud from the diary that had been found with the body. 'It was a moving and gallant document,' Kempson recalled. 'An extraordinary documentary revelation of monomania and determination of purpose,' recorded Warren. Shipton wrote: 'It was as if the man himself was speaking to us, revealing his secret thoughts. Outside our shelter there was complete silence as the snow fell in large fluffy flakes.'

> As I listened to the strange, intimate story, I soon had little doubt of the writer's sincerity. The motive behind his wild venture was unusual. It was obvious that he had little liking for the mountains, and he certainly claimed no spiritual uplift in their presence. At the same time I did not feel that he was striving for personal glorification. He believed that he was guided by some kind of divine inspiration to deliver a message to humanity. His implicit faith in his destiny seems to have been with him to the last.

Wilson's project ought not to be judged from a mountaineering standpoint, Shipton said. Nor did he – Shipton – have any touchstone by which to judge Wilson's arrogance, so clearly revealed in his diary. Such a characteristic, he supposed, may well have been essential to his kind of faith. 'We cannot fail to admire his courage,' was all Shipton would say.

Wilson's diary was brought back to England, where it found a home eventually in the Alpine Club library. It is still there. Would that the same could be said of poor Wilson in his crevasse. Unfortunately, that unquiet ghost surfaces with macabre regularity. Chinese mountaineers found him in 1960, and again in 1965. Since then, there have been frequent references to a diminishing bundle of bones not far from Advanced Base Camp.

It is not surprising that interest still flares around this quixotic figure: war hero, disciple of Gandhi, modelled on Biggles, a mystic, an ascetic, and in touch with The Beyond. Most people, like Shipton, applaud his tenacity, but his dottiness has brought about murkier speculation.

One story that recurs persistently concerns a secret 'sex diary'. The existence of such an item is unproven and altogether unprovable – or so I think. Nevertheless, rumour has it that both Shipton and Dan Bryant, who were on Everest in 1935, have referred to a second diary, or notebook, that retailed Wilson's erotic fantasies; and the playwright Barry Collins used this as the starting point for a moving drama about

Wilson's last tormented days. *The Ice Chimney* is a haunting study of a man *in extremis*, his faith gone, being forced to face his own obsessions, but what truth there is behind it, if any, can no longer be verified. Shipton and Bryant cannot tell. Both are long dead.

Similar rumours have circulated that Wilson, when found, was dressed in women's clothing, that he was a fetishist, that Chinese mountaineers discovered a lady's high-heeled shoe in a prewar camp . . .

In 1984 an American living in Oregon, who described himself as an artist/writer and the world's leading authority on Maurice Wilson, contacted the Smithsonian Institute in Washington to say he had 'evidence' to support the possibility that Wilson had reached the summit of Mount Everest twenty years before Hillary and Tenzing. He intended to go to the mountain the following summer to carry out archeological and forensic investigations.

Nine months later Charles Warren received a letter, also from Oregon, requesting details of the discovery of Wilson's body, and I had one about the so-called 'second diary'.

The curious thing was that although all these letters appeared to have emanated from the same individual, the name inscribed at the end was different in each case. I wrote to my correspondent:

> The story of the 'second diary' is very curious. There is no way, as I see it, that a further notebook (or items of women's clothing for that matter) could have been found with the body of Wilson unknown to any one, two or three of the four people present at the discovery. I have read the diaries of both Dr Warren and Edwin Kempson and they are very explicit about what was found and what Wilson was wearing.
>
> Neither Shipton nor Bryant, as far as I am aware, ever committed to paper anything other than the 'official version'. The fact that word-of-mouth stories circulate to the effect 'Shipton told me . . . so-and-so . . . ' at a time when Shipton himself is no longer alive to confirm or deny the truth of such a story, is to me very suspicious. I don't believe there was any 'evidence' found on the mountain to suggest transvesticism or any form of fetishism. I am extraordinarily doubtful about the woman's high-heel shoe story, too, but that could I'm sure be checked out with the CMA.

The only way, to my mind, for there to be a grain of truth in these rumours would be if incriminating evidence about Wilson turned up somewhere other than on Everest. For instance, he had spent several years in New Zealand, where among many jobs, including that of door-to-door salesman and a manufacturer of quack medicine, he had at one time run a ladies' dress shop in Wellington, a flourishing establishment by all accounts, but one which he left rather abruptly. That might have provided the impetus for the women's clothing stories. Perhaps, too, Wilson's flair for getting into the newspapers was something he had always had, wherever he was, whatever he did. There could well have been gossip in New Zealand, maybe even another diary. Certainly he had romantic liaisons there, which included one or two wives. Dan Bryant came from New Zealand. You can make connections, but they are sheer speculation.

All this, in any case, was of only marginal interest to the Oregon mystery-man since his prime purpose lay in re-examining how high Maurice Wilson had climbed on Everest. He felt the wrong conclusions had been drawn about the body and the tent found at Camp III.

Wilson wasn't in his tent because he failed to climb the Ice Chimney, so he believed, but in his Sherpas' tent because he *had* ascended higher and then abandoned all his gear (including tent and sleeping bag) on the way down.

It fitted the facts as neatly as anything else. Warren had been puzzled at the time why no sleeping bag was found with the body, or, indeed, why Wilson died when he was within 200 yards of a food dump he knew to exist. He could not understand the Sherpas' claim not to know what had happened if they had waited at Camp III while Wilson made his last futile attempt on the North Col's slopes. The tent in which he died would have been visible to them and within hailing distance all the time. But supposing Wilson had climbed higher, disappeared from view? If he were gone some time, wouldn't the Sherpas have felt perfectly free to go down and wait in the valley?

As I heard nothing more from this man, I assumed he'd been unable to go to Everest in 1985, and thought it conceivable we might bump into his 'forensic expedition' while we were there in 1986. Later, by chance, I learned that he did come to Tibet as planned, but was taken ill below Rongbuk. In Lhasa on his way out he met the Basque mountaineer Mari Abrego and charged him to carry out the search for Wilson. Abrego found the remains, took photographs, picked up some items and a jaw bone for identification, and sent them off to Oregon. In 1987 he was telephoned by some Seattle journalists asking for confirmation of the story, but has heard nothing since. I never did find out if the book and screenplay the American was writing saw light of day. But the story continues to fascinate: others follow it up.

Funny, isn't it, I thought, how these old Everest mysteries can still generate so much interest, and breed such dedicated fanatics burning to unravel them. Did I count myself as one of those? More to the point, did anyone else?

★

I spent a lazy day, dozing and reading in the sun. I felt fine, if not frisky. Ken, though, had spent a wretched night and grew worse as the day passed. He was put on to oxygen that evening and the next, but did not improve, and had to go down.

On the 14th, a small group set off with some Sherpas for the North Col, but was turned back by a lunchtime storm. In another attempt the next day four Sherpas recolonized the camp on the Col, though Mike Yager had to retreat when he lost one of his gloves. Sue started getting her kit ready to climb up with the next party on the 16th. We knew this would be our last big push. There was a desire to keep all 'the family' together for this and everyone fit enough in the lower camps started heading up again, including our Base Camp Manager, Al Read.

All that night the wind savaged the tents, shaking them like a terrier with a rat. The Sherpas on the Col had a wild time of it. 'Snow as high as the tents,' they radioed down in the morning. There would be no movement up or down from there today. It was pretty deep where we were, too. Once more we'd had to dig ourselves out in the morning.

An Unending Silence

FROM ADVANCED BASE you can just see the summit of Everest. Although the view is compressed by foreshortening, it looks impossibly distant. It could be another world. No wonder Tibetans and Sherpas think gods and demons live up there. How could anyone go so high without being changed, without receiving some special cosmic flash of insight? What must it be like to see the summit glinting just ahead, to take those last few windy steps to the rooftop of the world? What do you feel? Climbers provide only tantalizing clues, for tradition demands they maintain tight-lipped restraint over matters of great drama or high emotion. In any case, I suspect the real sweeping euphoria comes not on top, but later, once they are safely down again, reaping the congratulations.

Ed Hillary, when he'd inched himself up what has become his eponymous 'Step', helped Tenzing to his side and led off along the snakelike undulations of the final summit ridge. A patch of shingle barred his way. This, too, he clambered wearily over, continuing on round the next bump. Only then did he realize that it was the last bump of all. Ahead the ridge dropped steeply before rising again in a great corniced curve to the top. Out in the distance he could see the pastel shades and fleecy clouds of the highlands of Tibet.

> It was too late to take risks now. I asked Tenzing to belay me strongly, and I started cutting a cautious line of steps up the ridge. Peering from side to side and thrusting with my ice-axe, I tried to discover a possible cornice, but everything seemed solid and firm. I waved Tenzing up to me. A few more whacks of the ice-axe, a few very weary steps, and we were on the summit of Everest.

His first sensation was one of relief. And then astonishment. And in the end came quiet satisfaction. Tenzing was grinning beatifically behind his oxygen mask and all the icicles in his hair. Hillary made to shake his hand, but Tenzing would have none of such formality, flinging his arms round Hillary's shoulders. They hugged and thumped one another in mutual congratulation. American mountaineers who came next to the top admitted to tears as they embraced, tears running down their oxygen masks and turning into ice.

Doug Scott and Dougal Haston arrived by way of the South-west Face, reaching the last wide whaleback ridge late in the day. Scott noticed that his mind seemed to have split in two. A small rational part was directing operations from somewhere behind his left shoulder. It warned him when he was getting too near the cornices, when to slow down to avoid stumbling through brittle snowcrust, and generally bolstered his confidence all along the way. He and Haston were rewarded with one of the finest summit moments granted to any of the elite band to have reached that special spot. A truly glorious sunset cast a 200-mile shark's-fin shadow upon the russet plains of Tibet. But they were late, too late to make it down to their last camp before dark. In a cold night of bivouac, while fighting not only to survive without oxygen but to preserve the quality of that survival, it was not just Scott's brain that hived off to an independent life of its own; his feet too discussed with him what should best be done to save them from frostbite. Brummie Stokes and Bronco Lane were assisted through a similar high bivouac by the presence of a mysterious third, a guardian spirit with whom they shared their last dribble of oxygen.

Reinhold Messner has been twice to the top of Everest without artificial oxygen. He also found his brain able to detach itself and override the body's protestations. It issued the orders, took decisions almost on its own, leaving his soul receptive to spiritual sensation. On top – 'that little point, where all the lines come together' – he was washed with overwhelming peace, even though his breathing rasped dangerously like someone who had run the race of a lifetime. He could rest now, he felt, for ever.

His companion, Peter Habeler, struggling up in his wake, felt that someone else had taken over the effort for him. Floating free, a short distance behind, attached only by a line, he watched this *doppelgänger* with mild curiosity until a sudden cramp snatched him back to a suffocating fear of death. 'Lord God,' he prayed, more fervently than he had ever prayed in his life, 'let me get to the top, but give me the power, too, to remain alive. Don't let me die up here.' Again, he saw

Through the seracs of the East Rongbuk glacier to the North Col

Sitting out the bad weather at Yak Camp – Al Read, Tom Holzel, Audrey Salkeld, Ronnie Faux

Filming climber's arrival on the North Col

Audrey Salkeld and Sue Giller at 21,000 feet, with the North Col behind

Ed Webster's remarkable photograph, taken from Changtse, of sunrise over the North-east Ridge of Everest and the North Col, the summit in sunshine

David Breashears with Kee-Chak, the Tibetan driver, and kite-flying on the last morning

George Mallory and
Andrew Irvine aboard
ship on their way to
India, 1924

Pumori and the
Lingtren peaks seen
across the Rongbuk
Glacier from the high
moraine above Base
Camp

himself crawling upwards, 'below me, beside me, higher and higher. I was being pushed up to the heights, and then suddenly I was up again on my own two feet: I was standing on the summit!'

He arrived to find Messner whispering into his pocket tape-recorder. 'I am nothing more than a single, narrow, gasping lung, floating over the mists and summits,' Messner croaked.

When next Messner climbed here he was entirely on his own, on a summit day overcast and gloomy. Again his body resisted every movement and willpower alone drove him on, and even that was fizzling away in utter weariness. 'I think nothing, feel nothing. I let myself fall. I lie there. For ages I remain completely lifeless. Then I take a few more steps. At most it can only be another ten metres to the top . . . Above me is nothing but sky, although I sense it rather than see it – as I see only a little of the world beneath me through the mist . . . '

Unsure whether he is on the top or not, he stumbles into all that is left of the metal tripod placed there by Chinese mountaineers. So that's that. Still he feels nothing, wants nothing but to rest and let the world slide away. He has climbed himself to a standstill.

Crowning his long Everest years with success, Chris Bonington struggled towards the summit at the age of fifty, breathless, panting, apprehensive, his companions out of sight ahead. He found himself emboldened for the last painful expenditure of effort by the almost physical presence of Doug Scott. 'I could see his long straggly hair, the wire-rimmed glasses and could sense his reassurance and encouragement. It was as if he was pushing me on.' Les, his father-in-law, popped up as well and, between them, the pair steered him safely to the top of the Hillary Step, and along the airy ridge to rejoin more tangible companions on the little billiard table that was the summit.

Stephen Venables approached the summit alone, without oxygen. On the Hillary Step he had fancied himself in a pub, with an open fire, a pint of Guinness and a beautiful girl with long golden hair beside him . . . Then it (and she) vanished, leaving him cruelly alone in the grey cold. At least, once over that obstacle, the going was easier and he had only to plod gently on. There was no doubt now that he would make it even if it meant taking a rest at every third step, as he strained convulsively for extra air. Approaching the last few feet, he once more saw figures, sitting erect right on the summit. They would not return his greeting. Must be soldiers, he told himself, the British Services expedition. Better speak to them in their own language: 'Are you going to fucking talk to me or not?!' That brought on a fit of coughing, and he thought to make a joke when he finally did reach them, something about having to give up smoking . . .

It was only as he pulled close that he saw there was nothing there but a few empty oxygen bottles stacked in the snow and, disappointed, he flopped beside them. 'There was a dreamlike sense of disbelief at being in this special place . . . It would be nice to say that it was the happiest moment of my life and that I was overwhelmed by euphoria; but . . . there was only a rather dazed feeling of . . . "So this is what it's like".'

Venables could see how easy it would be to remain forever in 'this bewitching dreamlike place', but knew he must resist. Drawing on his last reserves of will, he fled 'back down to Earth' before it was too late.

With careening emotions after such sustained and draining effort, we should not be surprised that physical description of the scene is often disappointing. Of that unique perspective, granted to the person who stands highest of all, we learn little more than that it is 'absolutely staggeringly beautiful . . . beyond superlatives', that you can see 'easily 100 miles in every direction . . . as though in a hot-air balloon, peering down on the tops of cumulus clouds two miles below'.

> All of a sudden, damn, I was looking right down the north face, and I was looking down the east face, and I was standing right on the summit! You could see Annapurna, Dhaulagiri – all the Himalayas this way. And then, Kangchenjunga, and Jannu, and Makalu was just chiseled – the peak that sticks out there. And there wasn't a cloud through Tibet. You could see all those little – just brown – hills with a little white fang, a little tooth sticking out of it . . . [Chris Kopczysnki]

Always it is the inner sensations that are the strongest. Habeler described his confusion:

> After the crying and the sense of redemption came the emptiness and the sadness, the disappointment. Something had been taken from me; something that had been very important . . . I now felt exhausted and hollow . . . no feeling of triumph or victory . . . I saw the surrounding summits, Lhotse, Cho Oyu. The view towards Tibet was obscured by clouds. I knew that I was standing on the highest point in the whole world, but somehow, it did not move me. All I wanted now was to get home, back to that world from which I had come – and as fast as possible.

★

Walking along the high spine of the East Rongbuk glacier on the way up here, you gain an excellent and complete view of the pioneer routes. Clearly, on the skyline, are outlined those steps made famous by Odell's last sighting of Mallory and Irvine. The oblique angle at which they are presented suggests a distant projection of the line of sight Odell himself would have had from the face. You think he must have been right in believing – as he did initially – that it was on the Second Step he saw the pair, for it is hard to imagine, even in drifting cloud, there being any confusion. The Second Step is the dominant feature, the First from this angle appearing scarcely larger than other bands of outcropping strata on the ridge.

The same conclusion was drawn by David Breashears and Steve Shea when they looked up from our Camp V, situated high above the North Col at 25,700 feet and offering a viewpoint even more closely resembling Odell's.

Something else struck them up there. Climbers on the West Ridge could be seen clearly, tiny certainly but demonstrably moving figures, from a distance far greater across the full sweep of the North Face than had separated Odell from his friends. It scotched any idea that he might have been mistaken in what he saw.

Throughout his long life, Odell was constantly sought out by people interested in the disappearance of Mallory and Irvine. It must sometimes have seemed to him that his own life, his mountaineering and academic achievements, counted for little. All anyone ever wanted was to hear about the events of those few distant days in the summer of 1924. The persistent questioning was both a chore and, at times, an irritation to him – especially as it is doubtful that he was ever able to add the slightest detail to his original account of what happened. It says a lot for his Edwardian courtesy that Odell continued to receive researchers and answer their many enquiries up until the day he died.

He always professed not to understand what the fuss was about, and perhaps it is hard to see why this one mountaineering incident should be universally remembered above all others. Arguably, it was Odell's last sighting that made Mallory and Irvine into such enduring heroes. Their loss would have been no less tragic, no less mysterious, had they vanished unseen, but it is doubtful if their memory would have remained as green. Precisely because Odell's image of two small figures, defying all odds and steadfastly pressing *together* into the unknown is so perfect, epitomizing as it does the noblest qualities in the human spirit, has it been etched so deeply into public consciousness. You could say it was that which had drawn me here, and it probably inspired a good many others of our team as well.

I had known Odell for several years and long thought him indestructible. He was a tall man, upright in every sense of the word, a year younger than Captain Noel – well into his nineties therefore, although he looked much younger. Perhaps his ponderous manner was the secret of his longevity; it was as if he had eked out his vigour. Those who climbed with him used to be driven to distraction by his extreme slowness in dealing with his kit and completing camp chores. Secretly, they believed this must have been why Mallory decided to partner young Irvine on the fateful last climb. Odell was infinitely better qualified, but Mallory was a creature of impatience and action: he would have found it intolerable to hang around, waiting for Odell to emerge from his tent in the morning. All the same, Odell was a goer. He would plod on and on, inexhaustibly, and be fresher twelve hours after the start than anybody else. His profession as a geologist had taken him around the oilfields and universities of the world, but in his retirement, he was made an honorary fellow of his old Cambridge college, Clare, and lived in a small flat to the south of the city. David Breashears and I organized a long filmed interview with him before we left for Everest.

'This American Everest fever is catching our press now,' Odell commented – over the goat we had selected from the 'Greek Day' menu in the University Centre – while lights and cameras were being set up in the lounge next door. 'The Sunday Times were on to me earlier this week. All the usual questions of Mallory and Irvine's fate, whether I thought they reached the top – all that.'

He seemed pleased to have given them little encouragement. The contemporary urge to pry under every stone found no favour with Odell. In his book, a colleague deserved the same button-lipped loyalty after he had been dead sixty years as he did in life. No one needed to know a man's private business. He deplored any insinuation, as was often made, that there may have been something more than friendship binding Mallory to young Irvine.

'Mallory was a good looking chap and a great friend of many people in Cambridge,' he said. 'There's been all sorts of horrid things said about him – wicked things . . . really wicked things . . . One filthy fellow wrote a book about Cambridge, saying that George Mallory was a homosexual. Nothing of the sort! He never was anything approaching

100

it . . . That family, as a matter of fact, was a rather religious one . . . '

We were going to have to steer cautiously with our questioning. It wasn't that we wanted to touch upon anything indelicate, but Odell would need to feel comfortable that we had no such hidden designs. I need not have worried that the old man might find a long session distressing. Odell sat staunchly on, oblivious to the hot bright lights, chatting as freely as if the cameras were not there at all. Only occasionally would he pass a cupped hand across his brow, or run a long tongue along his upper lip, gestures as much to gain time for deliberation, it seemed to me, as indications of any discomfort. It wasn't in Odell's nature to answer concisely, and as the afternoon wore on, we ran out of film long before he ran out of breath.

David wanted him to describe the make-up of the early Everest parties with their preponderence of gentlemen travellers and what a later Everester liked to call the 'bloody soldiery', men good at managing animals and porters, and some who even paid their own way, but numbering among them very few who – like Mallory, like Odell – justly warranted the term mountain climbers.

'Was there any feeling that this was the best type of person for the job?' David asked, rather ingenuously. 'You didn't take any working-class climbers on your trips back then, did you?'

Odell bridled. 'Some of us of course had been fortunate socially to be able to go off to the Alps and practise climbing on our own, and it's true we were the ones to be selected by the Everest Committee. But as far as a "working class" is concerned, that's a very invidious term. We all have to work nowadays and always have. I've been very much a workman. I worked in the Cornish mines while I was still a boy . . . '

We were not going to get far on that tack either! We had better stick strictly to standard lines of questioning.

'What were their spirits like,' I asked. 'What was the feeling when Mallory and Irvine set off?'

'When they left Camp IV, they seemed – well, if not subdued exactly – to be taking the whole business quite seriously. There was no bantering, nothing like that. Neither of them was of a jocular disposition. Irvine, perhaps, had a bit more humour than Mallory. But there were no jokes that morning.'

Two days later, climbing in support of the pair, Odell caught that famous last view of them: 'I saw two figures moving on a snow slope well away up towards the final ridge leading to the crowning pyramid

101

of the mountain. Unfortunately clouds had come down and it was very difficult to see the actual relationship between these two moving figures and certain rock pinnacles that stuck up from the final ridge. At the outset I thought they were at what we called the Second Step. Later, I could see it might very well have been the First . . . I've never been clear from that day to this which it was . . . but one figure got up more quickly than the second. The second followed in his steps, and, as far as I could make out, joined the first. Clouds prevented any clear view.'

Odell always took exception to suggestions that he might have been mistaken in what he saw. We know now that he retained astonishingly keen eyesight to the end of his days; he was still driving a car without spectacles in his late eighties. But at the time contemporaries wondered if he could have seen cloud shadows, or rocks, or even Alpine choughs flying across the face and fancied them to be people. Odell was adamant.

'I had no hallucinations. They were *moving*, actually, *moving figures*. My records, my diary, my specimens of geology . . . are all consistent one with the other, and with what I saw. I tell you they were climbers!'

'And that night, you watched for them to come down? You saw nothing, no lights at all?'

'No light.'

'So you were getting very worried by this time?'

'I decided I must go up and look for them.'

From Camp VI, Odell had signalled down to Hazard on the North Col by means of sleeping bags placed in a prearranged position on the nearest patch of snow. This meant their companions were nowhere to be found and it must be concluded they were lost. Hazard relayed the news by further signals to those waiting below in Camp III, Advanced Base. Norton called everyone off the mountain.

Sitting at Advanced Base, watching as the wind whipped snow off the North Face, it was hard for me to imagine climbers ever moving about up there with anything like the 'alacrity' Odell described in his last sighting. We might have convinced ourselves that he saw them on the Second Step, some four or five thousand feet distant from where he was standing, but his own colleagues and the climbers of the 1930s plumped instead for the First Step. They knew the Second to be too difficult to surmount in the five or so minutes Odell described seeing the first of his climbers reach the top.

That was a difficult point we had to address. To explain away so quick an ascent, we had to suppose that Odell first started watching the pair not at the foot of the entire Second Step – quite an extended feature – but somewhere nearer to its crest. The final rocky upthrust harbours a snow ramp, probably varying in height according to season, but leaving some eighteen feet of very difficult climbing at its top (grade IV to IV+ Catalan climbers have estimated) before the snowy dome of the step is reached. This last is probably where climbers would break on to the skyline.

All we had to go on in surmising what happened, all that sixty-two years had produced were the three clues: Odell's vision; the ice-axe found in 1933; and the body allegedly discovered by Wang Hong Bao. That is to say, we had one bit of 'hard' evidence (the axe), and two that can only be called 'softer' bits (the uncorroborated sightings). The main difficulty in deciding what to make of these clues is construing a theory that could simultaneously accommodate all three.

The usual supposition is that Mallory and Irvine, roped together, fell from a spot more or less where the ice axe was found. The Chinese discovery of a body, lower down but apparently in line with the axe, fits neatly with this, except that only one body was mentioned. If the two were roped, you would have expected two bodies, still roped; or at least for there to have been mention of a portion of the rope still being attached to the body that was found. A broken rope is such an evocative symbol, if it existed it is hard to imagine it being omitted from an eye-witness account, even if (as in the Chinese case) that account was described in sign language.

Odell's sighting, wherever it was, placed the pair at a point higher than the axe was found.

The simplest way I could see of relating all the clues was to abandon the idea put forward by Frank Smythe in 1934 – that the axe marked the spot where a roped leader fell. In Smythe's scenario the second man knows he must hold his companion but having no firm snow into which to drive his axe for a belay, puts it down in order to seize the rope in both hands. Failing to stop his partner, he is himself dragged down, leaving the axe behind. I favoured considering that the axe was dropped or abandoned – on the way up or down, it did not matter, the point being it did not of necessity have to represent the deaths of two climbers. The climbers need not have been roped together. (Others had not done so on this ground.) This opened the way to contemplating not one but two accidents.

There! From my initial resistance, I now, like Tom, allowed the possibility of separation. It did not have to mean Mallory was so blinded by summit fever that he abandoned Irvine to his fate – the idea which traditionalists assumed underpinned Tom's theory and, understandably, found so abhorrent. It did not have to involve oxygen cylinders changing hands. There were any number of eventualities that could bring about the voluntary separation of two climbers, as misadventure could effect involuntary separation.

I asked Odell what he felt about an expedition going to look for more clues to what happened to Mallory and Irvine.

'It seems an extraordinary decision to come to after all this time,' he said. 'Why on earth hasn't anybody wanted to do it in the sixty years between?' He paused, 'I would prefer, I think, that nothing was ever found, that it remained a mystery.'

Well, he was not alone in that. Captain Noel, by contrast, could barely wait for something to be uncovered. 'It is knowledge necessary for all the world to know,' he would declare, producing a string of ideas to help us in our search.

One ruse was for a narrow-gauged auger, with which to bore into the ice and snow in the quest for bodies, or even a camera, for as he said, with some reason, 'You couldn't expect Sherpas or yourselves to have the vigour and strength to dig with spades at the foot of the final pyramid. You would be operating from the highest camp man has ever built, and you would need to be there for at least a week.'

To excavate any crevasse or gully where relics might lie, small hand-grenade devices should serve. 'You could let off a succession of little eggshell bombs, one after the other – gently, until you had carved away the ice.'

I smiled now to think of his enthusiasm. He and Odell had both consented to become honorary members of this expedition, although Captain Noel grew very disgruntled when the women joined our team. This he saw as lack of commitment to the search.

He was right about the public interest. Everest belongs to everyone. From the time the first expedition was announced, people have felt impelled to offer advice on how it might be climbed. These ingenious and often elaborately detailed solutions were not always received by the Mount Everest Committee in the same spirit of generosity.

In 1922 a Mr Wallace wrote to Hinks, the tetchy secretary of the Committee, suggesting that to overcome the difficulties involved in the last 5,000 feet of the climb oxygen could be shot up in advance of the climbers. The obvious disadvantage that shells might bury themselves too deeply in the snow or ice he felt could be avoided by employing expanding devices or firing linked shells from a pair of lightweight guns. Carry the guns on wooden mandrils, he advised, to avoid transit damage, and break them down into numerous small containers . . .

By return, Hinks leased off a sniffy reply. 'I do not know if you have calculated the probable rate of diffusion fired from shells in the way you propose . . . '

Wallace found it hard to conceal his exasperation. 'I can only suppose you accuse me of suggesting the oxygenation of the Himalayan atmosphere at large,' he retorted, 'sufficient to right the conditions in the alveoli! I had gathered that the final difficulty was in essence one of transport and whether you shoot up oxygen or a ham sandwich is all the same . . . '

Others propounded pressure suits (like diving dress, necessitating two climbers to carry between them a small air compressor and petrol engine with which to pump up the suits), or Japanese pocket ovens, or canned oxygen briquettes. One wellwisher from Hindhead recommended rubbing legs and feet with fish oil, and a celebrated American aviator and wing-walker offered to land a plane on Everest. Yet another extolled his secretly patented 'Hydro-Aerocar'.

Lieutenant-Colonel Martin Martin of Sleat, with a thought for human frailty, proposed an engine to haul climbers up to 28 or 29,000 feet. Now that sounded just what I could do with! Like a model aeroplane, it would measure six feet long, and instead of wheels be provided with 'tripods for launching'. Coming down steep sections, the device could be employed rather in the nature of a parachute, with 'breeching under the armpits and the engine pulling vertically upwards'. Body weight, the Lieutenant Colonel promised, would only just outweigh lift and the climber would be lowered gently down – unless of course the engine cut out, in which case he and his toy plane would land in a crumpled heap at the bottom.

★

The taunting question of why Mallory should have selected Irvine for the last climb, rather than Odell, does not seem to me satisfactorily explained in the generally accepted response. The intention was to use oxygen; the apparatus was notoriously temperamental; therefore that made Irvine, the mechanically adept tyro, a better choice in Mallory's eyes than the sound and experienced mountaineer, Odell, who was just coming into an astonishing peak of fitness.

That smacks more of justification than reason. It leads one to think that Mallory preferred not to climb with Odell. Maybe it really was because Odell could be so cussedly slow and methodical. There is little to suggest the two men were ever close, and nothing to indicate Mallory even considered taking Odell, that a choice was made at all.

Somervell, when asked if he knew what lay behind the final pairing, said that he always had the suspicion Mallory was keeping a promise to young Irvine. Mallory certainly seemed to be fulfilling a promise to himself. From the beginning, he had visualised Irvine and himself reaching the top together.

We know that Irvine cherished the idea of climbing to the summit, that he was a stout companion, strong as an ox, willing and uncomplaining. We also know that towards the end of the expedition he was far from fit. Diarrhoea, breathing difficulties and a sore throat had dogged him. The sun and wind on the North Col, where he spent much of his last week, had flayed his fair skin to an agonizing rawness, as he wrote on June 3: 'A most unpleasant night when everything on earth seemed to rub against my face, and each time it was touched bits of burnt and dry skin came off, which made me nearly scream with pain.'

His diary for this period is interesting also in that its brief entries reveal several uncharacteristic spelling and other lapses – 'Camp was reached about 3 a.m.' (he meant 'p.m.'); 'Throat is rather soar'; 'Face was badly caut by the sun' – which incline me to wonder whether he was also suffering altitude impairment. Major Hingston, the expedition doctor, felt, 'Neither of them is fit enough for so great an effort; unless the oxygen is of greater value than we expect.'

How much was Irvine swayed by Mallory's enthusiasm? Did he have any say in the matter? Did he want any, or was he game for anything? Geoffrey Young had once told Mallory with uncomfortable prescience, 'your weakness, if any, is that you . . . do not hold back from allowing yourself to sweep weaker brethren, carried away by their belief in you, to take risks or exertions that they were not fit for'. Odell was clearly troubled by a similar reservation, which he sought to dispel when describing the pair's departure in the expedition book.

Who with the fighting spirit of Mallory, or with the long-tried obsession of attainment of the greatest goal of his ideals, could be otherwise than impatient to be off on the culminating challenge of a lifetime, nay even of a whole generation of active mountaineers! And Irvine, though through youth without the same intensity of mountain spell that was upon Mallory, yet was every bit, if not more, obsessed to go 'all out' on what was certainly to him the greatest course for 'pairs' he would be ever destined to 'row'!

When the call came from Mallory for 'this one last effort with every means at our disposal', Odell believed that Irvine, however much he wished the attempt were without oxygen, 'saw the necessity of foregoing any personal preference in the matter, and welcomed almost with boyish enthusiasm a chance that he had little thought would come his way.'

Odell returned to the theme (and to a rowing allusion) later in his chapter on Mallory and Irvine's attempt.

I know that Mallory had stated he would take no risks in any attempt on the final peak; but in action the desire to overcome, the craving for the victory that had become for him . . . an obsession, may have been too strong . . . Irvine I know was willing, nay, determined, to expend his last ounce of energy, to 'go all out', as he put it, in an utmost effort to reach the top: for had not his whole training in another hardy pursuit been to inculcate the faculty of supreme final effort?

Irvine's willingness is borne out by his diary entry for the day he and Mallory returned to the North Col in order to 'be ready to fetch sick men down, or make an oxygen attempt ourselves'. He said, 'I hope they've got to the top [Norton and Somervell], but by God, I'd like to have a whack at it myself.' This, from a man of few words, was a clear sign of intent.

How little we know of this young man, Irvine, who joined the expedition on Odell's recommendation. Looking for candidates for a sledging party he was leading to Spitsbergen in 1923, Odell had been struck by a tall oarsman on the tideway at Putney, training with the Oxford boat. In a moment of inspiration he invited him to the Arctic, and had no cause afterwards to be disappointed, for Irvine proved hardy, game and resourceful, a splendid companion for a rugged venture. Upon his return, Odell wasted no time in commending the 21-year-old engineering student to the Everest Committee, and within a matter of weeks Irvine was one of the team. He was fourteen years younger than the average age of the party, sixteen years younger than Mallory.

His modest assurance endeared him to everyone ('neither bumptious by virtue of his "blue", nor squashed by the age of the rest of us', said Somervell), but he must often have felt isolated from their experience and conversation by his youth and lack of intellectualism. He must have longed for a friend of his own age to confide in and relax with. Odell has commented on how withdrawn he became as the Everest show progressed.

Irvine was in charge of equipment, but the amount of time he spent improvising and mending went far beyond the call of duty. He repaired stoves, torches, stools and tables; made rope ladders and lantern shields. At all times, in camps across Tibet, Irvine sought refuge in his 'tinker's shop', tapping and braising away until late into the night. His contact with his fellows largely took the form of performing odd jobs for them. I don't know if this was simply the result of a general helpfulness and good nature on his part, or the easiest way he could see to make overtures to older companions. There may even have been an unconscious sense of hierarchy at work, a hang-over from public school or military days, which saw the youngest, rawest recruit as school fag or batman. Of course Irvine knew he was here for his engineering skills, and the others may have been impractical to a man. Still one is appalled by the amount of work they expected or allowed him to do, bringing him their crampons to fix, cameras to mend, films to develop . . .

Perhaps my response was coloured by the fact that I had a son of similar age. Were he in the place of Irvine, I would not want to think he had been used, or that nobody ever considered his welfare. Whisked away by the glamour of the enterprise, I could not help wondering if Irvine really appreciated what he was getting into. It is certain that his parents did not.

'Poor Mr and Mrs Irvine . . . are terribly broken down,' Mallory's mother wrote after the tragedy. 'I don't think they had in the least realized how great the risk was.'

I could understand the anger his younger brother still felt sixty-two years after Irvine's death, and which he directed particularly towards George Mallory for leading him on that final climb.

Some corporate madness must have been at work when Irvine was selected for the team on such slender mountain qualifications. He and

Odell had undertaken one day's climbing together on the Spitsbergen trip. Otherwise, all that has been recorded is an Easter weekend in North Wales, and some 'glacier-skiing' in Switzerland – this after a three-week crash course on basic turns from Arnold Lunn. For a long while I wondered about that glacier skiing. Perhaps it was an extended tour of the Oberland. And then I found it had been written up by another member of the party, Antony Knebworth. In a letter to his father, the Earl of Lytton (and published in the Earl's memorial to his son, *Antony*), he tells that after a night spent at the Egon von Steiger hut a two-hour run was made the next morning down to a village whose name the young Viscount could not remember ('Platte or Blatter, or something – we called it Blotto'). There they 'found the pub very quickly and all got completely tight for 2 francs'.

> We entertained the village, and sang songs to them for about an hour – in fact we had a real good orgy, and then went on and tried to ski. It's the funniest feeling in the world trying to ski when you're blind. The snow comes up and hits you in the face! Old Fritz [their guide] went first, waving one ski round his head, and sitting down every few yards. One had no idea of the contours or the bumps or anything, and it felt too queer for words. I got down to Goppenstein at about 1.30.

Sandy Irvine slewed in about half an hour later. It had been a jolly jaunt, but the skiing was 'extremely disappointing' and, as useful mountaineering experience, counted for little. Even so, to suppose Irvine an innocent victim of Everest is, I'm sure, to do him an injustice. Every climber's imagination has to be fired somewhere along the line. Without too much difficulty, one could as easily see Mallory propelled towards the Everest adventure on other people's dreams.

Geoffrey Young, for instance, was an inspirational figure to Mallory throughout his adult life, as he was to many mountaineers. Young had a penchant for Arthurian legend and knightly chivalry; he saw mountaineers as latter-day knights errant, swinging ashen-shafted axes in place of swords. A poem he wrote on this theme ended with the words:

> Brothers till death, and a wind-swept grave,
> Joy of the journey's ending:
> Ye who have climbed to the great white veil,
> Hear ye the chant? Saw ye the Grail?

A clear reference to the loss of Mallory and Irvine you would think? But the words were not written in 1924, the year of Mallory's death. They appeared in a 1909 collection, the year Geoffrey Winthrop Young met the youthful and impressionable mountaineer and bestowed upon him the nickname 'Galahad' for his pure and questing spirit.

It was Young who encouraged Mallory to go to Everest. Let us hope his protégé needed little persuasion, for otherwise it is a short jump of the imagination to see Mallory compelled to live out the older man's fantasies.

Alone of the 1924 party, Odell believed Mallory and Irvine had died of exposure, benighted on the mountainside. Perhaps they had been unable to rediscover Camp VI in the dark, it being tucked into a narrow cleft of rock. Odell never saw any reason to alter this conclusion, and never wavered in his conviction that the two reached the summit before they perished.

Norton did not care for the idea that the two could have missed the tent which he and Somervell had erected, however poor the visibility. He was sure a slip by one or other caused them both to fall and sought to reassure the victims' families that death from such 'a purely mountaineering accident' would have been instantaneous.

'It is hard to invent any hypothesis which will cover the facts entailing the idea of a lingering death from exposure,' he wrote to Ruth, 'nor is there any reason to suppose that any defect in the oxygen apparatus could have been the cause.'

George Mallory's mother, who before she learned the news had dreamt that her son was dead, took more comfort from Odell's version. She preferred to believe 'the messenger came for them in their sleep, like the going of Moses'. It was all a great mystery, she said, after Odell had visited the family to describe those last days on the mountain, 'An unending silence'.

Death in the Morning

THIS WAS MY fourth day up here at 21,000 feet, and I wasn't in good shape. My throat and bronchial tubes were on fire – from all that gasping in the cold air coming up – and my limbs felt very heavy. At night tormented dreams and sudden bouts of feverishness kept wrenching me awake, but with such long nights and nothing to do but loll about during the day, how much did that matter? In this thin air the breathing passages exude such copious amounts of mucus it becomes a full time job coughing it all away. Your body must be trying to dissolve more oxygen for your lungs, but runs the risk of drowning you in the process.

I don't think I was sick; I had no headache; but I had no idea either how well or badly I ought to feel. Anyone who has been to altitude before comes to recognize the system's limits. It didn't seem to me that I was deteriorating beyond control, especially as in the daytimes I felt so much better. All the same, I worried I wasn't brighter. My secret dread was of finding myself forced to go down just when climbers were urgently needed up here. The last thing I wanted was for someone to have to escort me back, and I knew I would not be allowed to trudge off on my own. When I heard that Mo was going down that afternoon with the British camera team, it suddenly made sense to head out with them. I wasn't ready to go, didn't want to leave at such an exciting time, for not only were our Sherpas tenuously clinging to the North Col camp, but in the same hurricane winds, two Britons, Harry Taylor and Trevor Pilling, were fighting for their lives high on the North-east Ridge. They had hoped, in one last desperate push, to get through the Pinnacles before going home.

Having swallowed a quick lunch in the Sherpas' kitchen I said goodbye, and in a fierce wind plodded off behind Mo. The cameramen would follow.

111

Goodness, there was a lot of snow about! I kept tripping over as I struggled to keep up. Every time Mo looked round I was floundering about in drifts. I could imagine him thinking, What the hell have I landed myself with here? All he said was, 'Are you sure you want to go down in this?'

But I'd started now. And I'm very stubborn. My mind was already switched into now-or-never mode. We pressed on.

'We can give it another forty minutes,' said Mo. 'See how far we get. What we can't risk is being stranded between camps.'

We wouldn't be.

Mo was very patient. He kept stopping for a smoke to enable me to catch up. He took my camera and snapped some shots. In the pictures I am so far in the distance I can hardly be picked out, even in my red jacket. I couldn't understand why it was taking so long to get *down*hill. Any slight rise in the ground all but finished me off.

I became convinced the Corridor was endless. The old British accounts used to talk of a glacier lassitude affecting people in here . . . something to do with stale air being trapped by the ice. While we were cut off from the worst of the wind, there was enough air swirling about for it not to be stale, but lassitude had made lead weights of my limbs. The snow was even deeper here, and every few steps I hung over my ski stick wanting nothing but for sleep to take me.

Threading the moraine-hills was no less interminable for there was more deep snow, even on the medial crest, not the shattered black rock I had hoped for. What a difference a few days can make.

After six hours, and just as it was getting dark, round a bend Yak Camp hove into view. Mo steamed ahead and put on a kettle, then came back to take my pack and help me up the last hill. There were no lamps in the mess tent and I collapsed on to some packing cases and stared vacantly.

Tony Riley and his camera crew staggered in a short while later and we ate a cold dinner in the dark. This dismal, draughty tent, which was sagging so badly, bore no resemblance to the cheerful staging post where I had so recently spent a week. There was precious little water for another brew, and no-one felt like going out to chip lumps off seracs in the dark. So we sat on, broodily, coughing up our lungs.

It was another tempestuous night, one of the worst so far. Why on earth had our team pitched tents on such an exposed ledge? Up here, where the glacier takes a sharp bend, we were the target of every wind that blew. Again, there was no sleep to be had for coughing and struggling to breathe. The mucus was getting thicker and more racking to shift, like hawking up pennies. 'Beware the green-lungers,' Cathy used to say of altitude coughs. Couldn't tell the colour by torchlight, but I could taste I was coughing up blood with these. Surely that was just the constant rasping, I told myself, so don't panic.

When the sun came up, I wobbled weakly down to the mess tent and started trying to jack up all the poles that had collapsed in the night. I lit the gas under the old stewed tea as a gesture towards breakfast. What the hell was the matter with me? I ought to have been feeling better, having lost a couple of thousand feet. Why wasn't it working? When Tony Riley shuffled in, I said, 'I'm having trouble breathing.'

No sympathy there. 'I'm having a heart attack,' he countered. We resumed our coughing.

Later, we set off down towards base, leaving Mo to pack up the camp. Before long I had lost sight of Tony and the others among the moraine heaps. I sat and waited, and when they did not come, supposed they must be somewhere ahead.

I reached the river at the wide crossing the yaks use. It was partly iced over and I crossed without difficulty. Before long I was back in the ruins of the pioneer camp, where I stopped for a drink and a bite of a fruitola bar. There was no sign of the others in either direction. At least the going was easier now, with no snow on this side of the river. The track I knew quite well from my afternoon walks.

Already it was 4 o'clock. I don't know why everything took so long. I missed the path once and had to make a weary scramble back up on to it. On these wonky legs skirting the exposed bits was even worse than usual. Slowly I made ground.

Somewhere down that last passage between the Main Rongbuk glacier and the earth towers, Tony Riley passed me. So he and the other two had been behind all the time.

The tower with the eyelet right through it, which I always reckoned marked the halfway point of this section, steadfastly refused to come any closer. It was getting dark.

At long, long last, I turned the corner in sight of the camps. Figures trickled out across the moraine waste towards me. Ronnie Faux was the first to reach my side.

'Bad news, Audrey,' he said. 'One of your Sherpas was killed on the Col today. It's just come over the radio.'

★

Sue Giller had noticed some dark figures descending when she looked up at the Col that morning. The next time she glanced in that direction they were scurrying back up again. Probably very sensible, she thought, to sit it out a bit longer if the snow conditions were bad. Wait for all that new stuff to consolidate a bit more.

The weather at Advanced Base Camp was clear and cold with little wind. Above the Col the mountain was being battered by the full strength of the jetstream winds. It was the fifth day the four Sherpas had been stranded up there.

Early that morning, Andy and Nawang Yongden, the Sirdar, had spoken with them by radio as usual, and agreed that, with no prospect of climbing higher, the men should try to come down. Dawa Nuru led the small party that set out at about ten o'clock, while Andy and Nawang anxiously watched their progress down the fixed ropes until only one Sherpa was still visible, the others having dropped below the rise in the glacier which concealed the lower third of the slope.

This man they saw stop, and presently two of the others climbed back towards him. Andy had his radio switched on, but it was only when the two ascending sherpas rejoined the last man, who carried their radio, that he received the alarming tidings that Dawa Nuru had fallen. A small avalanche had struck the Sherpa and borne him down the slope.

The news roared around camp. 'All people, quick, quick, go help!' the Sherpas shouted. David, Steve Shea and two Sherpas dashed off without loads, leaving Andy to supervise everyone else into taking up spades and ropes and other items of emergency equipment.

From Advanced Base to the foot of the Col is no great distance, but it rises gently and steadily. In the thin air, hurrying rescuers, themselves no longer in peak condition, were forced to stop every few minutes, hands on hips, to strain painfully after breath.

Twenty-five minutes after the radio alert David and Steve were at the foot of the Col. Altogether, no more than forty minutes had passed since the accident.

An arm was sticking out from a mass of tumbled snow and ice below the line of fixed ropes. They scrabbled in the debris, and quickly had Dawa free, but it was too late. His neck was broken. There was nothing anyone could have done.

Dawa's three companions continued clambering down, and before long had joined the shocked group at the foot of the slope. With their help, David moved the body clear of the fallen debris.

When the other rescuers pulled over the rise, Dawa, wrapped in a sleeping bag, was placed on an inflatable toboggan that Tom had brought up. The melancholy cortège then made its way back to Advance Base Camp, everyone drawn with sorrow, the Sherpas weeping freely. Dawa was much loved. He was an experienced climber, one who had reached the summit of Everest the year before with Chris Bonington and the Norwegians. He was perhaps the most devout of all our Sherpas, and could often be heard praying to propitiate the gods before setting off on a climb.

The exact cause of the avalanche was not clear. It seems likely that one of the Sherpas above Dawa Nuru on the rope triggered the snow slide that ripped him from his footing, carrying him over a sixty-foot cliff. A growing avalanche of large, compacted snow blocks followed in his wake, and it was probably the pummelling he received from these blocks, coupled with the weight of the oxygen bottle in his pack, that broke his neck.

The next day Dawa's body was carried on down to interim camp, and on the day following it was brought by yak to Base Camp, where we had cleared out the mess tent for use as a temple.

★

When I was coming down to Base Camp on the day of the accident, growing increasingly tired as the afternoon wore on, I had wondered if – like the famous marathon runner – I would collapse at the finishing post. My body was giving up on me. By this time my breathing was an asthmatic wheeze, one eye had fused shut for god knows what reason of its own, and when finally I reached the others, my voice, too, had vanished once more. Staggering drunkenly, I rounded the moraine bank into the arms of my friends and croaked a greeting. Concerned Sherpas hurried over to take my load – but that I had already dumped at Yak Camp. Ronnie Faux supported one arm, Roger Vernon the other and Tsintin, our young Tibetan cookboy, having welcomed me effusively with a huge hug, took both my hands and, dancing backwards, guided me over the stones. Clinging together we stumbled into the cook tent where I was immediately plumped on to a crate and plied with supersweet tea.

It was Roger's birthday and Mary Kay had been helping the cooks prepare a special banquet in his honour when they received the news about Dawa Nuru. Now, although the meal was still being cooked, nobody would eat it with any heart. My arrival had served as a welcome diversion. For a short while the misery could be forgotten as everyone gathered round, fussing, caring, giving me all the love and attention no-one could now extend to poor Dawa.

Within minutes, Philip Horniblow, the doctor, had taken charge. He ordered me into one of the larger frame tents, newly designated as our 'hospital', where Ken was already recovering from his stint at altitude. My temperature was taken and my bubbling chest listened to, then I was tucked up with a bowl of soup, a hot water bottle and an oxygen flask at the ready.

'You have bronchiolitis,' Philip declared, but without conviction since it usually only afflicted children under eighteen months!

Antibiotics were prescribed and sprays to relieve any spasms. Ken would keep an eye on me, and all through the night, whenever I wheezed, his would be the finger that reached the aerosol button first. Before I dropped off, Roger brought in a batch of mail that had just arrived. News at last of Peter and Tom at home, and two letters from Adam! Better than any potions. Clutching them tightly, I drifted happily to sleep – safe and snug. The rest could wait until morning. As the old Everesters would have put it, I had shot my bolt.

That next day remains a blur in my memory, a hazy, billowing, intoxicated blur. In waking moments Ken and I played tapes and talked. Nerve-ends raw, my emotions ran havoc to the music. Welling cadences conjured visions of green and birdsong. I floated on spring breezes. Waterfalls dripped amid verdant ferns. The beauty was almost unbearable. This was more than just a coming back to life, it was the heightened awareness of rebirth. From the sterile heights where death stalked, I was back in the world of the living. I had loved being up there, but felt an overwhelming sense of deliverance upon coming down.

Departing Spirits

DAWA NURU'S BODY was brought in to Base Camp. We clustered round as he was laid out in our 'temple'. The sherpas had supervised all the funeral arrangements, and Dawa was to be cremated in the ruins of the Old Nunnery the next day. Two lamas came up from Rongbuk to perform the rites for ensuring that his spirit detached itself from his body, and from all ties to his earthly relatives and friends, freeing it for rebirth. All night, as we tossed and coughed sleeplessly in our tents, we heard them at their vigil, humming and chanting, accompanied by the icy tinkling of little bells.

The most propitious time for the ceremony, it appeared, was at daybreak, and long before it was light, Dawa's body was taken further down-valley while the rest of us shivered in the frosty air, waiting for the jeep to return for us.

In a pink and turquoise dawn we bumped to a halt at the boulder mound which concealed the Nunnery. A full moon hung over the mountain wall to our left. It was crackly cold.

Still feeble, I lagged behind as the others surged over the hill in clouds of breath. Kee-Chak took my arm and helped me up. The two lamas were already there, as well as Nawang and some of our other sherpas. They had set up a little altar in one of the ruined buildings, and decked it with butter lamps and sacrificial *tormas*. Juniper wood had been brought up from the valley for the pyre.

Dawa Nuru was carefully undressed and placed naked upon the logs. As first light caught the encircling mountaintops, the fire was lit. A scrawny old monk capered round, pouring oils and other offerings on to the blaze, praying and humming. He wore coloured felt boots and a full-length, faded maroon *chuba*. The beads of his rosary swung at his waist.

We stood silently, huddled, close. Only Dawa's special friend kept

117

apart, pinched with loneliness. With the little pile of clothes at his feet, pathetic residue of a life, he watched as the flames licked the smooth, brown skin of his childhood companion.

The fire burned well in the still air, spitting, hissing, its red embers slumping and shifting. The corpse arched and blackened, thrust stiff, seared arms into the towering smoke.

In one hollow of silence, Andy stepped forward and addressed the flames. Softly he said, 'Dawa, you made our lives so much richer with your friendship, your cheerfulness, your ever-willing sense of adventure. Know that our love and our respect go with you to your new life – as we, always, will treasure your memory, will carry part of you with us in our hearts, wherever we go.'

After an hour or two in the blue cold we broke for a cup of tea. David and Andy took Nawang down to the Rongbuk Monastery to complete formalities. They were hoping to have Dawa's death horoscope cast to indicate what his transition would be like, and what further rites should be observed, but the chief lama was still away and nobody could find the special astrological book.

The rest of us stood on at the dwindling fire, seeing Dawa through to his next existence.

When we left, only ashes remained. The Sherpas would come down later to retrieve these, some to take home to his family, some to cast into the river in a private ceremony. Now that Dawa's spirit had started its long journey through *Bardo*, the between-life state, we were not to mention his name any more. Nothing must be allowed to deflect him from his passage. Reincarnated, his spirit should return to Earth within seven times seven days.

★

The heightened goodwill which had bound us so closely during the last weeks was wearing thin. I couldn't bear it. This team, which I had come to regard as a family, showed serious signs of schism. Of course everyone was worn out, disappointed at our lack of success, bitter at the death of Dawa Nuru. All of us were operating on shortened, highly volatile fuses. Tempers flared, tears flowed with little warning. We grew increasingly irritated with each other's less attractive qualities. One evening, after too much wine at dinner and upon hearing that those left at Advanced Base were getting ready to evacuate, Andy and David bemoaned our lack of purpose. I went to bed. I didn't want to hear such things, even if it was just frustration talking.

The exodus had put paid to last hopes, though there was still talk of David and Steve going up again, if only to recover expensive film equipment. We really had been unfortunate. The weather had shown us no quarter all season, with never more than a week clear at a stretch. It was of little consolation to learn afterwards that it had been the worst autumn this century, with monsoon storms running right through to the onset of winter. The pattern persisted. After the success of Loretan and Troillet at the end of August, no-one else on any expedition managed to climb Everest again until Christmas of the following year.

Sue arrived back in Base Camp the next day, and spent a long, acrimonious de-briefing in Andy's tent. We crept around outside listening to the raised voices without being able to tell what was going on. The good news was that the Brits had finally decided to broach the barrel of beer they had been brewing throughout the expedition. We were invited to help them drink it.

'I don't believe it!' said Andy in some exasperation as Mary Kay came smiling through the door, bearing a plate of popcorn. 'You're supposed to be at Yak Camp, manning the radio!'

'Oh, I've made tonight's call,' she said sweetly. 'I'll get up early and go back for the one in the morning.' She didn't like being alone up there with the yakmen, that's what it was – that and the fact she could never resist a party.

The Brits were in fine fettle. From their mongrel beginnings, they really had welded into a relaxed and happy team. Brummie welcomed us expansively. He looked wilder than ever, bewhiskered, hair bleached, startling eyes – near-white in their lightness. Horniblow had shucked out his tweed hacking jacket, but had no intention of dispensing with the green desert turban he always wore as last of the Great White Explorers. Beside him: Harry, solid, stolid, benign; Ronnie, whose thigh-slapping joviality boosted a natural resemblance to Bluff King Hal; Paul Nunn, identified (as always) by his booming, inimitable guffaw; Joe Brown, down salopettes leaking feathers; Mo, gamin, gap-toothed, rumpled, badgery sideburns escaping from under his cap. Cross-legged on the table, he was telling ribald stories. 'Like a Breton sailor,' Horniblow said. 'Don't you just love him?' No hint then that Mo wouldn't go on for ever.

They dived into the popcorn, spitting, throwing it at one another like schoolboys. When the cigars lit up, I fought through the smoke and took my tickly throat to bed. You could think yourself in a

119

mountain sanatorium here at night, as consumptive coughing echoes from tent to tent.

The end-of-term madness continued to build. Mary Kay burst into my tent one morning, thrusting a sealed pack of smoked salmon at me.

'Guard this!' she instructed. 'With your life.'

'Why, what's it for?'

'Got to save it for the Sherpa party, and I don't trust *anyone* but you. There were three packs yesterday, and now this is all that's left!'

Best not to tell her I had joined in the gobbling with everyone else. I stuck it under my mattress.

All manner of stores were running low. Already we'd had to go cap in hand to the Brits, begging toilet paper. And very scratchy old Army stuff it was too – more like cardboard. It didn't suit the Americans at all.

'When the food's all gone,' I asked Ken, 'do they start eating the oldest or the youngest first?'

'We won't wait around to find out,' he said. 'Be ready to hi-tail it out of here before that moment comes.'

Roger, Ken and I went down to the old pioneer base to recreate Captain Noel's famous photograph with the long sunset shadows – hard to match exactly as this was a different time of year. We had much more snow, too, but it would be close enough to allow a dissolve from black and white into colour to give a sense of time in the Mallory and Irvine film. The river was almost frozen over now, so we were able to cross to the high-level moraine on the other side for an oblique look into the entrance of the East Rongbuk Valley. Should we need it, this was the shot to illustrate the approach that Mallory missed.

It is very secretive and insignificant. Really, we ought not to be too surprised that he overlooked it. Yet where else should he have expected to find a way to the other side of the North Col if not up the nearest valley? He is a puzzle, that man, but you cannot fault him on gusto. The amount of reconnoitring he and Bullock got through in 1921 is phenomenal. When you scramble up these steep cliffs of jagged scree, or look over the tossed seracs of the Rongbuk Glaciers, if you remember how turbulent the rivers are, and icy when swollen with snow-melt, then you appreciate the sheer distance and ruggedness of the terrain they covered. This mountain, up whose plinth we were now labouring, was one of many they nipped up for a better view of the glacier configuration on this side of Everest. And almost all the viewpoints they reached, Mallory or Bullock went back to again, to rephotograph them once they learned they had messed up their first set of pictures.

From up here our camps looked so small. We could hardly make out figures – even through the camera lens we could not identify who was who. Only the British and we were left now. Air-Over-Everest had been forced to give up. On the day I walked up to Yak Camp their leader Steve McKinney made a flight from 20,300 feet on the West Ridge down to the Rongbuk Glacier. He took a swig of oxygen before launching himself into space and landed safely on skis. Encouraged, the gliders were set up on the Shoulder for further flights, but the storms and high winds that pinned us in Yak for a week and continued to interrupt climbing for the rest of October, frustrated that expedition too. In the middle of the month the camp was dismantled and the gliders brought down. Catherine Freer and Andy Politz made one last attempt at the Hornbein Couloir, but conditions there had deteriorated seriously since the Swiss climb and that too was abandoned. The expedition pulled out a few days later.

The river we could see was almost white with ice, a loose, white-fringed plait. Halfway between the two camps a giant bonfire consumed rubbish. Brummie's lorries were expected that afternoon.

We were up early next morning to wave them off. Nobody envied them on the back of their trucks, bundled in all their down gear. Stiff with cold already, it would be two or three hours at least before the sun came up. This spelt the end for our expedition as well, and we began clearing camps.

There was a straw poll to see who should go up and man Yak Camp radio that night. Andy kept the short straw, and we never knew if this was his way of volunteering for an unpopular task. While he was away we raided the last of the booze, then went wild on the empty food chests. Their resonant polythene made them perfect native drums, we discovered.

One of the store tents had been taken over as mess; it had not seemed right to continue using the old one after Dawa had been laid out in there. We sat among the sacks and boxes and hanging relics of meat, thumping the chests between our knees. The noise bounced off the mountain walls, and reverberated over the empty moraine.

David clambered on to the table, and swung round the tentpole to our best renderings of 'The Stripper'. Catherine Freer immediately jumped up to show him how it should be done, exotic dancing being just one of many talents this exuberant mountaineer employed to earn the pennies that kept her climbing. Cheese told tall stories. Yager's eyes crossed as he drummed himself into a frenzy. And Tom's normal no-nonsense manner was tossed to the winds as he pummelled and sang with the loudest, his red hunter's cap cock-eyed on his head, his raffish new beard glistening in the lamplight.

Sue retired early to bed, distancing herself from such dissolute behaviour. The Sherpas shook their heads and kept quietly out of the way, fearing we had all gone mad.

We had. By the time we were finished we had all but emptied one storage bin of wine and beer, and hurled the barrel into the night.

Luckily, there was sufficient left to hold the party for the Sherpas the following night. Everyone was down. We danced and sang until night-cold and tiredness drove us to our pits. Once more the dome tent span like a pinwheel when I tried to lay my head.

All too soon, the last days passed. Base Camp grew desolate and empty as tents were demolished and loads stacked into piles. We finished filming the interviews we needed, and almost all else on our 'shopping list'. Our lorries rumbled towards us over the stones a day earlier than we expected.

This was it! Bed tea at 6 o'clock, then frantic last-minute packing and trading with the yakmen for bells, saddles and yak-hair rope. Fires were lit inside the engines of the lorries to thaw out their frozen works. Just one sequence remained to be filmed of a Sherpa flying a kite, and we gambolled on the stones, getting the thing aloft. Just as we were wrapping up, Ang Nima accidentally let go of the string, and our kite soared away into the blue. The trailing line must have snagged a rock for when we pulled out of Base Camp an hour or so later, we spotted a brave little red dot, endlessly circling high on the mountain wall.

★

A sacred spring spills across the path just above Rongbuk. We pulled up so that Kee-Chak could fill a bottle with holy water. At the monastery we stopped again for David to present his sunglasses to an old nun. All the time we had been here this bent little crone had squinted at us from behind old-fashioned Chinese snow goggles with glass in only one eye. She could not believe this fancy new pair was really meant for her. When David returned to Everest the following year, she still wore them proudly, and she recognized him at once, cackling with delight to see her friend again.

Kee-Chak brought the jeep to yet another halt in the first village along the road and leaned on his horn. Children tumbled out to greet him, followed by their elders. He was clearly a well-known and popular visitor, and as his travelling companions the welcome extended to us too. We were tugged into one of the houses to be given sweet milk-tea. Now I understood why Kee-Chak had insisted I collect some of the water too. The mother of the house poured the precious liquid carefully into a jug to be used in the daily devotions to the household gods. In exchange, we were given fresh chang, measure for measure. We toasted the view from the top of the Pang La – a horizonful of peaks like breaking surf, Everest in the centre, clearly the tallest, trailing a long plume of blown snow as if it were smoke from a volcano. We toasted Everest. We toasted us.

A few miles further down the road we stopped and did it all again!

In the Xegar compound dismal reality reasserted itself as we waited for those in the lorries to catch up. This was our last evening all together before the expedition divided. I was one of four who had cannily exchanged places with those in the Kathmandu party so as to go out a different way.

The food did nothing to raise our subdued spirits and we took ourselves off to the local bar in the Tibetan quarter, a real hole in a real wall where, for a while, the villagers could forget the constant blare of public loud-speakers. Cheerful, cramped, smoky, it called to mind the high altitude saloon in *Raiders of the Lost Ark*. Customers (all men) had the dashing air of brigands with their wound braids, turquoise ear studs and gold-glinting smiles. We ordered chang and watched them playing an oriental version of shove-ha'penny. When politely invited to have a go, we disgraced ourselves by performing so badly that it took an hour to clear the board. The longer it went on, the more embarrassed we became until finally, with three fine if flukey shots, Ken finally brought the game to a conclusion and we disappeared into the night.

The chang had succeeded only in making us sulky. I scuffed back to the blockhouses feeling miserable and hungry. Already I was missing Nima Tenzing's cooking. We raided the lunch-food boxes for cheese and chocolate and made one last feeble attempt at partying. A surprising awkwardness had grown between us, as if, now that our long isolation was at an end, our separate worlds were clawing us back. Families, careers, other friends beckoned and the bonds were breaking apart. Two and a half months ago most of these people had been strangers to me. That seemed impossible to believe now. Maybe we would never more grow as close. Some I might never see again. Still, I knew these were my foul-weather friends, friends for all seasons, friends for life.

There seemed nothing to be salvaged from this cold night, and with an early start promised for the morning, I slunk off to bed where I shivered under extra blankets.

The goodbyes were painful. In the bleak yard I hugged Sue and Andy, and then Tom. I shook hands with Kee-Chak, my first Tibetan friend, and – clinging desperately to a faltering smile – hugged Roger and Ken before clambering into the cab of one of the lorries. Waving goodbye, we swung out of the compound, back over the river, and headed westwards across the high plateauland of Tibet towards the Nepalese border. All the way to Tingri, I sat squeezed between the Chinese driver and Nawang Yongden with tears distorting the view.

Scattered settlements, rainbow cliffs, ruins of temples and fortresses on the most inaccessible of crags swept by. Sandstone pillars masqueraded as the stumps of old Mongol forts – or was it the other way round? After a doughball lunch, David joined me in the cab and slept his way through the most beautiful high desert country, deep russet in colour and rimmed with snowy himals. Once over the high Thong La pass, a bristling cockade of a peak rose into view, hung about with glaciers. I could not allow him to miss all this.

'Wake up!' I nudged. 'Isn't that Shisha Pangma?'

'Mmmm?'

But when he opened his eyes he at once sat bolt upright and began picking out its possible routes. It was an astonishingly beautiful mountain.

The route was downhill now, all the way into Nepal. This may seem strange if you think we hadn't yet crossed the Himalaya. That would be achieved by threading through a series of deep valleys draining south. We dropped off the dome of the plateau and into the first incision.

At once vegetation began to appear – scrubby little bits and pieces at first, then bigger shrubs in autumn tints. Soon the air was syrupy and we were into gorges luxuriant with tropical forest, just like those of my fantasies when I came down from the high camp. I longed to be out on the back of the truck instead of shut up here in the front. No matter that those who were riding up there with the luggage had to keep dodging branches and outcropping bits of cliff, or squealed with alarm as we rounded exposed corners. Outside Khasa vehicles had backed up in both directions behind the scattered debris of a rockfall, which drivers, passengers and villagers were contemplating gloomily ...

'Come on, you guys!' David and Steve began trundling a huge boulder towards the drop at the edge of the road.

Suddenly everyone was shouting instructions, pushing, pulling, levering stones out of the way. Before long a passage was cleared, sufficiently wide to let the traffic through. We followed the truck in front, holding our breath lest anything else come down. A short distance below lay the little border town where we were to spend the night. These steep hairpin loops on either side of Khasa are notorious for their landslips. The cliffs above are marbled with fresh scars, below which trails of felled trees indicate the passage of thundering rock. With the road continually doubling back on itself, a single chute of rubble can block it in several places. We saw one house with a gaping hole front and back and were told that a sleeping family was wiped out there a short while ago. The boulder had not even stopped, but ploughed on to wreak more havoc lower down.

Months earlier the road between the checkpost in Khasa and the river bridge which marks the actual border had slumped away. No one was in any hurry to repair it while men and boys of the village were provided with work portering. After passport and customs formalities, lorries proceeded as far as the landslip, where their contents would be off-loaded on to straining backs and transported down the slippery slopes to a waiting vehicle on the Nepalese side of the bridge. A bus was coming up from Kathmandu to meet our group on the far side.

With us, this far, had come Tsintin, the young Tibetan yakboy who took over in the kitchen when Anju fell sick. He had worked so well that Nima Tenzing made him the offer of employment in Kathmandu. There was one snag: the lad had no passport.

'We can give you a lift to the border,' Andy had told him. 'But we daren't risk smuggling you across without papers. There, you're on your own, I'm afraid, Tsintin.'

To him, it seemed worth the risk. He slipped back to his village the night before we left to say goodbye to his parents. There was no telling when, or even if, he would see them again. If he were successful and made it into Nepal, as an illegal immigrant he could expect just as much trouble getting out again. I worried. The boy was still so young. Not a week before he had scalded himself in the kitchen and whimpered with pain and fear; almost a child he seemed then. I had grown extremely fond of him and hoped life would be kind.

Light at the End of the Tunnel

NEXT MORNING WE gathered at the border. The Friendship Highway appeared to be living up to its name. Cheerful Western classics blared from the loudspeakers rather than the usual propaganda. At the first strains of the 'Blue Danube', Jed and I stepped into a Viennese waltz, egged on by our friends as cameras clicked. There was barely time to become dizzy before a Chinese official pounced.

Snatching Mary Kay's camera, he ripped out the film with great flourish. 'Passport!' he barked, holding out his hand until she gave it to him.

'What the hell's this all about' 'What's the matter?' The cries went round.

No dancing, no photographs . . . that was the gist of it. To the Chinese, the border post represented a military installation, frivolous behaviour an insult to their authority.

The man looked round for more cameras, insisting he had seen at least two people taking pictures. If we did not submit our films, he said, we would be searched. No one would be allowed through. We would be held in detention until the matter was sorted out.

Our protests were brushed aside. An aide ran to fetch the man's superior. Taking advantage of the confusion, I slipped behind one of our lorries and changed the film in my own camera. I did not want my last pictures of the high plateau sacrificed to this petty tyrant. The little can of half-exposed film I passed surreptitiously to Jed, who slid it into a pocket.

The Border Guard was gesticulating now at our lorries. Oh my God! He wasn't going to strip them down, was he? He'd get all our precious films then, everything we'd taken on the whole expedition. Why the hell had I been so foolish as to lark about here?

I let the bastard see my camera.

'Give!' he commanded.

I gave.

He opened the back. To my horror, I saw that in my fumbling haste I had not properly engaged the new film. Instead of winding it on half-way, as I thought, there was the end flapping loosely inside. Our friend guessed at once what I had done, tore it out and shouted some more.

The man's superior strode up and eyed us coldly, then inclined his head to receive the tirade of his minion. He scrutinized our papers. When he looked up it was without hostility. We clearly weren't spies in his book. 'No more photographs,' he said at length, handing Mary Kay back her passport.

The guard stammered in protest. He pointed at me and my phony film, but he'd been overruled. The matter was closed. With two of our films lying in the dust honour had been satisfied. We were waved on.

This border is known for its tight security. Recently the Chinese had caught and given long gaol sentences to a couple of Western gold-smugglers trying to slip into Nepal by way of the river. Tsintin was right to be apprehensive. In the Sherpa lodge the night before he had been lighting one cigarette after another. This morning he had disappeared entirely. I imagined he was off to find a way over the mountains.

At the landslip when David and Nawang Yongden were apportioning loads from the back of the truck, they were amazed to see a familiar face in the crowd waiting to be hired. In all the hubbub with the guard, no one had noticed Tsintin slip into No Man's Land with a group of porters: had we planned it, we could not have given him better cover! We knew we must show him no recognition. Even if he got over the bridge safely, there was still the Nepalese Security on the other side.

When, finally, we and our kit were all across and aboard the bus, setting off for Kathmandu and tucking into the blueberry pie and champagne provided for us by Yager's wife, who had come to meet us, there, grinning broadly at the roadside, waiting to be picked up, stood Tsintin.

Next morning, in Kathmandu, I scarcely recognized the immaculate figure in new jeans and tee-shirt, wearing a smart red baseball cap. There was no need to have worried for him. He wheeled a bicycle. If he kept going at this rate, Tsintin would be driving a Mercedes in no time at all.

*

During the first weeks and months home, I continued to breathe the rarefied air of Everest. It was impossible to put it from my mind – Everest, Everest, Everest! It coloured my every day. On and on I chattered, trying to make sense of the experience, to reconcile what we did and found with the mountainous hopes and expectations that had preceded the trip.

Had we come any closer to knowing Mallory? Any closer to answering the perennial questions – why was it young Irvine he took on that last climb, not Odell; what misfortune befell them up there; and had they trodden those summit snows?

Many of Mallory's closest friends were always convinced that with the summit in his sights, he would not, could not, have turned back. 'With the only difficulty passed . . . it would have been an impossibility,' declared Winthrop Young, who had been Mallory's early tutor in the Alps and mentor over many years, and who thought him 'unconscious of the impossible'.

'He was mentally ill over Everest,' Captain Noel used to say. 'Thought of nothing else, day and night. He could see the top of that mountain and he wanted to see himself there. It dominated him.'

'What about Irvine,' we had asked him. 'could he have reached the summit?'

'Bit overweight, but yes, he was fit and very strong. Perfectly capable . . . '

'Even of climbing the Second Step?'

'They got to the top. I know that!'

This was something Noel told us frequently, authoritatively, and always with a great play of mysteriousness. At first, he would add, 'Don't ask me how I know – I can't tell you!' Later he confessed to having hung on to a personal article belonging to Andrew Irvine through which a 'psychometric impression' could be elicited. With its aid, he said, a Tibetan lama had been able to 'see' Mallory fall into a crevasse.

'Are there any crevasses on the North side of Everest?' Noel demanded. Then without waiting for a reply, 'No! I have examined the mountain very accurately with my longest telescope and my 20-inch camera lens – none on that face! But on the final slopes, within the last five or six hundred feet, right where the summit pyramid starts to rise from the mountain's crest, possibly there you'll find a crevasse. That is where you must look for George Mallory.'

Well, we had not made it anywhere like as high as that. And in any case, what about the body that Wang Hong Bao, the Chinese climber, was said to have found? That was a lot lower down at 27,000 feet, although even that was still higher than our expedition had managed to get. What were we to make of that? Could we believe in its existence when we only had a secondhand press report to go on and the matter was vigorously denied by the Chinese authorities?

A British climber was once present when a Chinese mountaineer had been questioned about Wang's find. 'There is no body!' the man announced, but afterwards he had whispered to the Briton that it was not something on which the Chinese Mountaineering Authority was eager to encourage speculation. There might have been a camera on the body, and the CMA did not want a picture to be found that could prove Chinese climbers were not the first to ascend from the north.

Nobody could ask Wang, of course. He had been killed climbing to the North Col in 1979 – curiously on the day after imparting his story to a Japanese mountaineer. At least we could check out the facts with this man, Hasegawa Yoshinori, and some months before leaving for Everest, Andy arranged for another Japanese climber to question him. Hasegawa would have preferred not to go into it all again, he said, but was at last persuaded to write down for the first time what had passed between himself and Wang. A translation arrived of Hasegawa's letter, in which he apologized for his memory being so unclear on some points. The events were a long time ago. Please remember also, he said, that his only language was Japanese and Wang spoke only Chinese; neither of them had any ability in English.

'Our conversation was made by very simple words,' Hasegawa explained, 'by characters written on the snow and for the most part by gesture . . . Only the word "English" – Wang pronounced it as "Engleese" – had already become common between us through our conversation when we passed across the remains of the camp of the English team near Camp I.'

Hasegawa had become very interested in the story of Maurice Wilson, and this prompted him, when they arrived at the site for Camp III on 11 October 1979, to ask Wang if it was where they had found Wilson's corpse four years before. Wang immediately answered 'Yes', but showed little interest in the body of Wilson, beginning instead (Hasegawa wrote) to speak of another body.

. . . pointing up to the northeast edge with his finger (from this spot we could command the whole north-east edge and the last slope

129

leading to the summit), he said to me, '8,100 metre Engleese', and he made a gesture to sleep.

This gesture of sleeping was made in the way that you put your palms of both hands together against your cheek, and incline your head to one side with saying to children, 'Now let's go sleep' . . .

Then Wang opened his mouth, pointed his finger to his cheek, pecked it slightly with his finger, and whirled it as if to catch a dragonfly. He also gestured at his clothing, picking at it, moving his finger to his mouth and blowing off it.

Hasegawa interpreted this to mean that the victim's mouth was agape, the cheek perhaps sunken or pecked by birds, and that it was an old body with clothing so blown and weathered it was nothing but tatters. He was sure they also discussed the posture of the body and the exact position in which it was discovered, but these details had now vanished from his memory. What remained clear was that Wang gave a big nod when in Chinese characters Hasegawa wrote with his axe in the snow: 'A body of Englishman at 8,100 metres'? (Chinese and Japanese characters are common in some instances, and the translator of Hasegawa's letter confirmed that they were so in this case.)

In 1980 Hasegawa returned to Everest, where this time his team discovered the body of Wu Song Yu, one of the 1975 Chinese party. It was lying at 8,200 metres in a line with the First Step, and this was enough to convince him that, if Mallory or Irvine had fallen from the ridge, they too would still be lying on a terrace somewhere on the upper part of the North Face. If he had entertained doubts before, Hasegawa was now certain that Wang Hong Bao had indeed stumbled across one or other of them.

And several years later, he too was heard no more. I feel that this is some kind of fate. I cannot say anything about what it does mean for us to discover the bodies which are finally settled in the place where they will rest for eternity. But if others are going to try again to discover their bodies with such purpose, I pray for them to fulfil their purpose safely. Please give them my best regards . . .

After monsoon season, the Choma Lungma is covered with thick snow, and everything may be hidden under the snow. I am afraid that the search will be very difficult. One more thing I must mention is that the slope of the North Col in autumn is very dangerous and dreadful. Please advise them to be very careful.

'I would like to finish this letter with a prayer for all the souls who had died in the Mt Choma Lungma,' Hasegawa concluded, 'especially Wang Hong Bao.'

Here, then, was confirmation of Hasegawa's earlier account, but not of course of Wang's. No one could now confirm that. Yet Tom Holzel had pinned great hopes on finding someone else, besides Hasegawa, to whom Wang confided details of his macabre find. He wondered whether to visit Wang's widow, if he could track her down in Beijing, and in Base Camp Tom spent much time questioning our liaison officer, Mr Song, who had been a member of the expedition on which Wang was alleged to have made his discovery. We filmed them together, Mr Song animatedly prodding a sketch of the upper slopes of the mountain with his finger.

'Yes, of course I have heard the Wang story,' he told Tom through an interpreter. 'None of it is true. Wang never report finding the body of English mountaineer.'

Tom's spirits were dashed. Later, he tried other approaches in case he had phrased the question wrongly, but the answer kept coming back the same. Wang told no-one anything about a find. Song was a terrific character – we all liked him – but he was also in the employ of the CMA. Was he saying to us, 'No body – that is a fact', or was it, 'No body – that is official'? We couldn't be sure. Tom showed Song a copy of his article defending the much-disputed Chinese claim to have climbed Everest in 1960. The West had taken a long time to accept this ascent: official reports at the time had been sketchy and their blatant recourse to Party rhetoric stuck in the craw.

Among references to the strategic thinking of Mao Tse-tung and the shining light of the motherland, Tom homed in on a small topographical detail that proved beyond doubt, he felt, that they had indeed been to the summit. Song softened. He recognized faces of his friends in the article's accompanying photographs. Tom put it to him –

'Isn't it possible that Wang found the body and didn't report it officially? Maybe he just told his friends?'

'If that is so,' Song told him, 'I know who his climbing partners were. You can meet them on your way home.'

In Lhasa, Tom was introduced to Chen Tian Liang, Wang's Group Climbing Leader, but his story was essentially the same as Song's. No, Wang had definitely not found a body at 27,000 feet. 'I should know,' he said, 'I was with him all the time we were high on the mountain.'

In an article in *Summit* magazine, Tom has told how for five hours he grilled the Chinese climber, frequently feeling the need to apologize for such intrusive questioning. He simply could not reconcile the blank denials he was getting with the unsolicited detail in Hasegawa's testimony. Hasegawa had no cause to make it all up.

Chen said, 'If Wang find body, it could only have been Chinese climber he sent up to find, Wu Tsung Yue, who slipped – has heart attack maybe – near below First Step.'

That was clearly ridiculous, as Chen himself was quick to allow. Of course Wang would have recognized the body of one of his own party, and would have dashed back at once to his fellows with the news.

The interview dragged on, getting nowhere. Outside it was growing dark and Chen began to fidget. He wanted to get home.

In desperation, Tom finally asked, 'Is there anything we haven't covered? Anything at all?'

Chen thought for a moment. 'One thing,' he said at length. 'While resting at Camp VI, I have radio call tell me climb to bivouac camp, Camp VII, and look for missing climber.'

'Did you take Wang with you?' Tom wanted to know.

'No. I go with Tibetan porter.'

'So Wang was on his own at Camp VI all day, while you climbed up to VII?'

'That is right.'

'Isn't it possible, Mr Chen, that Wang discovered the English body during that time?'

Chen fixed Tom with a long look before replying. 'Yes,' he said. 'Is possible.'

'Was anybody else at VI that day?'

'Zhang Jun Yan,' Chen told him. 'He live in Beijing.'

Tom was elated with this small victory. Next morning he pressed the liaison officer to set up a meeting with Mr Zhang as soon as they reached the Chinese capital. He had almost given up hope of hearing anything, however, when on the afternoon before he was to fly home, a telephone call came through at last from Song to say Zhang would stop by at the Bei-Wei Hotel that evening. Tom was uncharacteristically nervous waiting for his guest. He had bet so much on the Japanese report, and come away from the expedition with so little to prove, or disprove, his theory.

'What if Zhang simply gives me the same story that I've heard from

132

everyone else?' he asked himself. 'That would change a quixotic journey into a foolish one.'

They sat down to dinner. Zhang struck Tom as a tough-looking customer; he saw no point in beating about the bush.

'What happened that day you and Wang were alone in Camp VI, and Chen went up to look for the missing climber?' Tom asked.

'I stay in sleeping bag,' he replied. 'Wang go for walk. He gone twenty minutes.'

That didn't sound very long. What could he do in twenty minutes? Tom asked, 'Did he say he'd found anything out there?'

'Yes. He tell me he find body of foreign mountaineer. Not say at time, but on way down. He tell others too.'

Tom gaped in astonishment. There it was! The corroboration he had been looking for. Short of actually finding a body, this was the next best proof that there was one up there. And it could only be that of Mallory or Irvine.

'Mr Zhang,' Tom said. 'Do you drink champagne?'

★

I have a photograph of the summit of Mount Everest, a telephoto taken from the North Col in the course of Michael Spender's carto-graphical survey in 1935, on which are marked his calculated heights and contours. The picture encompasses the final ridge of the mountain from just below the Second Step. Immediately under the summit pyramid is another bump on the ridge, prominent from this angle, a Third Step therefore, which is shown to rise from the 28,500-foot contour. That makes it 400 feet higher than the foot of the Second Step.

In coming to the decision that Odell must have seen Mallory and Irvine on the Second Step, our expedition explained their apparent speedy ascent by supposing them to be already near its top when he first saw them. And to his satisfaction, Tom argued away the belief that they were four hours overdue on their estimated time of reaching there by examining the climbing rates of sixty-nine Everesters over the years. From these he concluded that Mallory and Irvine would not have been late in reaching the Second Step at 12.50 – the time of Odell's sighting. With their oxygen functioning correctly, the Second Step was precisely where they should have been at that time.

Odell's early descriptions of his vision claimed that for a few moments 'There was a sudden clearing of the atmosphere, and the

Summit of Mount Everest from the North Col

entire summit ridge and final peak of Everest were unveiled.' Later, he qualified this by adding, 'Owing to the small portion of the summit ridge uncovered I could not be precisely certain at which of the two "steps" they were . . . '

If indeed he was granted only a brief tear in the atmosphere, I wondered was there any possibility he could have seen them on this Third Step?

The idea had much to commend it. Despite its appearance of prominence from below, it does not present a major obstacle to climbers; it could perhaps be surmounted or bypassed in the five or ten minutes Odell described. Lying beyond the Second Step, it neatly diminishes or dispenses with any suggested lateness on the part of the climbers. There are snow slopes below and above it. It was important to re-examine Odell's exact words in his earliest dispatch home.

'The place on the ridge mentioned is a prominent rock-step at a very short distance from the base of the final pyramid . . . ' he said.

That could be said to describe the Third Step more accurately even than the Second, whether or not glimpsed through a rent in the clouds.

Just supposing it was on the Third Step Odell saw them, it would be inconceivable they did not go on to reach the summit.

★

The film was edited in Manchester. It meant a lot more time away from home, days and nights on end, until it seemed that even the dog would cease to recognize me and all friendships lapse through neglect. David Breashears returned to the upper slopes of Everest the following spring for more footage of the First and Second Steps. Then, almost a year to the day after our departure, Alistair's and mine, we left the cutting rooms, the film complete bar the final sound mixing. We had rattled no skeletons in Mallory's cupboard, nor photographed any corpses. There were no metal detectors, no deep-frozen cameras – just a reassessment of known facts and supposition, based on modern knowledge of the mountain and of high-altitude physiology.

And that was that. The albatross (for such it had become in those last frantic weeks) was lifted. Peter, my son Tom and I put on our rucksacks and bought rail tickets to France. When we looked to be far enough south, we would get out and walk. Not far, not fast, but sampling vineyards and olive groves as we journeyed, and crossing paths with a minstrel or two, we hoped. It may not be the Himalaya but it was close to Arcady, and we were in need of some pastoral relief.

Tom Holzel could not wait to get back to Everest to continue his search. He looked around to see if he could attach himself to someone else's expedition.

Eighteen months went by before an invitation finally dropped on his mat. He was so excited the morning it arrived that he forgot to shave. It was to be a spring attempt, just what he wanted, the best season for a search. I was amazed when Holzel turned down the offer. It had not been an easy decision to make, he admitted, but increasingly he was coming round to the conviction that he should not let this old Everest enigma take control of his life. More important, he should not put his family through the ordeal of another expedition. They were, after all, innocent partners to his preoccupying quest.

By the time I saw Tom again, two years after our Everest trip, he professed relief that the episode was over. He could get on with other things now, enjoy his children growing up. So far as he was concerned the ghosts of Mallory and Irvine were laid. I was holidaying in New England with my family when the Holzels invited us to dinner. David Breashears was there, so was Sue Giller, and before long the table talk turned to Everest. We spoke of the oxygen relics we had found, the Finch bottles and also an encrusted soda-lime canister that came from an early closed-circuit apparatus.

Suddenly Sue said that she had found something interesting once, on the East Face in 1981. 'It was a bit of metal with a sort of strap. I didn't know what to make of it at the time. I was on my way up and I put it on a rock, meaning to collect it on the way back. I wish I had. Looking back now, I'm pretty sure it must have come from the carrying frame of one of those old sets.'

Tom looked thunderstruck.

'But if it were . . . ' he said, 'and nobody had climbed on the east side before, it must have come down from the ridge . . . from near the summit . . . And if that's so . . . it had to belong to Mallory . . . or just maybe Irvine . . . for nobody else was on the ridge before the War . . . with oxygen . . . And that means they . . . oh my God! That means . . .'

He was off again. The ghosts were not going to let him off the hook that easily.

*

For a long time after she received the news of her husband's death, Ruth Mallory found herself clinging to the hope that it might, after all, be a ghastly mistake, an error in transmission perhaps; that when the team sailed home there George would be, smiling, among his companions. Coming to terms with her loss would be so much easier, she felt, if she could know whether 'it was his time'. She placed great store by this, telling Mallory's confidant, Geoffrey Winthrop Young, that it was not difficult for her to believe George's spirit was ready for another life, and his way of going to it was very beautiful. What grieved her almost beyond enduring was that their three small children would never know the extent of their loss, but it was 'irreparable'.

She attended bravely to all the necessary formalities of death and comforted George's parents, while all the time keeping her own feelings tightly under control. Never one to be openly demonstrative, she now appeared to her volatile mother-in-law as 'almost too stoical'.

'She reminds me of a stately lily with its head broken and hanging down,' George's mother said.

Not long afterwards Ruth received a letter from a close friend, Will Arnold Forster, who had known George a long time and was convinced he had been in touch with him through 'table-turning'.

Will told Ruth that when asked by neighbours 'Do you ever sit?' he had not known what was meant, and even once the process had been explained, was not sure he believed either in it or for that matter in the immortality of the soul, but he was curious enough to give it a try.

Thus it happened one evening that he sat with his fingers on a table watching as it moved and tapped out words and messages through the medium of one of the other people in the circle. Just as the session was coming to an end, the table lurched once more.

'G-E-O . . . ' it spelt.

Will said, 'Is that you, George?'

'Y-E-S.'

The full text of the 'conversation' that followed has been lost, but Will told Ruth that he had asked the spirit where he was when his soul passed on to the next life.

'T-H-E T-O-P,' came back the answer.

'George, is there anything I should tell the Everest Committee?' Will wanted to know, and held his breath as the letters stuttered out in reply,

"O-R-G-A-N-I-C E-X-H-A-U-S-T-I-O-N.'

Ruth wasted no time in going to Cornwall to stay with Will and his wife, Ka. The three sat together in the little cottage near Land's End that years later was to become Ruth's own home and tried some table-turning of their own. Hands resting gently on the table top, they waited. Within minutes the table began to tilt and move, and George once more identified himself.

'Do you know who is here?' Will asked.

'R-U-T-H.'

Ruth wanted to know of her lost husband whether he was aware when she was thinking about him, and if he could tell what she and the children were doing. The answers to both – which gave her great comfort – were that he did.

'And are you active and busy?'

'Y-E-S.'

That was it! Her beliefs confirmed! There had been something 'better' George was ready for, some service for which he was required on the other side. She had an explanation for his death. Now it was for her to prove her love for him by being content to let him go; to be thankful, as she said, for her 'share of happiness'.

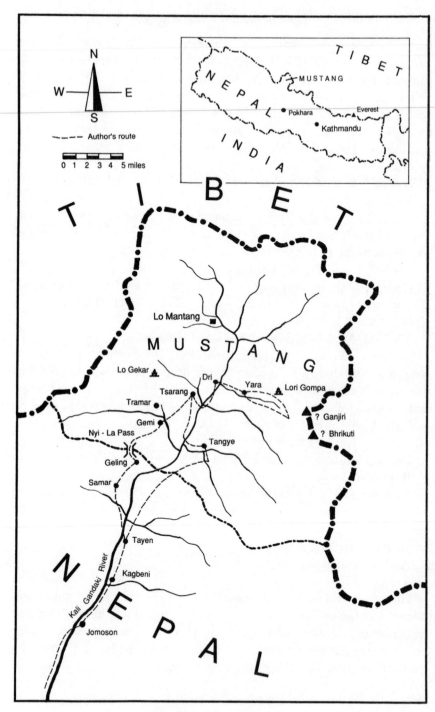

The Route into Mustang

TO CROSS THE
FORBIDDEN DESERT

Chance of a Lifetime

> Surrounded on all sides by a garland of white mountains,
> with perpetually flowing streams of cascading waters, clear
> and clean like a crystal orb, such is the palace of the King
> of Mustang.
>
> -Kun-dga' -grol-mchog, Jo-nang (1507–66)

'BEST YOU DON'T go out tomorrow,' Lhakpa warned. 'There will
be demonstrations. Could be bad in the streets. Best you stay in
your hotel.'

'Why, what's it all about?' I wanted to know.

'National Democracy Day,' he explained. 'The Nepali Congress
will be out in force.'

I was no wiser.

'They students, mostly – want to bring down government,' Lhakpa
said earnestly. 'Really, is very serious. Maybe some shooting. Could
last several days. Best you stay right away.'

It comes as a shock to hear of unrest in Kathmandu. Even knowing
Nepal to be the sixth poorest nation in the world, it is all too easy for
us from the West to persuade ourselves that Himalayan peoples have
access to a mystical serenity which elevates them above the material
dissatisfactions of the rest of mankind. We even imagine it is something we can pick up from them as an antidote to our own cluttered
lives. Romantically tripping the oriental trail in search of cosmic
enlightenment, we too lightly forget that one man's Shangri-La can be
another's hopeless existence.

Especially unreal seemed any hint of trouble when sitting on an
immaculate lawn, being served tea like a potentate by waiters in
white tunics. Finding myself in such a position was a surprise in itself. I
had not expected to be met at the airport, but waving frantically at the

barrier were Elaine and Lhakpa, one blonde, one dark head, two wide grins. Elaine grabbed one of my bags, while Lhakpa fended off the crush of porters and taxi drivers, ploughing a path to where his cousin was waiting outside with a car. 'We've booked you into the Shanker!'

I had already telephoned a reservation to the more modest Tibet Guesthouse – but no matter! I could always transfer downmarket the next day. After all, staying in the Shanker Hotel was a gloriously decadent way of starting any trip as it was one of the old Rana palaces of Kathmandu, all gleaming white stucco and ornate as a wedding cake. Inside, a decor of elaborate Newari wood-carving blended happily with turn-of-the-century kitsch.

From the riot of cottage-garden blooms in the flower beds – poppies, marigolds, sweet peas, geraniums – it was hard to believe this was still only February, the middle of winter. Over the pilastered front porch an orange trumpet vine hung like a vivid curtain. The head-gardener stood guard over a magnolia which he told me proudly was more than 150 years old. Ranks of salaaming doormen gave the impression I had strayed back to the heyday of the Indian Raj, and it was certainly worlds away from what I had come here to find. I was to join Elaine and Lhakpa on a rugged trek beyond the Himalayas to the high passes and arid valleys of Mustang.

Few outsiders had ever penetrated this tiny, forbidden kingdom on Nepal's northern border with Tibet. Tucked into the rainshadow of Dhaulagiri, geographically you would expect it to form part of Tibet. Certainly, its people – the Mustangis or Lo-pa – are ethnically and culturally Tibetan, and for years Khampa guerrilla fighters found it a safe haven from which to harass Chinese occupying forces across the frontier. It is because of the political sensitivity of its position that visitors have been kept out so rigorously, and there are plenty of cautionary stories to deter those unwise enough to force a way in illicitly. Several travellers have met mysterious deaths there in the last decades. Others have disappeared without trace.

After my trip to Everest I longed to return to the Himalaya. It was as if the sights and smells of High Asia had been carried on darts deep into my flesh, from where their slow-release potency continually provoked and tempted me. Yet years passed and there seemed little hope of going back until one day I received a breezy and unexpected call from Elaine Brook, inviting me to join an exploratory trek she and Lhakpa were putting together.

'We have a permit to attempt Bhrikuti,' she said.

I was impressed. 'You're really to be allowed into Mustang? Elaine, I can't believe it!'

Eric Valli, my French explorer friend, had been trying for years to get in. He'd been several times to neighbouring Dolpo, which is also restricted, and always Mustang's red and violet rock towers beckoned him from a distance. I was sure he'd give his eye teeth for a chance like this. I should not, could not, pass up the opportunity.

'I'd love to come!' I told her.

It has to be said there was still a lingering whiff of uncertainty about the trip. The precious enabling papers had yet to be handed over to Lhakpa by the Tourist Ministry, but he was confident nothing would delay our departure from Kathmandu the following week. He and Elaine scurried off for more top-level negotiations, while I decided that if I really was to be grounded for a day or two, I had better make the most of this afternoon. It was nearly midday when I wandered into town.

★

It is odd how conspicuous you feel in unfamiliar surroundings. I had no wish to get out a map and advertise that I had only just arrived, but it couldn't have been any secret. People shouted 'Hallo!' and 'Engleesh? Engleesh?' as I walked past and the rickshaw-pedallers matched their speed to mine, vying for my custom. I kept the wall of the King's Palace to my left, encouraged to notice that fruitbats still hung like ill-wrapped Christmas parcels from the branches of the tall pine trees inside. Strangely, this was my most enduring memory from the couple of days I spent in Kathmandu on my way home from Everest four years ago – one sign of constancy in a changing world.

Before long I recognized the Rani Pokhri Lake opposite the entrance to the narrow streets of Thamel, and headed off eagerly into the warren of bazaars. The heat, the clamour and the violent incandescent colour come as no less an assault on the senses second time round. Perhaps, like the piles of rotting refuse, these are things you never get used to. You resist it, but it remains hard not to blench at the smell. Everything, everyone seems so indescribably grubby – and so tightly packed.

Even the tiniest children try to sell me things. In one street a row of small boys with bathroom scales offer to speak my weight and a very persistent, very pretty Indian youth dances at my side imploring me to buy a peacock-feather fan. There are flute sellers and urchins with miniature pots of tiger balm. You long for more money to spend, not because you want the merchandise, but because bargaining is such fun. One young man leads me up narrow stairs to his first-floor shop.

'Mind your heads!' he cautions, ducking under a low beam, then like a conjurer begins pulling out his collection of cotton patchwork trousers, clown trousers in brilliant colours, one after the other from stuff bags. There is scant space to hang much on display, and in any case everything fades so quickly here.

'Best for yous,' he advises, 'buy plenty. Three, four, five pairs – best for yous – very good price!'

Best for hims too, I guess, but do not feel the need for more than two pairs. The price is not that good.

★

Lhakpa had said everything would be on strike the next day – Sunday. Shops and taxi-drivers had all been threatened with bricks through their windows and windscreens if they defied the strike-call. A few unmarked cars were waiting in line in the drive outside the Shanker Hotel, and I was able without too much difficulty to persuade one to take me and my luggage down to the Tibet Guest House in Chetra-pati. A general warning had gone out for all tourists to avoid, among other places, the New Road area, only a few blocks away from my new base, but the man on the front desk did not consider this meant I ought to stay in.

'If you see a crowd, just walk the other way,' was his advice.

There was certainly a strong military presence. Riot police in steel helmets and primitive corrugated flak jackets lined the approaches to all the bigger road junctions. Some were armed with guns, others with stout staves, or *lathis*, to break up any assembly. Soldiers paraded in twos and threes. Lorries crammed with more armed men rumbled up and down the lanes and around the squares. I could see machine gun posts on some of the flat-topped roofs, barrels disconcertingly trained on us, passing below. If trouble flared quickly, it was easy to see there would be many innocent victims among the usual crush of people on the streets.

Although the shops were officially closed, some bookstores (of which there are a great number in this part of town) had their grilles only at half-mast, so that customers could still duck inside and browse. Every so often youths would hurtle down the narrow streets, shout a

142

warning, and the shutters would clang right down, imprisoning us inside until it was considered safe to open up once more.

'What will come of all this?' I asked one bookshop owner. In the face of such an intimidating display of force I could not think many protesters would be willing to make themselves conspicuous. Already there had been widespread arrests and rumours of police beatings.

'Oh, we will win in the end,' the man said. 'However long it takes. All the people want democracy.'

It is true that *Democracy Now!* slogans were appearing all over town. I had seen them scrawled on the university building, which was shuttered and barred, the students sent home in an attempt to defuse the situation. The last serious pro-democracy demonstrations here in 1985, had collapsed when a tourist was killed by a bomb in the smart Annapurna Hotel. Such violence shocked everyone, and with the economy of Nepal utterly dependent on tourists, it made no sense to frighten them away.

But then, the desire for democracy does not go away either. I wondered if people here had heard of the success of the democratic uprisings in Eastern Europe in recent months, and whether that was affecting the mood. But news is hard to come by in Nepal. The press is strictly monitored, and when underground papers have sprung up in the past, editors have swiftly been locked up as soon as they said anything critical of the system. Some foreign-language papers are imported for the tourists, and every morning in Thamel groups of Westerners can be seen clustered round those stores with newspaper racks outside, trying to catch a glimpse of the front page of the *Herald Tribune*. But in those early days of the disturbances we knew only what we could see. Later the most reliable reports filtered back to us from outside via foreign news sources and phonecalls home. *The Times* and the *Guardian* both appeared to have correspondents inside Kathmandu.

Political parties were outlawed under the existing tiered *Panchayat*, although general elections were held and there was a degree of representation. Local five-man councils chose delegates to serve on district *Panchayats*, which in turn sent nominees to the national assembly, the *Rashtriya Panchayat*. The system was claimed as already democratic by its supporters, and held to be less divisive than full or 'plural democracy'. Ultimate power rested with the monarch, although in practice it was wielded by his appointed ministers and military advisers. Corruption was widespread. Censorship and the country's economic difficult-

143

ies exacerbated discontent, as did the acute fuel shortage following a long trade dispute with India.

King Birendra, an Old Etonian and a shy remote figure, appeared to be held in affection by most of his subjects, even if the display of his and his Queen's photographs in all the land's business establishments was more a requirement, or an insurance policy, than any outward sign of this affection. The Nepali Congress showed no wish – as yet – to depose the King. It was calling for a constitutional monarchy, but had seen the advantage of forging an alliance with Nepal's recently united communist factions whose loyalty to the monarchy was far less secure.

Unlike her husband, Queen Aishwarya was almost universally mistrusted. As a descendent of the deposed Rana clan that governed Nepal for 104 years until 1951, she was believed to wield too great an influence on affairs of state. Her striking physical resemblance to Imelda Marcos did not go unremarked. A story circulated during the troubles of how the Queen 'in a rare act of charity' visited some of the injured in hospital. When she stopped at the bedside of a young student who had been arrested and then raped by police, the woman spat contempt for a regime that allowed such outrages to happen. The Queen departed hurriedly – but not before issuing orders for the girl's execution.

Rising Nepal, a pro-government English-language paper, carried a Democracy Day message from the King, reminding people that they should thank the 'democracy' introduced by his grandfather, King Tribuvan, in 1951 for opening the way to modernization. The setting up of the partyless Panchayat in 1960 had consolidated that progress. 'The joint efforts of the Monarch and the people in bringing about the dawn of democracy,' he said, 'are entirely in conformity with the Nepalese tradition of collective endeavours.'

Democracy demanded respect for the verdict of the majority, but there was no reason, the King suggested, why anyone should feel alienated from the national mainstream.

*

With little or no motorized traffic on the streets, I was able to cover ground quickly and spent most of the afternoon getting used to the layout of the city, following advice and keeping out of trouble. I took my bearings from the two rivers that encircle the capital and must have crossed and recrossed almost all the bridges, including a long contraption of bouncy planks hung on steel cable. Alarming gaps on either side made it no place for the faint-hearted, for you had to press to the edge whenever you met – as invariably you did – motorcycles or a flock of sheep coming the other way. The poorest parts of town are by the riverside, where shanties line both banks. People squat in the mud, breaking stone for building – women, children, everyone. There is very little water in either the Bisnumati or the holy Bagmati, but a lot of rubbish. Pigs rootle in the malodorous ooze, and buffaloes huddle in dumb groups. There are snow-white ibis and swooping vultures.

It was overcast for most of the day, with even a few spots of rain, but the sun broke through towards evening to give a rainbow and glorious sunset. From one of the bridges, snowy mountains shone into view briefly before muddling with the turreted clouds.

An unfailing delight in Kathmandu is the richness of names bestowed by the Nepalis upon their business ventures. Auspiciousness is clearly the main criterion, but with undertones of professional pride and sheer, pink-spectacled optimism. So we have: *Glory Hairdresser, Jubilant High School, Dewy Dawn English Language School, Twinkle Tailors, My Son Electrical Store, Smiling Roses Child Care, Surprise Boarding School* (not a bad surprise, I hoped), and *Optic Nerve* (his prices perhaps were too high). Public injunctions are collectable, too, for their quaint turn of phrase, or quainter spelling – *Be happy be cleanig your city, Police Beat Petrolling.*

During the night I had heard the occasional stutter of gunfire, and in the morning more places were closed than on the day before. The unrest was clearly widespread. Reports told of other towns and outlying districts affected as well as Kathmandu, and extremists had begun calling for the King's assassination.

Elaine telephoned me at the hotel: a policeman had been hit on the head with a large brick and killed. There were stories, too, that a government official had been kidnapped. But so much was rumour. We had no way of discovering the overall picture. Several hundred dissidents, we knew were rounded up before the start of the campaign, and many more arrested yesterday. Official word had it that in Kathmandu seven people had been injured in clashes with the police. Opposition sources claimed 150 around the country. *All India Radio* reported ten dead. A group of Americans in the hotel this morning were arranging to get food and emergency supplies to those being held in appalling conditions in detention.

A quick turn round the block confirmed that riot police were out again in force, but still nobody appeared to be staying in on their account. Instinct told me that, if there were trouble, the more witnesses to it the better. I wasn't going to place myself in the middle of any skirmishes, but neither would I hide away. I joined the crowds thronging into Durbar Square, where it was peaceful enough – as you would expect with the police headquarters in one corner. The New Road, too, seemed normal except for the large numbers of riot police and all the closed shutters. Even the money-changing touts and marijuana hucksters were out, hissing at tourists behind the backs of the police.

I tagged behind a line of sightseers with a guide, heading through a carved doorway off the square, and found myself in a courtyard under the window of the Kumari, or living goddess. She appeared twice and regarded the group incuriously. It is a lonely life being a virgin deity: she has no playmates and may only leave her apartments for a few religious festivals in a year. Even then her feet must not touch the ground. She is paraded through the streets in a palanquin. A kumari's term ends on reaching puberty, when she receives a rich endowment that it is hoped will secure her a good marriage. That doesn't always follow, for it is widely believed that an ex-goddess brings only bad luck – and an early death to her unfortunate spouse.

A small dark-eyed street-boy offered to take me to the Monkey Temple, and we set off at cracking pace down Pig Lane towards the bouncy bridge over the river. A mile or so ahead Swayambunath swam like a hazy Mont St Michel high above vegetable fields.

The boy's name was Uddab, and he was thirteen. He had lived alone in Kathmandu ever since his father was killed felling a tree two years before. Where his mother was he didn't know, for she had taken off on a pilgrimage immediately after the accident and not been seen since. There was no longer a family home. For four hours each morning Uddab attended school where, if his excellent English was anything to go by, he must have been the star pupil, then in the afternoons he conducted tourists to earn enough money for his room and his education. A French benefactor, he said, sent gifts from time to time, otherwise he supported himself.

'What are the people like who you live with?' I wanted to know. 'Do they keep an eye on you?'

'Nobody keeps eye on me!' he retorted with fierce pride. 'I look after myself.'

We reached the temple and climbed the 365 stairs without pausing for breath.

'A drink, you like?' Uddab asked outside a Coca-Cola booth on top, and taking that to mean he wanted one, I purchased two foaming bottles.

We gulped them down – Uddab was not one for hanging about – then took a quick turn round the stupa (clockwise, of course, in Buddhist fashion), pausing briefly to look out over the Kathmandu Valley to the airport, and at the King's Palace. He haggled with a Tibetan pedlar for a miniature mani stone for me, and then clattered down the steps once more, hurrying me back to Durbar Square. With luck he could get in another tourist before teatime. If he needed to, that is. Clearly, I proved a soft touch, for a short while after negotiating his fee and gravely shaking hands on the deal, I saw Uddab again as I walked back to Chetrapati. He waved to me grandly from the seat of a rickshaw.

★

A charming dark-eyed boy serves tables at the Tibet Guesthouse. One morning I went in to breakfast to find I was the only person eating. I was sure other guests would soon join me, but the morning ticked by and nobody appeared. The boy stood to attention beside my chair, my solitariness clearly bothering him for at length he broke the silence.

'How old are you?' he asked solemnly.

The question caught me off guard and I giggled foolishly. Vaguely I said, 'Oh . . . in my fifties.' Why I couldn't come straight out with 'I'm fifty-three' or 'I'm nearly fifty-four', I have no idea. It's not that I mind people knowing particularly; just, I suppose, that I don't like facing up to the fact myself.

'In Nepal,' the lad said, 'that's old.' He paused. 'Maybe not Kathmandu. My village, that very old.'

I laughed again. 'Believe me,' I told him, 'there are times when it feels very old wherever you are!'

He was eighteen, this young man, and had been working at the guest house for two years. His family came from a village outside Kathmandu and every so often at festival times, he was able to get back to see them. He was a very sweet boy. Proudly he showed me a small bamboo wall-hanging he had bought at a religious fair. WELCOME, it said, with great flourish.

'That's nice,' I told him. 'Where are you going to hang it?'

He shrugged. 'No have place. Maybe one day I get room my own . . .' And rolling it up, he returned it to the small wooden box, which

147

with sudden shock I realized must contain all that he owned in the world.

My young friend slept on the floor of the breakfast room after all the guests had gone to bed, one of an estimated seven thousand 'restaurant boys' living this way in Kathmandu. They were the lucky ones. Much smaller children slept in the street with the stray dogs, picking scraps from skips and lighting rubbish fires in an attempt to keep warm. Two little boys I remember, brothers I should think and aged perhaps five and eight, lay curled foetally together one cold night like Yin and Yang on a pavement not far from the King's Palace.

★

Lord Shiva has many forms. He is both Destroyer and Creator, the reconciliation of all opposites. He is cruel, yet mild; evil, yet good; an abstinent and an ithyphallic. He is the shepherd of souls and a haunter of graveyards. But in Nepal, the manifestation by which he is most revered is as Pashupati, Lord of the Animals and guardian of the Kathmandu Valley. Legend tells that he once roamed the forests around Pashupatinath in the guise of a deer.

For Shiva's festival, Maha Shive Ratri, pilgrims and sadhus swarm to Pashupatinath to keep an all-night vigil in his honour. They huddle around fires and votive oil lamps and at intervals throughout the night take ritual baths in the turbid river. Marigold garlands are flung over the famous *lingams* or phallus symbols by which Shiva is worshipped, and which sprout rampantly all round this holy place. At dawn begins the recitation of sacred texts, giving way later in the day to chanting and the singing of sacred songs.

The temple area, when I arrived on the morning after Shiva's night, was swarming with people, and riot police were everywhere blocking paths with human chains, marshalling crowds in determined patterns but without discernibly easing the crush. Beggars lined the roads and stairways. Lepers and hideously emaciated fakirs – every manner of mutilated individual – clawed at the air. One man with no legs had been fastened to what looked like the feet of a music stool. A line of pilgrims, waiting to file past Shiva's bull in the golden temple, stretched down the Jacob's ladder of steps, round the banks of the river, over the bridge and up the white staircase carved in the hill opposite, almost to its top.

Groups of turbanned holy men, in saffron and red, sat cross-legged on the hillside, singing themselves into a trance. '*Om namo shivaya. Om namo shivaya.*' For hours already they had thumped the beat with tambourines and rattles, uplifted way beyond bodily distractions on wafting clouds of ganja smoke. Fascinated tourists pressed close, thrusting long lenses into their faces, to be met with glares fierce enough to compel them to add to the pile of rupee notes on the rug between the worshippers.

I was happy to sit, mind-abandoned, in a holy grove, watching the pilgrims pass to and fro. Monkeys skittered round the dappled steps of old temples and I made the mistake of sharing a biscuit with two baby animals. Before I knew it, a huge male sprang out and grabbed my arm, wrestling me for my bag. Hissing, with bared yellow teeth, his face had a look halfway between skull and demon. I was saved from an ugly and doubtless rabid bite by some youths hurling rocks and driving the fiend off.

Police with staves and batons hurtled suddenly from the woods, grabbing two young men from a tea booth at the top of the steps and frog-marching them out of sight into trees on the other side. Everyone stood helplessly by, and a sullen, resentful air seeped through the crowd. As the afternoon progressed, the troops grew increasingly jumpy, and a number of skirmishes developed.

On riverside steps, opposite the ghats where four stone platforms overhung the water, I watched as one cremation was completed and the ashes brushed into the river. Men with rakes waded into the water to direct the ashes downstream, after which the platform was swept and washed clean, and blessed for the next ceremony. Already two funerals were beginning on other platforms, and long, white-shrouded bundles lay in line, waiting their turn.

For a Hindu, the most auspicious way to meet death here is with feet immersed in the sacred Bagmati, a tributary of the Ganges. Up and down the bank families clustered round sick loved ones, dipping them into the soupy green water to assist them through their last moments of life.

'Many man die,' commented a serious young man at my side. 'Six man die today. Very sad life, man-life.'

Maybe there is something ghoulish in sitting, as I was, watching the grief of strangers. All I can say – if it's any mitigation – is that foreign tourists made only a small part of the audience, most were Nepalese and all separated from the obsequies by the width of the river. No-one – Westerner or local – was treating the occasion lightly. The impression I formed was of an intimate leave-taking, a far more tender and appropriate conclusion to life than the clinical way we go about things. Always it has struck me that there can be nothing more false or ridiculous than the sight of a coffin gliding through swishing curtains to the cheap strains of canned music.

★

Lhakpa had been seriously ill as a small child. Medicines, prayers . . . nothing was of any help. People said he must be under the influence of a malicious demon, but not even his father, who was the village shaman with the power to call up earthbound gods and spirits, could discover what was needed to drive the evil away. An air of resignation set in, as it does in these remote communities when all their limited means have failed, so that even the child, tossing on his blankets, knew that he was expected to die. There was no use struggling against it. He, too, waited for the end.

Then one day came the sound of shouting outside and his mother rushed from the house to discover that Sir Edmund Hillary had arrived in the village, looking for a place to build one of his celebrated Sherpa schools.

'There's a doctor with him,' neighbours told her excitedly. 'Maybe he can do something for your Lhakpa!'

She ran at once down the hill to beg for help. Even today Lhakpa's family do not know what ailed him then, but he turned the corner from the moment of the doctor's visit. Within weeks he was scampering about the village, completely restored and up to mischief with the other children. He has no doubt in his mind that he owes his life to Sir Edmund Hillary.

Not only that, but the most famous of all Sherpas, Tenzing Norgay, was an uncle of his. It is no wonder that Lhakpa grew up to believe that the path to Everest, if not paved with gold, led at least to opportunity and influence. All his life he had seen crocodiles of well-heeled Westerners traipsing past his village on their way to Everest Base Camp. Sherpas who worked as guides and porters for the foreign visitors came home with smart new clothes and radios, piles of climbing gear and money to splash around. Lhakpa could hardly wait to embark on a lucrative career like that. He knew that to be successful with climbing and trekking parties, he would need to speak very good English, and begged his parents to send him to the Hillary school along with his older brothers. But they had different ideas for their third son: he was destined to enter the monastery.

Poor Lhakpa! Religious discipline he found impossibly irksome and the last thing he wanted in life was to be a lama. He kept running away, and to earn sufficient money for private lessons, would undertake all manner of jobs around the village. But because he stayed up so late over his studies, he was always too sleepy to concentrate properly and one morning, chopping wood, succeeded in cutting off his thumb.

At the age of ten, he left home and made his way to Kathmandu. There, he teamed up with Sherpa friends Ang Dorje and Sungdare, living by his wits until he was old enough to be taken on as kitchen boy and porter for climbing expeditions.

To a Sherpa, climbing has a certain macho glamour, but its main attraction is that it pays better than other available work. Most Sherpas regard employment with expeditions as a step in the ladder to independence. They work until they have made enough contacts and saved sufficient money to start up their own trekking agency or to open a restaurant. Expeditioning is inherently risky and it is irrefutable that Sherpas bear the lion's share of the danger. Probably the most hazardous part of any expedition to the south side of Everest, for instance, is going up and down the Khumbu Icefall. Sahib climbers try to limit their journeys to once up, once down, but Sherpa porters must ferry loads up the treacherous ice repeatedly. They are in a position of maximum vulnerability far longer than their employers, but have less opportunity to select their own route or time of going. Of the first hundred people killed climbing Mount Everest, 41 were Sherpas and five were other Nepalese employed as 'Sherpas' (Gurungs, Tamangs and the like) – making 46 in all. Japanese had the next highest toll with ten deaths, and there were eight British fatalities.

Lhakpa went with expeditions to Kangchenjunga, Makalu and Ama Dablam, and finally to Jannu. One morning he and two friends were carrying oxygen for a group of sahibs who had pulled ahead of them and were clambering up the ridge above in high expectation of making it to the summit that day. Without warning an avalanche swept the slope and engulfed all three porters. When the dust settled Lhakpa was the only one left alive. He lay half-buried in the debris, blood oozing into the snow, and unable to move anything but his eyes and mouth. The climbers on the ridge appeared not to have noticed and continued slowly upwards.

All day Lhakpa lay there, staring at the sky, convinced that he would die. In the evening Sherpa colleagues came up from Base Camp looking for their friends, and they dug him out. Once more it had turned out not to be his time for dying.

The sahibs had a good day. They reached their summit and could count the expedition a success. Coming down, they passed very close to where Lhakpa was imprisoned in the snow. They didn't stop.

Lhakpa doesn't care to be employed on climbing expeditions any more. He first met Elaine Brook when she took a blind friend trekking to Everest and engaged him as their sirdar. A misunderstanding over how many porters should accompany the party clouded the first days of their journey. Lhakpa was relieved to find that Julie – the blind girl – had few problems on the rugged trails of Solu Khumbu. It was the independent-minded Elaine who spelled trouble. Elaine, for her part, steeled herself against Lhakpa's good looks and disarming charm, suspecting them and his smart Western clothes for the trappings of an opportunist. Only later, in their shared concern for Julie, did they come to know and respect each other, and on their next trek together, with a party of Americans, it was clear to both of them that they had fallen in love. When Elaine returned to England that time, Lhakpa went with her.

They were married in a registry office and later returned to Lhakpa's village for another wedding with full local ceremony – and lashings of home-brew. They make a striking couple: Lhakpa, dark-skinned for a Sherpa, chunky; Elaine a true 'lily-maid' with long blonde hair, small and slight. They divide their time between a home in Herefordshire where Lhakpa enjoys being a village gentleman, and trekking in Nepal where they run their own highly individual programme of walking holidays off the beaten track.

Elaine has been described as 'a British woman with a serious case of wanderlust'. She first went rock climbing as a fifteen-year old, since when her life has been one long series of adventurous trips. She has climbed throughout the Americas and in Nepal, skied in the Rockies, and walked the length of the Himalaya from Gangtok in Sikkim to Srinagar in Kashmir. She has learned to speak both Tibetan and Nepali fluently. To hold her own in the male-dominated outdoors world she adopted a feisty, assertive front which from time to time has led her into conflict. The British climbing establishment has subjected her to the sort of cool-shouldering that Julie Tullis experienced, though her entry into the arena at a much earlier age was also seen as a threat by a scheming Eve to the cohesive intimacy of male climbing. Elaine's reaction was to undertake many of her climbs and expeditions with other women. In Yosemite she climbed with Jill Lawrence and Cathy Cullinane, in the Rockies and the Andes with long-time friend Judy Sterner.

I had known Elaine since 1983 when she and Julie Donnelly were planning their trek to Everest and she had just returned from a trip to Tibet that changed her life. She had gone with Doug Scott to Shisha Pangma as the only woman in a small, competitive climbing team. Increasingly she found herself at odds with the others, especially once it dawned on her that what they really wanted was for her to keep quiet and concentrate on cooking, pot-washing and general atmosphere-sweetening. Not Elaine's style at all!

Doug confided that he and Alex MacIntyre had both promised their partners back home that they would not sleep with her during the trip. 'As if it was their decision, not mine!' Elaine snorted with indignation. But the real and unexpected barrier to asserting equality on this trip was not her companions' egocentric attitudes but the fact that Elaine herself had ceased to feel the same commitment towards climbing that she once did.

'Whatever it was I had been seeking for the last ten years in the headlong pursuit of higher summits and harder rock pitches, I was no longer finding it. I caught myself attempting to justify my motives for climbing and realized suddenly that I did not need reasons for *being*. I was now looking for a way out of the layers of self-justification.'

After some untidy squabbling, she broke free of the expedition and made her own way back across Tibet, staying with families, dodging Communist officials and coming joyously to terms with her new-found persona. She has never looked back.

The Long Walk to Annapurna

THE MAP OF Nepal shows a loop in the northern frontier that thrusts like a tongue into Tibet. It is where the Kali Gandaki river makes its way down from the high Central Asian plateau towards the Himalayan chain, which it cleaves in two. The land contained within this loop, and thus surrounded on three sides by Tibet, is the ancient kingdom of Mustang, or – as it is more traditionally known – the Land of Lo.

At first you might think it a geographical accident that this arid region should ever have been regarded as part of Nepal, so different is it from the rest of that country. Then you notice that a rim of snowy mountains separates it from Tibet also, and it becomes clear why it remained independent for hundreds of years before a negotiated border treaty between its larger neighbours committed it formally to Nepal.

Before the middle of this century, little was known of Mustang by the outside world – or indeed of any of the other isolated centres of Tibetan culture along Nepal's northern border. Then a handful of anthropologists and scientists visited the region and published delighted reports of their findings. They had discovered what to them was the equivalent of Tutankhamun's tomb, a time-capsule that preserved in perfect detail the richness of an ancient civilization. Yet this was more wondrous than the pharaoh's treasure for it was no *lost* civilization: it lived still. Mustang's remoteness, and a way of life that kept such perfect balance with its environment, had allowed it to survive intact, unchanged, for centuries. With the sealing of the Tibetan border by Chinese overlords, suffocating vital trade links, that timelessness was now threatened.

The peak of Bhrikuti on Mustang's eastern border was officially opened to expeditions eight years ago, but few had been granted

154

permission to attempt it and little was published afterwards of their achievements. Short notices would sometimes appear in the American Alpine Journal asserting that it had been or was subsequently learned not to have been – climbed. Conceding Bhrikuti as a mountaineering peak did not represent any relaxation in the policy of keeping Mustang firmly closed to outsiders. The authorities expected climbers to make an approach from the south-east, from Manang, which would not necessitate parties descending into the valleys of Mustang at all. But Mustang is a long way from Kathmandu and its precise geography remains vague to most bureaucrats there. No two sketch maps agree. By cannily requesting that we climb the north-west face of Bhrikuti, the side giving on to Mustang, Elaine and Lhakpa – as much to their surprise as anyone's – were successful in having many of Mustang's villages listed on their climbing permit. It was an astonishing coup!

Technically, then, we were on a mountaineering expedition, although you would never have thought it to see the party that finally huffed out of Pokhara. Our credibility rested with a few Sherpas who had climbed mountains before. The plan was that with Elaine and Lhakpa, they would launch their attack from a base camp on Bhrikuti, and the rest of us would merely hold ourselves ready 'in support'.

★

When we gathered in Kathmandu, I had been relieved to see that this time I was not to be the group elder. Several women were 'of certain age' – men too. I fancied I ought to be able to hold my own. One person I underestimated, as indeed did all of us, was the liaison officer assigned to accompany our group.

Mr Kanharya Basnyet had the sleek, well-fed look of a man of standing. He was a senior policeman, the highest caste of Chettri, plainly used to getting his way by the merest snap of expressive fingers. We wondered why he should want to accompany us. Clearly it was not for the money since, as he was prompt to inform us when Lhakpa introduced him in the bar of the Shanker, he owned several properties in Kathmandu. Nor did we gain the impression that walking held special appeal for him. We imagined him wheezing along, only too willing to settle comfortably into the first village in Mustang, leaving us to rootle around the countryside at will. So much for first impressions. Our man was deceptively fit, his plumpness melting away with the first days' trekking. Very quickly and easily, he walked the rest of us off our feet. Admittedly he travelled light, carrying only a towel –

for mopping of the brow – and a radio-set, which he wore like a shoulder bag and kept remorselessly at full blast.

'Very important for a policeman to keep up with what's going on,' he would tell us. 'Especially during these troubled times.'

Up hill, down dale, all day along the trail, that accursed radio blared forth, delivering – it is true – the occasional bulletin of news, but mostly pumping out the latest Indian pop songs. It was just as well he walked so far ahead of the rest of us.

I wondered why it was taking me so long to get into my stride. The early morning starts were grim and cold, but I certainly wasn't skimping on sleep. We would tuck up in our bags soon after supper each evening, cuddling drinking-flasks of hot water to our chests. Soon it dawned me what the matter was. Insides! Everything boils down to how your stomach feels. By that alone is landscape coloured. On queazy, disordered days, all is grey and barren. Dreary trails lead ever upward. But when you wake bright as a Bile Beans advertisement, every boulder sparkles with crystal and exquisite miniature flowers peek from under every stone. Effortlessly you bound along, eating up the miles.

Each morning, before daybreak, a mug of smoky, milkless bed-tea arrives through the flap in the tent and my stomach heaves, just as if I had morning sickness. Sweetened or not makes no difference, I had never yet managed even half a mugful, but the nausea usually passes after an hour of walking, though it is then too late to catch up on a hearty breakfast. It meant I was falling down miserably on the job of keeping up my liquid intake.

This day began as one of the unsettled variety. Worse was to come. Shortly outside Ghasa, where we spent the last night, I turned my ankle and crumpled in a pathetic heap on the path. Miserably, I allowed Pemba, one of our young Sherpas, to take my pack from me.

★

Before leaving Kathmandu, Elaine had insisted on inspecting our kit, to see if it was capable of withstanding the winter cold we could expect as we climbed higher. She circled the group, fingering sleeping bags and jackets, while we watched edgily, feeling exposed, our effects on display like this. My special Everest gear passed muster, as I would have hoped. All I needed to hire were snow gaiters and a ski-pole. Laureen didn't get off so lightly.

'These really won't do.' Elaine dismissed her hollofill bag and jacket.

'They always have done,' retorted Laureen. This was her ninth trek and with some truculence she refused to replace the offending items. 'They were good enough on Kala Patar,' she said. 'They'll serve me now.'

Margaret, the peace-maker, diverted Elaine. 'If you're really worried Laureen won't be warm enough,' she whispered, 'let me hire an extra jacket. It can travel on the ponies, can't it?'

The moment saved, Elaine and Lhakpa continued the briefing. 'We must all try to drink four to six litres of liquid a day,' Elaine said.

'Forty-six?!' Colin was staking his claim as the wag of the party.

'And take plenty of small money on trek,' advised Lhakpa, revealing why his briefcase bulged so importantly. It was stuffed with bundles of 5-rupee notes (each worth less than 10p). For a few travellers' cheques, I was amazed to be given a wad almost three inches thick. Impossible to wear that in a money belt, I decided, stuffing the notes in my rucksack. Each morning I would peel off a few for my pocket.

'Any more questions?' Elaine wanted to know.

Those who had just flown in wondered how safe it was to walk the streets. Another democracy strike had closed shops and businesses.

'Oh, I've sussed out the Revolution,' announced Colin, 'it's set for after tea.'

'No, next week – after we've gone!' Lhakpa countered.

We all laughed. What Lhakpa did not tell us was that when he had gone to the bank for the trek money security forces were spreadeagling everyone against the wall and searching them with rough diligence. Those intent on withdrawing large amounts of cash were singled out for special attention as there had been rumours that dissident groups were being funded by the Chinese ... or by the Indian government ... or by Western powers ... some foreign force exploiting the situation for its own ends. Even if it were true, it is hard to imagine the money coming in through banks, but the authorities were taking no chances.

Counter-rumours claimed that the government itself was orchestrating the violence in an effort to discredit all opposition ... For a week Nepalese newspapers had been urging people to expose troublemakers and malcontents; and elaborately engineered statements of loyalty were published by one Panchayat after another. At one rally in Jaleswar, *Rising Nepal* claimed 125,000 people had shouted: 'Our King and Country are Dearer than Our Lives! Our Language and Our Dress are Dearer than Our Lives! Long live His Majesty the King!

Long live Her Majesty the Queen! Long live the Panchayat System! Long live Panchayat Unity!' And in Solu, to the same slogans was added, 'Down with Foreign Alliance!' From the scale of propaganda alone, unrest did not look as if it were proving easy to bottle up this time. The King had retreated from the capital to his well-guarded Summer Camp in Pokhara.

★

Pokhara was our own first destination. We travelled there by bus on 26 February, a propitious day for a journey as it was *Losar*, the Tibetan New Year. Lhakpa's auntie had baked us special Losar cakes for a ride that took most of the day, a drowsy, jogging journey of heat, but with the oasis of lunch by a jade-green river in a beautiful gorge. Around us large butterflies flopped loosely, like tossed exercise books. One sat on a mud bar masquerading as a beech leaf, then opened its wings to reveal the rich and luminous blue of those butterfly pictures that were all the rage in the 1930s.

There was rafting on the Marsyandi, and a flock of vultures pecking at something in the water – not, I hoped, a rafter. A huge dam was under construction, partly financed by the Chinese. We had to be signed through several checkposts, and gradually the landscape changed from near-barren hillsides to verdant farmland, with banana trees and the waxy red flowers of bombax and coral tree gracing bare branches. Triumphal arches lined the last twenty miles into town, bearing such encouraging greetings as: *Pokhara Leo Club heartly welcome you*. We unloaded our baggage on a patch of wasteland, observed with curiosity by the local children, before plodding in dull and lessening light to a campfield in Hyangja.

I shared a blue ridge tent with Reiko, as I would for the rest of the trip. A Japanese businesswoman and veteran in the Himalaya, Reiko travelled regularly with English groups. I loved her at once. She was a year or two older than me, infinitely good-natured, dainty and fluttery. She would squeak and burble in her bag as she tried to wake up in the morning. The early starts came no easier to her than they did to me. By some fluke she had wangled two kitbags instead of the regulation one, and these were packed with miniaturized luxuries, and goodies for birthdays or pick-me-ups. First thing each morning she would read the temperature both inside and outside the tent, and check the altitude, recording the results meticulously in a little notebook. She would photograph every campsite. When the rest of us wrote up our diaries, days late, we knew we could always go to Reiko for the names and heights of passes, and all the important details that had blurred in our memory.

When tea came round that first morning, and we struggled up so as not to appear laggards in front of the others, I pulled out a bottle of Johnson's baby lotion and dabbed at my nose and cheeks, my Everest answer to keeping clean in adversity.

'No, no!' Reiko piped, 'Water coming.' And she mimed washing her face. As an old hand, she knew the routine.

Sure enough, a minute later, two little bowls of steamy hot water, the size of pudding basins, appeared at the door of the tent. We were soon adept not only at strip-washing in these, but afterwards rinsing through our smalls as well.

It was a fine morning and the mess tent had been struck early. Breakfast was taken at long tables in the open with the most breath-taking vision of Machapuchhare, the fish-tailed peak, slightly flushed, towering before us. Our own tents were dismantled as we ate and loaded with our kitbags on to mules. This left us free to travel lightly, with only the daily necessities in our packs – drinking water, suncream, camera and a few spare clothes. Before leaving, I peered over a wall into the next paddock where stocky white birds strutted to and fro, pecking at scraps. They had the hook-beaked, cold-eyed look of seagulls, but were infinitely larger. Egyptian vultures, I surmised, but a long way from home. Already I was regretting leaving bird and flower books behind. Why had I not thrown out some clothes to make room for them?

On the first day our path criss-crossed a new road being built up the Seti Khola – again with Chinese money. Those who had been here before bemoaned the way the valley had changed. 'Oh, you wouldn't believe . . . this used to be the most beautiful village,' they would say, where now a raw gash sundered houses one from another. Whole sections of track were destroyed. It was hard to see the new road bringing any benefit to the people who lived here; they had lost far more than they would ever gain. Trekkers will simply bypass this section when the road is open, taking their trade with them. The villagers will not be able to afford to drive the road, and their ancient trackways will have been lost to them for ever.

We climbed steeply through woods to the Naudanda ridge, where we found a large blue tarpaulin spread on the ground and our Sherpas busy at their stoves. Lunch, we soon learned, was to become a craved-for, morale-boosting ritual. In Chotare, our head cook, Elaine and Lhakpa had discovered a marvel. Anywhere, anytime, he could conjour delicious meals out of thin air. There would be a fruit drink to come in to, followed by at least four or five items on an amply loaded plate – very often to include chips or *pouris* – then salad, a dessert and cups of tea. The performance could take place at any time between eleven and two o'clock, there was no way of knowing. Chotare would leave camp in the morning long before everyone else and, unladen, scoot ahead to see what the countryside had to offer. Where necessary he negotiated with landowners or teashop proprietors to use their facilities. His kitchen-boys followed as fast as they could pack everything together, usually overtaking us about an hour out on the trail.

Chotare did not select places merely to suit his own convenience. It was a matter of some honour with him that picnic spots should be perfect in every detail – comfortable, with shade if there was any, and a good panoramic view. We were soon programmed to scan the landscape upon breasting every brow or col, and when we spotted the heavenly blue of the lunch 'tarp', would slaver and salivate, and lunge ahead like Pavlov's dogs.

That night, and the next, we camped on narrow terraces in hillside gardens. This section of the route was regularly trekked, forming part of the Annapurna Circuit, with frequent teahouses and resting spots along the way. Long before the trekkers came, it was one of the most important trade routes of Nepal. For years people have sought to earn spiritual merit by providing comfort for travellers. Shady platforms were built with linked banyan and piple trees, ledges provided at just the right height to take the weight off heavy loads. The track looped and climbed, followed airy walkways, meandered through villages and buffalo byres, clambered across landslips and skirted terraced barley-fields. It was just as I imagined Nepal should be. On the third day, we climbed steeply all day, out of spring and into winter. This was the famous 'Staircase' between Tikhedhung and Ghorepani. Our picnic was served on a sunny, grassy hill amid scented daphne bushes and golden mahonia. Primula plants were just coming into flower in the grass, and when we disappeared into a thicket to relieve ourselves, we found delicate white pleony orchids nodding in the moss of a tree-trunk.

In the afternoon we walked through an enchanted rhododendron forest, hung with tree moss and watered by crystal streams. It grew colder as we climbed, and patches of snow began to appear, until at last

The mule trail to Ghorepani

The village of Tsuk nestling at the foot of
a massive cliff wall hundreds of feet high

Left: Looking down on the three chortens near the Mustang border, with lines of weird needle rocks climbing the slope opposite

Sue, Geoffrey, Susan and Colin at a rest stop on the trail. Mr Basnyet watching over the party (inset).

Right: Above Tsile, looking south across the Kali Gandaki riverbed to the Himalaya beyond

Griffon vulture with pony carcass

Man-made caves in horizontal mud-vein, 100 feet above the river

we were beyond all blossom. By the time we made the last muddy plod up into Ghorepani at 9,300 feet, it was sleeting and cold, and we were glad to be welcomed around a blazing fire in one of the lodges. Chotare cooked, and we ate, indoors that night. Some even risked the famous teahouse fleas to sleep under a dry roof. It was still drizzling when we went damply to bed.

★

For once, it was us who wanted to be up early since 'the thing to do' at Ghorepani is to climb Poon Hill at dawn. Then you are rewarded with a view of Dhaulagiri and all the Annapurnas flushed pink with first light. Sad to say, even at such a prospect, Reiko and I did not wake as early as we wished. A quick glance outside established that it was no longer raining, that the clouds had lifted, and we scrambled into our clothes, grabbed cameras, and puffed up the hill behind camp.

We were just too late to reach the top in time, but Annapurna South and Putha Hiunchuli, to the side of us as we climbed, blushed a delicious shell pink, and the view of the south face of Dhaulagiri, once you do get high enough, is stupendous whatever colour it is. For us, it was a gleaming primrose rising out of the dark shadows of jungle beneath. Large stretches of snow lay up here, and the famous rhododendrons which provide one of the most popular tourist images of Nepal were crisp with hoarfrost. For a view like this, it was worth clicking away a roll of precious film. We scurried back downhill for breakfast.

There was no more climbing that day, the route being the mirror image of the day before – downhill, at times steeply, for six hours or more. It was hot and dry. As we approached Tatopani, to join at last the sacred valley of Kali Gandaki which would lead us all the way into Mustang, we saw people carrying sick and aged relatives. They were being taken down to the healing waters of the famous hot springs. Crossing the river on a fine suspension bridge, we followed a white marble path, polished by the feet of centuries, between walled citrus gardens into the village.

Tatopani (literally Hot Water), as the steep, narrow valley here dictates, is a linear village – a single street of mainly guest-houses and stores, geared to the tourist traffic. Here you can buy anything you require on a journey from corn-plasters to flashlamps. You can trade in your paperbacks for other people's cast-offs. Travellers' books acquire a very individual form. They get folded inside out to be read one-

Across the gulch opposite the 'Golden Staircase' people waved from the village of Gyagar

handed in bed, become dog-eared in a daypack, ring-marked as mug-stands, crinkled from damp. After a week their splayed pages can never more be made to close. A row of well-trekked books occupies twice the space on a shelf as the same number of new ones, and their titles bleach to invisibility in the sun.

Our camp was in a small compound behind the last house in town with a view upriver to the shapely peak of Nilgiri, which effectively sealed the valley. The woman who owned the campsite used to have, she said, a dozen other houses and paddocks further upstream. These were all washed away in disastrous floods some years ago. From being one of the richest landowners in the village, she was reduced in an instant to one of the lowliest. There is no insurance here.

'Where are the hot springs?' I asked those who had arrived first.

'Next track along to the right. You go down on to the riverbed and then around the corner. You can't miss them, you'll smell the sulphur!'

It was true. A number of brackish pools and seepages gave off the sickly sweet brimstone smell, and the squeals of other trekkers led us to two pools concealed behind a buttress of rock.

'Come on in! This is the cooler one,' someone sang out from where several were already poaching gently in the first of the carved-rock basins. The other was almost invisible for steam.

I dipped a toe into the piping water. Wow! If the second were hotter than this, it must boil you alive. I marvelled at those who were immersed up to their necks, and very gingerly lowered myself in to join them. We hung round the edge of the pool, legs floating inwards, like mussels on a breakwater, or a ring of Busby Berkeley swim-belles. Aches and pains floated away, but it was impossible to bear the heat for long.

Our cabbage-porters, two young maidens from Tsum, were too shy to share our pool. They braved the hotter one. Amid much giggling and hiding of downcast faces, they detached layer after layer of dusty clothes and unwound several wrappings of shawl, before dunking themselves, still modestly shrouded, in the scalding water. Their apple-red cheeks shone rosier than ever.

We washed our hair, scrubbed our clothes, and trooped back for a beer in one of the saloons before dinner. Reiko found a kimono at the bottom of her kitbag and wafted elegantly. Chotare excelled himself: he produced a delicate ginger soup (several servings each), and popcorn, a six-dish main course, apple-pie and we rounded off with tea or hot chocolate. It had been a long day. We all tucked early into bed.

★

I couldn't help wishing I had seen Tatopani before it became so well-visited. Too often the provision of tourist amenities robs a place of its individuality and natural advantages. Though the landscape is striking, and God grant it will stay so, popularity cannot avoid lending a tawdriness to the place. How I envied all those explorers who came to Nepal in the 50s and 60s when it first opened its doors to travellers. Yet things will change even more, and in a sense, everyone passing through Nepal's valleys and villages, now as then, is privileged in seeing something rare and transient. With a fast-growing population, forests are vanishing year by year – visibly – and in heavily trekked areas, a desire for hot showers on the part of visitors has exacerbated the problem. A giant hydro-electric scheme is planned for Tatopani. One day, without doubt, a road will be forced the whole length of the Kali Gandaki into Tibet.

No-one can begrudge the Nepali people their 'progress'. It is easy to see why Sir Edmund Hillary – and a good many others besides – have felt prompted to devote their lives to bringing schools and medical services to remote rural areas. Far too many children are still dying in the villages, almost half of them in some places, and this largely from contaminated water. Natural disasters, such as floods and landslips, are facts of life.

No landscape can be preserved at the expense of people who have so little. The best chance for achieving sympathetic long-term development is offered by such schemes as the Annapurna Conservation Area Project, which is being run with the support of the World Wildlife Fund–U.S. and active local participation in the husbanding of natural resources over an area of a thousand square miles contained within the Annapurna Circuit.

The high, enclosing valley walls, grey and steep, make Tatopani a gloomy place in the evening and early morning when the sun is too low to find a way in. We left first thing the next day, beckoned on by splashes of sunlight on the high cliffs ahead. The early flights in and out of Jomoson, further up-valley, shattered the silence. These can only operate in perfectly still, fine-morning weather, before the notorious Kali Gandaki winds blow up later each day. It is a one-plane service. A Twin Otter shuttles back and forth, between Pokhara and Jomoson,

163

with never enough seats for all the people hoping to save the long trek in one direction at least. Any extra flights that can be squeezed in on good days greatly reduce the log-jam.

Walking was relatively easy-going along this gorge, though the landscape was wild and tracks at times dizzying. Sean stopped to take photographs. It was getting warm, and he removed his leather waist-coat. By the time he remembered it again, he was already some distance from where he had set it down on a rock, and though he dashed back at once, it was gone. With it had vanished his wallet and a Georgian silver tobacco tin, a family heirloom. We had passed a couple of trekkers that morning, a mumbling lama and a trader with a string of mules. It could only have been one of these who had taken it, but by now all were well on their way. He would have to accept the loss.

A beautiful object, Sean believes, is at its most precious when performing the function for which it was made. A tobacco tin, however old, was for tobacco, therefore, not putting behind glass. It fitted Sean's character perfectly to risk it on a rugged trek. He was a romantic traveller. His outfit, which never varied – broad brimmed hat, riding jacket, check shirt and bandanna – was straight out of Indiana Jones. In his time, Sean has tramped many of the world's wildest places. He has been a horse-dealer in Pakistan, still owns a farmhouse in Swat, but having at last 'settled down' with a wife and young family, lives now in London, where he runs a busy travel agency.

Sean is a tireless supporter of the Tibetan cause. He acts as chauffeur for the Dalai Lama when he is in Britain, and is himself a Buddhist and a Tibetan scholar. In the normal way of things, you would never find him on a trekking party like this. He is a lone wolf. But there was no way of going alone to Mustang, and the lure of seeing a Tibetan way of life that since the Chinese invasion has been all but obliterated from Tibet itself, drew him – as indeed it drew all of us – on this journey.

All the same, Sean was restless. He took every opportunity that was offered to slip away from the main group and make informal contact with the villagers. He would let it be known that he was willing to trade; would ask to see inside gompas; would seek out chang houses with Laureen, who became his regular drinking partner. With Mr Basnyet he enjoyed an uneasy relationship: sometimes they would be the best of quaffing pals, telling tall stories and slapping each other on the back, but at others our liaison officer resented Sean's independence. His instructions after all were to see that we did not exceed the terms of our permit, and he was determined to ensure that not one of us questioned his authority. It led to several clashes.

Below Kopchepani, we crossed a side-river by a narrow suspension bridge. Beneath us, on rocks dampened by the foaming water, were sprays of white flowers. I was sure they must be orchids, but it was impossible to get close enough to see. Still, if there's one bunch, I said to myself, there's bound to be more, and I kept my eyes skinned. Sure enough, further upriver, I saw more clumps of gleaming white below me among a tangle of rocks by the waterside. Dumping my rucksack, I scrambled across the boulders towards them, finally fetching up under a huge rock over which flowed pendulous clusters of exquisite yellow-lipped blossoms. They were beyond reach and the light was dim, but leaning backwards I was able to take a wobbly photograph that I hoped would permit identification later.

This part of the trail is heaven to a naturalist. In the forest, Lhakpa had announced that some fibrous balls, which looked like small rolls of horsehair, were droppings of the red panda, and for all I know, he was right. Perhaps you can tramp through Nepal long enough not to be overtaken with wonder at every turn, but it is hard to imagine. Perhaps, if we had come a month or two later and found ourselves fighting armies of leeches – or ferocious lychees, as one Kathmandu guidebook warned – some of the glory might have waned, but even then, I suspect there would be plenty to delight. It was a struggle to keep your eyes on your feet, to remember to stop first if you wanted to look around you. On airy, narrow tracks, one stumble is all it takes to tip you into a ravine from which you could never find a way out. There are plenty of tales of trekkers who have simply disappeared without trace. Geoffrey and Susan in our group each had lucky escapes. While flowers threw me into ecstasies, they were ticking off exotic birds when a brilliant pheasant or spiny babbler too many caught them off guard. Geoffrey injured his ribs in one tumble, and his wife fell full on her face, putting her teeth painfully through her upper lip. Her smile, from then on, had a very lopsided look to it.

In books about Tibet, or Dolpo, you often read how travellers have camped on the roof of the headman's house, gained by means of ladders made from notched logs. I had not imagined we might do the same, but in Ghasa, a village built along a narrow valley, there was no other level place to camp. The Sherpas set up our tents among the doves and drying pumpkins on the flat mud roof of (aptly enough) the Mustang Hotel. Tent pegs could not be anchored deeply, so we had to hope for a calm night. In the dark we would need to take care not to fall over the edge or down the smoke hole. The roof shivered as we walked about on it.

Zoe, our oldest member – amazingly in her early seventies – took one look at the perched log and blanched.

'You surely don't mean us to sleep up there?' she challenged Elaine. 'That's ridiculous!'

'No, no! The Sherpas will help you. Really, you won't have any trouble getting up and down.'

'And if I want to spend a penny in the night, will they be there then? No, it's out of the question.'

She stomped off to find a guest-room. Certainly, to climb the log in the dark was not going to be easy. All right for the men: if they were taken short, they could just pee over the edge.

'Well, we could too, if we positioned ourselves right,' suggested Susan.

'You're not to try!' Geoffrey was alarmed. 'Susie, I positively forbid it. We've had more than enough accidents already!'

She was right, though, she confided with some satisfaction the next morning. It was perfectly possible.

'Susan, you didn't!'

She smiled her swollen smile.

Over the Hump

BETWEEN GHASA AND Tukuche the Kali Gandaki slices through
the main crest of the Himalaya, and the mountain scenery is
the most dramatic of the whole walk-in. Passing between the great
masses of Dhaulagiri and Annapurna – their summits only a few miles
apart – the rise from riverbed to mountain-top can be as much as
20,000 feet. To know beforehand that this is the deepest gorge in the
world is to yawn at one more dry statistic; but to be here, the
excitement of so much raw geography makes you giddy. Sad then that
on the day we walked this stretch I was hobbling miserably behind
Pemba, seeing everything through jaded eyes. This was the morning I
twisted my ankle and allowed the young Sherpa to take my rucksack
even though he already bore one of enormous size. Mine he slung, like
a baby koala, across his chest.

We had been walking for six strenuous days. I can only suppose my
body was rebelling against the unaccustomed effort. Even so, I could
not fail to be impressed as sub-tropical forests yielded to pine and
mahonia woods, which in turn thinned out to increasingly alpine
pastures. Clumps of pink primula and tiny, Athene-eyed gentian
dotted cropped grass. As the Annapurna summits and the Nilgiris
began dropping away behind us, to our left and ahead reared the
south-eastern ramparts of Dhaulagiri and Tukuche Peak, forming
between them an uninterrupted facade of evilly gleaming ice and
snow. Cornices overhung the entire length. The steep slopes were
raked with avalanche tracks. Dhaulagiri's eastern glacier tugged away
from the lowest notch of the ridge to spill chaotically over gentler
slopes at the foot of the wall. This was where an American expedition
lost seven of an eight-man trail-breaking party within days of its
arrival in the spring of 1969.

The climbers had just pushed to 17,500 feet, hoping to gain the

167

mountain's south-eastern ridge from the icefall. A wide crevasse barred the way ahead, but they had carried up logs from the valley with which to attempt to bridge it. The twelve-foot logs were pivoted carefully into position as all eight men clustered around the hole in the afternoon mist, engrossed in the problem.

After the avalanche had passed over them, only Lou Reichardt remained. He found himself in a world he could not recognize. Friends, equipment, even the snow on which he was standing had vanished, leaving instead a savage tumble of hard, dirty avalanched-ice, the trail of which continued on past him and over steep cliffs below. The scene was one of indescribable violence, yet at the same time uncannily silent and peaceful. He was left to make the loneliest journey of his life, back down the mountain to alert his colleagues, and shedding, as he was afterwards to say, crampons, overboots, and finally even disbelief on the way.

Reichardt was not the only man on that Dhaulagiri expedition to have had a miraculous escape. Al Read – our Base Camp Manager on Everest – owes his life paradoxically to a near-fatal attack of pulmonary oedema. Without it, he too would have been in the doomed party. A few of the team had arrived at Lete ahead of the main group, having forged up from Pokhara in four days, then gone straight on up to base camp at 15,000 feet. This represented a rise of more than 14,000 feet in five days, with all the men carrying their own loads. Al, as a young man, was fit and no stranger to altitude. He saw no cause for alarm. No-one did.

On the sixth day bad weather pinned the party in its tents and Al began to show the first signs of altitude sickness. He had a crashing headache, for which he took a pain-killer and tried to sleep. In the middle of the night his tent-companion was woken by loud groaning. Already in a coma, Al could not be roused. That he survived to make a full recovery is entirely thanks to the prompt action of his colleagues. At first light they began dragging him down the mountain, while the team's doctor, who had just arrived in Lete, set out from below to meet them. By the following nightfall Al was back down at 10,400 feet, where he was put on oxygen. That night brought another crisis. His pulse soared to 160 and his respirations to sixty a minute. Although there was some improvement by morning, his legs were still paralysed and his vision impaired. Throughout that day he made slow and steady progress, and was carried down another two thousand feet to the village of Kalopani, above Lete. From here, in a few days he was well enough to return to Kathmandu, although it took several months before his eyesight was fully restored. His companions returned to the mountain – and death.

Beyond Kalopani Mr Basnyet drew a line in the dust on the path. 'Congratulations!' he said, thumping each of us on the back as we crossed it. 'You have walked right over the Himalaya. Now we are on the other side.'

But still climbing, I thought ruefully, as we began the long pull into Tukuche. We were walking now along the stony bed of the Kali Gandaki river.

Himalayan rivers have enormous work to do. However dynamic their flow, the load of sediment they are required to bear is far more than any single watercourse can cope with. As the mountains on either side crumble under the assault of winds and frost, adding their detritus to the river's burden, shingle bars are thrown up. The stream adopts a shifting, braided pattern as channels sever and rejoin, carve and toss their loads, over the uneven bedrock.

In places this valley floor is as much as half a mile wide. I suppose at times of flood, channels must overflow, but surely the river can never fill the entire valley? Rising in the arid heights above Lo Mantang, the Kali Gandaki must be fed almost entirely on snowmelt since Mustang's rainfall is less than 500 millimetres a year.

We picked our way along the ribs and banks, making crazy detours to save getting our feet damp. Regularly walked paths identified themselves as pale streaks among the relentless, graded boulders. The long, low log-cabin teahouses which punctuated the route became welcome refuges from a stiff and constant wind. We were now in the heart of the district known as the Thak Khola, home of the Thakalis, an extraordinarily successful group who make their living as traders and merchants.

For centuries the Kali Gandaki has been the major corridor from Tibet into western Nepal, and on to India. Salt and wool were brought down from the high plateaux to exchange for grain that had come up from mid-Nepal. Tukuche was the main centre, and the Thakalis – by government decree – held a monopoly over all such trade. They became increasingly prosperous and powerful. Today, along the trail, we had been seeing grand houses and wayside inns left over from those days, sturdily built of dressed stone and decorated with elaborately carved wood balconies and window-grilles. But the days of their glory were over. Trans-himalayan trade has dwindled disastrously since the

Chinese took over Tibet, while new road and air links in Tibet and in Nepal have made a wide range of goods available to people who had been isolated for centuries.

Trekkers provide the main traffic along the Kali Gandaki today, and Hindu pilgrims making their way up to the sacred shrine of Muktinath. Many Thakalis have migrated down to Pokhara in search of work. Others run the modest *bhattis* or teahouses that still enliven the miles. In a few years this whole section of valley has undergone a swing of cultural emphasis, traditional Tibetan influence giving way to Nepalese.

There are still a few traders. We met three men from Dolpo who were coming down to where the first bamboos grew. They wanted baskets, and for these they offered apples, which they had presumably picked up on the way in Marpha by bartering something else. If we'd had our wits about us, we would have bought a stack of baskets when we had the chance, filled them with apples when we reached Marpha, and gone up into Mustang with those!

The first mountaineering party to come up the Kali Gandaki was Maurice Herzog's French expedition in 1950, which made Tukuche its headquarters. The climbers were unsure when they arrived whether they would be attempting Dhaulagiri or Annapurna for, beyond knowing that both were eight-thousanders, little information and only the sketchiest of maps were available. Their first month was spent reconnoitring the various approaches to both mountains before they crossed what they called the 'Pass of April 27' from Lete into the Sanctuary of the upper Miristi Khola, to launch a successful attempt on Annapurna I.

It was the first time an eight-thousander had ever been climbed and the ascent was made without oxygen, but at a terrible price. Herzog and Louis Lachenal, the two who made it to the summit, were both so badly frostbitten in an epic retreat that they had to be carried out from the mountain and afterwards lost fingers and toes, many of them before they reached home. There is a most gruesome chapter towards the end of Herzog's book of the expedition, in which the doctor Oudot performs operations in a railway carriage every time the train stops at a station. Poor Lachenal still has three toes to be removed when they reach Gorakhpur, where he has to change trains. Oudot snips away frantically, and seconds before the train pulls out of the station, Lachenal is helped clear. His friends are left to sweep out the compartment with a twig broom.

'In the midst of a whole heap of rubbish,' wrote Herzog, 'rolled an amazing number of toes of all sizes which were then swept on to the platform before the startled eyes of the natives.'

The three or so miles of boulder-trudging up the riverbed seemed interminable, a sense only accentuated by the valley's great width and the long views up and downriver. My legs were leaden. It had become very cold suddenly, cold enough to warrant anorak and woolly hat.

'Hang on, Pemba, I need to fish out my spare clothes.' He was still patiently matching his pace to mine, as he had all day.

With hat pulled well down over my ears, and roly with sweaters, I tramped on, locked in a private cocoon of weariness. Lammergeiers circled over high clifftops to the side of the valley, and in the river two griffon vultures squabbled over the sodden carcass of a pony: thank heavens I still had energy enough to press the camera button.

Once in Tukuche, I flopped, all interest in sight-seeing long since evaporated. I kicked off my boots, crawled into my bag and slept at once.

We were camped on a piece of waste land to one end of the village, which from Herzog's photographs I took to be the same site he used when he was here. Our 'loo tent' was erected – for some privacy – against a wall some distance from the tents. To reach it, one had to run the gauntlet of the many wild-eyed village dogs that milled every-where, challenging all strangers. One look at them had been enough to induce most of the group to book into the lodge where our Sherpas had set up kitchen in a courtyard. I joined them there for dinner a couple of hours later, but ate little, and soon returned to the tent to crash out again. Sue Byrne was among the dwindled band of campers, but when she zipped herself in for the night, she couldn't help noticing that among the chorus of dog barks outside, there was one more insistent than the rest, deeper, throatier, more menacing. She grabbed a polythene bag of belongings and streaked into the darkness to see if there was any more room at the inn.

I never did catch sight of this billy-dog-gruff, but a yappy little terrier snapped at my heels as I crossed to the 'privvy' in the dark. I had to shine my torch into his eyes to keep him at safe distance as I bared myself dangerously. Ang Pasang vowed to protect us if we were attacked in the night, and moved in next to Laureen, piling up an arsenal of stones outside the tent.

In the event, we spent a peaceful night. True, the dogs kept up their concert, but we were used to that by now. I don't know when I had slept so well or so deeply, and we were allowed to lie in until the sun was up. It was heaven. For the first time, I woke in the morning feeling really alive and refreshed. I chattered into my tape recorder –

5 March At my back the famous Kali Gandaki afternoon wind propels me along. Not perhaps as strong as I thought it would be, but we may not be properly into it yet. Certainly it's not a cold wind. The sun is out, and it's a shiny-bright, cobweb-blowing, spirit-lifting day. I have tied on my sun-bonnet with a scarf and am bowling happily behind our ponies and the kitchen boy with all our metal washing-up bowls on his back. A chicken is tied by its feet to the saddle of one of the ponies – dinner tonight. When I first saw it dangling upside down, I thought it was dead, but later the poor fowl managed to scramble up on to the saddle and sit out the rest of the journey stoically.

We have moved now into desert country. Trudging along, like this, in the wind and blown sand, scudding clouds above, is exactly how I pictured early travellers tramping High Asia . . . Mustang is only a day and a half away . . .

Outside Tukuche I noticed a number of willow saplings sticking out forlornly from among the river boulders. Most were dead. They had been planted, I learned, by contract labourers with no interest in whether the trees survived or not. Many were stuck into the stones without even removing the plastic bags in which they had come from the nursery. They leaned crazily, and it was small wonder the exercise had failed. Charlie Pye-Smith, in his entertaining *Travels in Nepal*, takes an ironic view of the effectiveness of many such environmental and aid programmes. The saddest aspect of this particular story is that a large number of trees from what little remained of the indigenous forest on either side of the valley had been felled to provide stakes for the hapless willows. Disaster twice over. How different the story of Marpha, a short distance higher up the valley.

Long before any houses hove in view, Marpha's famous fruit trees greeted us. Field after field of apple and apricot, just coming into delicate flower. Sparkling watercourses have turned what would otherwise be barren stonefields into successful orchards. They filled the valley with blossom. Everywhere looked tidy and cared for. Neat stone walls were topped for protection with Crown of Thorns, a cactus-like spurge whose barbed-wire branches ended in brilliant scarlet flowers like droplets of blood. We stopped at a roadside store for delicious apple juice, and bought fat packs of dried apple rings. These should last me throughout the trek, I thought, but when in five minutes I had munched almost through the first pack, I pulled a few more rupees off my wad and purchased some more. Marpha is the headquarters of a number of experimental fruit farms that were started here twenty-three years ago by a remarkable Sherpa named Pasang Khambache. Others are to be found in Mustang, Dolpo and Manang.

Pasang first trekked up the Kali Gandaki in 1956 with the British anthropologist David Snellgrove, who was studying Buddhist settlements in valleys close to the Tibetan border. Although he came from the Solu Khumbu, Pasang had been educated in Tibet, training as a printer and wood-block maker at the Rongbuk monastery under Everest, and later at Tashilhunpo in Shigatse. His religious background and fluency in Tibetan dialects opened many doors. In Dolpo, priceless old manuscripts were brought out for Pasang and Snellgrove to study, and in Mustang, where Snellgrove was forbidden as an outsider to travel beyond Tsarang, Pasang went on alone to survey the monasteries and frescos in Lo Mantang.

He remained in Snellgrove's employ for many years, working in England as well as Nepal. Altogether, he spent nine years in Europe, two of them studying viticulture in France. On his return, Pasang was made an agricultural supervisor for the Nepalese government and set up the first of his farms here in Marpha. Apples were clearly the most successful crop, although initially the locals had taken some persuading to turn their fields over to them in place of traditional buckwheat and barley. Now the village had to buy in grain, but in return, its cider and apple brandy were renowned throughout Nepal. Pasang also planted vineyards, but these had been destroyed in a flood some years before.

A whitewashed gateway led us into the clean little town with a swift-flowing stream beside the main street. After lunch in a sunny courtyard we were taken up steep streets to be shown over the gompa before continuing our journey. It offered a bird's eye view over the Marpha rooftops, a geometrized abstract in warm browns and ochres with the surprising exclamation here and there of solar panels among the piled logs.

By the time I pulled up the last hill before Jomoson, the Kali Gandaki wind had strengthened and was whipping eddies of stinging dust at my back. With relief, I crammed with the others into a tiny teashop on the brow of the hill. The inside was bare and neat, everything scrupulously clean. Open shelves on the walls held pots, pans and the metal beakers in which tea is customarily served. Tables were pushed into the corners to make more space, and a long, tin chimney conducted smoke from the wood stove out through the roof. It was a typical wayside *bhatti* except that the gloom was relieved by a neon light hanging incongruously from the ceiling. We were surprised that somewhere so isolated had electricity. Geoffrey had travelled on the plane to Nepal with a man brought out from England to find out what happens to the 25 per cent of Nepal's electricity that simply goes 'missing'. Well, if it's brightening the lives of people off the beaten track, I thought, so much the better!

Outside the little town was a wide flattened area among the boulders, which I did not immediately recognize as Jomoson's airport. Only when a bright splash of colour against the grey background resolved itself as a windsock was the game given away. Khampa soldiers are said to have levelled this short take-off and landing strip in the early 60s to enable the Red Cross to fly in medical supplies and other assistance for the armed 'refugees' deep in Mustang. The Nepalese, however, were quick to put a stop to such traffic as it was an embarrassment in their relations with China.

To troops deprived of medical facilities, even the small matter of toothache could be devastating – and that was something all too common among the Khampas because of the quantities of sugar they would devour for rapid energy. In *Hidden Tibet*, one old soldier described to the author, Roger Hicks, how the leader of a rebel band pulled a gun on his deputy and, handing him a pair of pliers, commanded the poor fellow to pull out a painful tooth. All protestations were brushed aside with an uncompromising 'If you don't, I'll blow your head off!' If not the cleanest of jobs, the service was duly performed, and as the two rode along together afterwards, the captain was laughing with relief through his mouthful of blood. Less successful was the soldier who used battery acid to try and dissolve away an aching tooth. He had to be restrained from blowing off his own head on account of the pain.

Unable to dislodge the Khampas, the Nepalese were anxious to frustrate any contact with Tibetan sympathizers, and so created an inner line near Kagbeni, beyond which foreigners were forbidden to go. Khampa headquarters were situated a short way up-valley inside the no-go area and their distribution centre higher still, at Tayen. From there over a thousand mules operated to keep the outposts supplied.

The Khampas controlled all trade in the Kali Gandaki, and any Thakali merchants unwise enough to challenge their hold were summarily frightened off.

Jomoson today is an important military and administration centre. There is a mountain warfare training school which was busy at shooting practice when we left the following morning, the sound ricocheting off the canyon walls all round. The present incumbent of the smart law enforcement office had been in town only four months and had so far found no one on whom to force his law. There is very little brigandry here these days. Our party had anxious moments as our trekking permit was minutely scrutinized. Mr Basnyet puffed importantly, but no authorization to proceed beyond Kagbeni had ever been seen here before, and the officer did not feel confident to accept the validity of ours without first checking back with Kathmandu. Even at this late stage, we knew permission could be rescinded. Until we walked up that river bed unchallenged, the known world safely at our backs, we would not believe in this bit of paper ourselves.

★

Kagbeni lay ahead, its square red gompa settled into the notch of the valley. An apron of fields stretched out before it, while behind jostled the pink, rose, and magenta coloured cliffs of Mustang. Further back still a line of snowy mountains suggested the border with Tibet.

It had been glorious, the walk up the valley this morning. Sometimes we were locked in by its golden sides, sometimes open to fine views in front and behind us. Sometimes we followed the river boulders, at others we took to crumbling trails on the honey-coloured banks to avoid crossing and recrossing infinitely braided streams. Our porters, with their great loads, opted for the flat, even if this did mean frequent wading. They shared the valley floor with the occasional flock of goats being shepherded from one side to the other, and horsemen galloping down from Mustang on sturdy Tibetan ponies with their blond manes streaming.

Last night was a chilly one. For the first time, I broached the stuff bag containing my down jacket and gratefully pulled its high collar well up round my ears. In bed, I spread it under my sleeping bag for extra insulation, and stayed luxuriously snug. In the hotel, where we ate, they stoked a hearth of coals under the table to keep our feet warm, the heat sealed in by a thick woollen tablecloth. Jomoson is a chameleon town: so beautiful in the morning, so bleak and deserted once the wind blows up in the afternoon. It has a long, strung-out main street, bordered on both sides by mostly single-storeyed hotels and saloons. Crossing by moonlight last night, from the hotel back to where our tents were set up in the courtyard of a guesthouse opposite, was like finding oneself in a Mexican movie. Hunched against a whining wind, dogs yowling all round the shuttered town, it wouldn't have come as a surprise to see outlaws creeping along the shadows, or feel tumbleweed bumping against one's knees. But this morning was warm and bright and still again, the streets crowded with people and livestock. All the fierce dogs had collapsed limply in the sun, legs sprawled. They might have been shot. You trip over them and they do not stir. All day they sleep soundly, only coming to slavering life again at night. Like vampires.

Leaving Jomoson, Nilgiri – to our right – reared ethereal in the early mist. At our backs now, the mountain has assumed slightly more substance, although with shadows the same pale blue as the sky, it could never take on completely three-dimensional form, existing purely as sunlit surfaces, a curiously polarized image, like a photocopy.

A few hours above Kagbeni lies the holy shrine of Muktinath, one of the most important sites of pilgrimage for Hindus and Buddhists alike. Around the temple of Jiwala Mayi a hundred and eight water-spouts, in the form of cows' heads, spew sacred water from which the faithful must drink, in turn. In the gompa, built against a nearby cliff, jets of natural gas supply living flame from the rock. All morning we had been meeting pilgrims on their way to or from Muktinath. One wandering sadhu in saffron robes and flip-flops arranged himself on a rock as Sue and I approached, and extended a hopeful hand.

'Kerala,' he told us.

'You've come all the way from Kerala?' I asked in astonishment.

That was in Southern India – more than a thousand miles away. And he had brought nothing with him besides beads, and a bowl, and faith in the goodwill of others to feed him on his journey. That surely warranted a few rupees from us, too; and I thought fondly of Don Whillans – a guru of sorts himself, you could say – who on encountering a naked, ash-covered pilgrim on the road to Shivling, had asked, 'On some kind of sponsored walk, are yer fella?'

How must he feel, I wondered, this holy man, to have come so far and to know that tonight, he would reach the destination of his dreams?

And how, after that, to have nothing to look forward to but the long march home?

Lost Horizons of Mustang

WE WERE TO GO no further than Kagbeni that day, for Mr Basnyet and Lhakpa had their own pilgrimage to make. They hired ponies to take them to Muktinath and back in the afternoon. Sean and Pat decided to go too, and I would have as well, except that a crumbling cliff path was probably not the best place to take up pony-riding. It didn't matter, there was plenty to see here. When they clattered back around teatime, we crowded round to hear how it had gone.

Lhakpa eased himself painfully from his wooden Tibetan saddle.

We clustered round him solicitously. 'What is it? Lhakpa, are you all right?'

'Damaged,' he moaned, endeavouring to straighten up. 'All my bones are broken!'

*

When we come into breakfast this morning, people are still asleep under blankets on the benches. With some embarrassment we squeeze past to line ourselves along both sides of the table. Not only does this narrow room double for eating and sleeping, it serves also as the family chapel or shrine room. The man of the house comes in to perform the morning rites. Into seven little offering cups set out on an altar shelf he pours fresh water and, murmuring prayers, sprinkles more water over some sacrificial tormas and the picture of Swayambunath on the wall. Someone drops by to trade, the business of the day going on regardless of us. It is as if they, the Tibetans, and we, the round-eyes, belong to two parallel worlds that only by chance occupy the same space. In a sense, I suppose, that's true. We pass our tea-kettles up and down the table, scrabble for chapatis and marmalade, wrap our toes in moleskin. Their concern is to keep the family fed and protected through one more day.

177

On a low plank bed in the middle of the floor under a great heap of rugs lies the old grandmother. She hardly stirs, except to cough weakly. She is dying. We have been told that it is many days since she has passed water. Margaret – our nurse – says this indicates cancer or kidney failure. Clearly, the poor woman cannot hold out much longer. She is in terrible pain, and her distressed family wept openly last night as they begged Elaine and Lhakpa to help. They seem to think we carry with us all the medical knowledge of the Western world.

'We have nothing for anything as serious as this,' Elaine had to say. Only hospital treatment could save the old lady, and there was no hope of that. This morning they are still agonizing over what to do for the best.

'We must give her something for the pain,' says Lhakpa.

'Yes – but what if she dies? We will have killed her with our medicine. That's how they'll see it,' worries Elaine.

In the end, it is agreed to tell the young man of the house that Lhakpa will be leaving some pills behind. If they want to give her any – and it is their decision – all that can be hoped is that her suffering will be eased. But she must be given them sparingly. To someone whose system is quite unused to drugs of any kind, even small doses of aspirin could be fatal. What a ghastly situation this is. Elaine, too, is weeping now at the sad hopelessness of it.

As we leave, we see the man bring the old woman a drink and tap her tenderly on the shoulder. She struggles on to one elbow and swallows her first tablet. Our only hope is that the end comes quickly, for we know what news will greet us when we come back this way in ten days' time.

3 March   At last, our day for leaving the tourist trail! Anticipating it to be a long one, we are away by 7.30 and quickly through the warren of houses to the end of town. A short scramble brings us down to the river bed. The air is sharp and the wide valley floor blue in shadow as we crunch our way along the shingle. A system of log bridges guides us across the web of waterways, then we hug the bottom of the cliffs of the right-hand bank. On a terrace across the valley the sun catches a tight-packed cluster of earth-coloured houses, Tingri. From here a trail leads off into forbidden Dolpo.

Over the past few days, while following the bed of the Kali Gandaki, we kept our eyes skinned for *shaligrams* or *marmoni*, which are the black fossil ammonites considered by Hindus to be representations of the god Vishnu. Prized as most sacred are those completely encased in stone, the fossil only being revealed when the pebble is broken open. I had seen these curiosities on sale in Kathmandu, the two halves – one with the fossil, the other with its imprint – kept together with an elastic band. Good specimens commanded very high prices. In Kagbeni, children tugged at our sleeves, trying to interest us in examples they had collected. The practised eye soon learns to pick out the stones most likely to conceal fossils, although we were taking time getting the knack of it: sometimes, a mark like a cogwheel would give away a partly exposed one. The best shaligrams are washed down a side stream from the black cliffs around Muktinath, but we were above that now. Still, similar shale-beds outcrop in other places along the Kali Gandaki – and indeed were probably responsible for its name, 'the dark, big river'. We kept looking.

Presently, we left the flood plain for a path that clung to the right-hand bank and rose steadily under cliffs and pillars of cemented boulders – worn boulders, river- or glacier-worn boulders, cemented into fantastical flutes and pipes. It was a long pull up, and on the way we overtook two women in long, black Tibetan dress. Between them, they helped along a small child, who grizzled with tiredness. The younger woman's *dokko* (basket), we discovered, contained a tiny baby, hidden under scarves and rugs. Three weeks old it was, the mother told Yu-Lha. They had been down to Pokhara for the birth. No wonder the little girl was so miserable. She could have been no more than three and had just walked as far as we had. Her grandmother asked us for sweeties to encourage her up the steep slope.

It suited us to consider we were in Mustang from the minute we passed beyond Kagbeni into that region where tourists are not normally allowed to go. In fact, we had been in the Mustangi district, from a Nepalese administrative point of view, since reaching Ghasa several days ago; and the Kingdom of Lo, the realm of the Mustang Raja, we would not be entering for another day and a half. Technically, now, we were in Baragaon, a series of villages between Thak Khola and the principality of Mustang.

From the top of a high rise, we saw our first forbidden village, Tayen, golden in the sunlight. We were not to stop. Lunch was to be in another village further on. We lingered long enough to photograph the chorten in the centre of 'town', a crumbling but still beautiful monument entwined with an ancient apricot tree. All round were

179

more old fruit trees with massive, crusty black trunks and a delicate froth of blossom, pink against the sky.

'How old, do you think?' I asked Reiko.

'Five hundred years, maybe,' she said. 'Some.'

Apart from the children, who called at us from the fields, the people here were shy, only peeping out at us from behind half-closed doors. Sheeps' skull charms were nailed over doorways to ward off evil spirits. The doors themselves were painted a warm rusty red. All the houses were whitewashed and beautifully kept, and a terracing of well-tended fields extended down to the river and for some distance up and down stream. They were fed by a system of irrigation courses. A ruined yellow fortress stood on a prominence over the river, similar to one we had seen in Kagbeni. The upper Kali Gandaki is often likened to the Rhine valley with its old forts and castles guarding every village. At one time feudal warlords must have squabbled and fought to protect their section of this important trade route, and no doubt the unfortunate traveller was forced to pay taxes to all as he passed through.

With mountain views in all directions, and towards Mustang magnificently fretted cliffs that looked to have been carved by Newari craftsmen, this seemed to us a most perfect and peaceful spot, where the only sounds were the squeals of the children and our own footsteps.

Again we climbed.

*

The view, once over the next hill, snatched our breath away. We had stepped into another world. There was a steep chasm in front of us, walled in on the right-hand side by streaked rock, and it harboured a curious garden of honey-coloured pinnacles, a nursery garden of infant pinnacles, so it seemed, arranged in tidy rows up the sandy hillside. The river plain below us was flat and silver, with a few strands of green water fanning across it. A tongue of sharper green projected in from the bank on our side, indicating the fields of the next village. And on the other side of the valley were arrayed more tiered and fretted cliffs, of bright reds and golds, continuing up-valley to seal the view ahead. From these cliffs blocks had tumbled, the size of blocks of flats but spilled just like children's bricks.

I scampered down the loose scree, planting feet carefully so as not to turn my ankle again. Yu-Lha whooped past at top speed, delighted at last to have picked up an ammonite, and Mr Basnyet appeared as it seemed from nowhere and overtook everyone, his towel flapping around his neck. A few more ups and downs brought us, puffed and exhilarated, back on to the river bed where a willow-fringed track led into the village. The chorten marking the entrance had broken open to reveal moulded clay memorial tablets (*taksis*) like those we used to find in the ruins of the Rongbuk nunnery under Everest.

All the villagers of Tsuk – or Chhuksang – turned out to watch us lunch in their dusty square. Men, women and children squatted around the blue tarpaulin for the show, giggling delightedly at our strangeness. Afterwards Elaine showed them the *National Geographic* article describing Michel Peissel's visit, and they crowded round for a close look at the pictures. Although twenty-six years had passed since he was here, some of the faces were familiar to them.

'We knew that woman,' someone would say, 'but she's dead now.'

'This little boy has grown up. He's got a son of his own that age now.'

And of course they recognized the different places. Very little changes in these villages over the decades – come to that, over hundreds of years.

The local health worker, who arrived from Kathmandu three years ago, was keen for news of the outside world. Proudly, he brought his wife and small son to meet us. His job was to look after six villages round about, where the main problems, he told us, were skin troubles and eye infections. This we could believe. The diet is poor and there's little water to spare for keeping themselves clean in a region where dung collecting is essential. Houses and floors are made mainly of mud, and every day the village dust is hurled round and around by ferocious valley winds. It gets into faces, and lungs, and clothes, the same polluted dust that has been swirling about these villages for centuries.

There was no time for a siesta. The kitchen boys urged us to drink up, so they could grab the cups. Swollen feet were squeezed back into dusty boots. The tarpaulin was folded. We waved goodbye. Dogs and children saw us out of the village. The full heat of midday, and a full stomach besides, are not the best conditions for walking. As the sun broiled our heads and necks we tramped uncomfortably back on to the river boulders, pulling hat brims down, sleeves down, collars up, to protect our flayed skin. Geoffrey unfurled his umbrella.

The sides of the canyon caught and bounced back the heat like a microwave oven. Eyes down, following the pair of feet in front of me, I did not notice until we were almost to the spot that the gorge ahead was blocked. A massive section of red cliff from the west bank, several hundred feet high, had toppled towards the rock wall opposite, where it now leaned crazily, forming a natural tunnel through which the river gushed. Making use of the constriction a smart new metal bridge had been laid across the current. In Peissel's day it had been one of logs. No further progress by way of the Kali was possible. Like our predecessor, we would have to cross here and leave the river where a narrow tributary gully came in, the Gyagar-chu.

A last look back revealed a strange perforated line high on the cliff opposite, under which we had just come. A row of neat, evenly spaced holes picked out a narrow, horizontal bedding plane of red-ochre some hundred feet above the ground; they were quite square, unlike other man-made caves we had seen coming into Tsuk, which all possessed semi-circular entrances. Throughout Mustang we were to discover many such cubicles carved in sheer rock. Every traveller has commented upon them, but with no real conviction about their origin. Maybe they really were the retreats of levitating lamas, as Christoph von Fürer-Haimendorf was advised by his guide.

The Gyagar gorge was steep-sided, with snow mountains visible at its far end. Peissel tells how he narrowly escaped death when rocks tumbled down upon his party in this ravine. We toiled instead up its right-hand bank towards the fortified village of Tsile (Chele), which occupies a commanding position on a high platform above. Here again we paused for no more than a breather, then continued climbing until the path brought us back to the rim of the gorge.

Across the chasm lay the very attractive village of Gyagar (or Jakar), precariously situated above crumbling cliffs. The bare earth on that side of the gorge was riven with dry gullies and craters, and in several places, huge fluted flakes had splintered away from the main cliff-edge, to teeter drunkenly before it. How on earth were we to get across? Suddenly, to my horror, I saw that, instead of plunging over the edge, our path swung to the right and in a golden staircase continued climbing straight up the cliff on this side of the valley. Gyagar, it seemed, was not our destination after all. Miles of steep uphill lay ahead.

At every level spot I made the excuse to stop and admire the view, but lacked the energy to get out my camera and capture it. Gyagar, as I could now see clearly, comprised a cluster of white houses with reddish timbers, and piles of brushwood on their roofs – very Tibetan, especially with prayer flags fluttering from every home. Field terraces extended behind and in front of the village and were surprisingly green

in this desert, although further down the slope others had been abandoned, clearly for lack of water. Individual plots, mostly oblong in
shape, were built up at the edges to hold in soil and any water. They
overlap, one atop the other, all up and around the hillside – a ramp of
open tobacco-tins. Children in the fields called out and waved, but
their voices reached us only in snatches.

I was surprised to see so many mature trees over there – cypresses or
juniper, to judge from their dark foliage. Clearly all the water for trees
and irrigation must come from snowmelt, from the high mountains
further up the valley, to my right. Beyond the village, sharing the
same terrace, lay a most intriguing series of dry, dome-shaped little
hills, mound upon mound upon mound. With the late afternoon light
casting sensuous shadows, they took on flowing body curves. Figures
in a landscape. A reclining of nudes, a fluidity . . .

A light wind blew up as we rose closer to the snow mountains,
offering some relief after this boiling day. The rock was now almost
daffodil yellow. It was not a bad path, this golden staircase, two or
three feet wide in places and carved out by the Khampa guerrillas –
wide enough to walk, but not to stumble. No place to feel dizzy,
although after so long on your feet, you do feel a bit light-headed and,
in the narrow spots, inclined to cling to the rockface so as not to get
too close to the edge. The drop, I imagined, was several hundred feet.
Every so often, a mule and pony train would come down in the
opposite direction. Fortunately, the tinkling of bells and the whistling
and cheery calls of the muleteers gave plenty of advance warning, time
enough to tuck into the best passing spot.

With all my view-admiring stops, I had fallen back once more
among the tail-enders. Pat wasn't enjoying this very much. She always
has trouble with heights and Yu-Lha was patiently leading her along,
holding her hand and coaxing her around the scariest bits. Geoffrey,
too, was keeping a close protective eye on Susan. The staircase went on
and on. Even once we had rounded the steep hill, there remained a
long pull up to a pass. With patches of snow lying, it was very cold and
getting dark. Towards the top, we were overhauled by a riderless
horse, which fell into step beside us.

We had hoped for a sight of Samar, the village of red clay for which
we were heading, and were disappointed to see on the other side
nothing but the path looping on around the mountain. No village, nor
any sign of the others, and only one crease in the landscape into which
we couldn't see.

'God!' I muttered, with what little breath I had left, 'I hope it's tucked into that, or I don't know what I'll do.' We had been on our feet for eight or nine hours this day.

Luckily, that's exactly where it was – a few houses and trees snuggled in a hollow. Never has a village been more welcome.

The horse turned into the first gateway, from where a moment later rushed an agitated woman, wanting to know what had become of the rider. We never did find out whether he had simply stopped for a chang and a gossip and the horse got tired of waiting, or tumbled off somewhere. So many stories are left hanging in the air when you're on the move like this . . .

Our camp was going up quickly in a walled garden to the delight of the local children. About thirty of them clustered round, peering, prying, giggling and fiddling with the zips. Although I was the last of the trekkers through the gate, the porters trickled in for some time afterwards. At the very end came the two well-laden cabbage girls, only now they no longer carried cabbages, for we'd eaten most of those. They were to have been paid off in Kagbeni, but they cried and pleaded so pitifully, were so desolate at the idea of being left behind, that the sirdar relented and kept them on. The ponies trotted in with our bags, and no sooner had we dragged our own to our tents than there was Chotare, Chotare the lifesaver, with his pot of milk-tea and biscuits to revive us.

If I were to come on another trek, I reflected, I would bring (besides the bird and flower books) powdered milk – my own private store. Black tea may well be 'the horse of the lonely traveller' – as Eric Valli told me once – but for me, here, milk-tea comes at a faster gallop. I don't know why we can't have it all the time. There would be no trouble keeping up on liquids then. It's strange, for I can drink black tea happily at home, but tastes and appetite change so completely at altitude that you don't even recognize your own likes and dislikes.

Another forty minutes and the demon-cook had dinner ready. We ate on the sheltered balcony of our host's house, overlooking an inner courtyard. This is typical Tibetan architecture and very practical: a square inward-looking, two-storey house, where stores and animals occupy the ground floor, and the family lives upstairs. Extra living and sitting space is provided by the courtyard, the balconies and, in fine weather, the flat roofs above.

★

184

There is little enough to read on Mustang before one goes there. The mountaineer H.W. Tilman has described a visit to the village of Tangye in 'Mustangbhot', which he made by crossing the Mustang La from the Manang side in 1950, but Michel Peissel is without doubt the traveller most readily associated with the area. He took a yak caravan the full length of the realm in 1964, and his experiences are contained in *Mustang, a Lost Tibetan Kingdom*. It is not an easy book to find after all this time; his well illustrated account in *National Geographic* magazine turns up more frequently in secondhand shops. We had copies of both with us, and wherever we went they never failed to attract crowds of interested villagers.

Peissel was still in his twenties when he made his journey, a young man open to adventure and ready to be astounded. If at times his story seemed to us over-dramatic, his life too often in danger, we would remind ourselves that this probably had less to do with a gallic flair for romanticism than that Peissel was in Mustang when the area was heavily infiltrated with Khampas, waging their war of harassment against the Chinese occupying forces across the border in Tibet. It was a tense and dangerous time. Peissel, then, was our primary source of reference.

There had been a handful of travellers before him, and since, but apart from one brief period in the 50s and early 60s, the area has remained officially off-limits to all non-Nepalis on account of its sensitive political position. The earliest recorded incursion into Mustang was by Hari Ram, one of the Survey of India's celebrated 'pundit' explorers.

These native Indians were trained to penetrate forbidden regions of the Himalaya disguised as pilgrims or traders in order to obtain the information necessary for filling in blank spaces on the Survey's maps. They were taught to walk at a standard 2,000 paces a mile, marking every hundredth step by the slipping of one bead on rosaries specially adapted to contain 100 rather than the usual 108 beads. The pundits recorded their bearings and the distances they walked in code on scraps of paper which they tucked, in place of ritual Buddhist mantras, inside their whirling prayer wheels. The need for such secrecy was a very real one: the pundits knew they risked death if their subterfuge was unmasked.

In 1873 Hari Ram came up the Kali Gandaki to Lo Mantang, the capital of Mustang, from where he continued into Tibet, gathering not only topographical information, but details of population, trade and taxation. The next known visitor, at the turn of the century, was a Japanese scholar and Zen monk, Kawaguchi Ekai. He, too, was bound for Tibet but on the way spent a year in the Mustangi village of Tsarang, where he studied Buddhist texts under the guidance of a lama of the Nyingma-pa (the Red Hat sect). Westerners gained firsthand knowledge of the country's remote North-west only in the 1950s when Nepal's borders were opened to foreigners for the first time since 1816. Then, explorers, climbers, geographers and ethnologists began making their way up the Kali Gandaki. Tilman visited Tangye, and the Swiss geologist Toni Hagen became the first European to set eyes on Lo Mantang. He was followed in 1952 by Giuseppi Tucci, whose journey is described in *Tra Giungle e Pagode*, a book that waited almost a quarter of a century to be translated into English.

Tucci, who was an archaeologist (President of the Italian Institute for the Middle and Far East, in Rome), spent only one week in the 'forbidden kingdom' and his experiences there occupy just ten pages, one short chapter, in the slim volume *Journey to Mustang*, yet I was delighted to have discovered it, not just for its enchanting descriptions of places and the people Tucci encountered on the way, but for the insights it allows – just occasionally – of the explorer himself. Tenzing Norgay, the Everest climber, once spent a year with Tucci, wandering Tibet shortly before the Chinese marched in. He said it was like travelling and going to school at the same time. Everything they saw was given history and meaning. Tucci was a serious man, absolutely devoted to his work, yet at the same time terrifically excitable. Everything had to be 'just so' or there was an enormous eruption. At first Tenzing was inclined to agree with fellow Sherpas who thought him mad to work for the strange, fiery professor, but in time, he said, he grew to like him as well as any man he had ever known.

In Mustang Tucci travelled with a doctor, who doubled as the expedition's black and white photographer, and a young woman, Signorina Francesca Bonardi, whose job it was to handle the colour photography as well as manage the food and transport. He could not have wished for stauncher companions: they 'eased the undeniable hardships and dangers of the journey by the conscientious way they carried out their duties'. In a coy preface to the English edition of his book, Tucci reveals that 'Signorina Bonardi of 1952' afterwards became his wife.

Tucci also travelled with us, in the sense that we took his book, along with that of Peissel, and at mealtimes would sometimes read

186

from one or other of them. We could have added the accounts of the
geologist Harka Gurung, who trekked into Mustang in 1973, and the
anthropologist Christoph von Fürer-Haimendorf, whose special study
of the people of the Kali Gandaki has incorporated a visit to Mustang
with his wife. These I picked up later in Kathmandu. Otherwise, there
are a few scholarly articles and booklets, and Peissel's account of the
Khampa rebellion – little else. All in all – Peissel apart – it amounts to
only a few thousand words.

Fountain of Fortune

ELAINE, LHAKPA, MR Basnyet and the Mustangi guide, Tsering Tamden, put their heads together to decide the best way forward. Paths and mountains, passes, villages and distances shifted like shadows as they spoke. Maps were drawn in the dust only to be smoothed over and redrawn differently. Tsering was doing his utmost to adapt the available geography to what he believed the others most wanted to hear.

'How many miles to Gemi?'

'No many miles. Today we there.'

'But we go to Geling first?'

'Yes, Geling first. No far.'

'How far exactly? How long will it take?'

'Two, three hours, Geling, maybe. Maybe four. Depend.'

'Depend on what?'

'Depend which way. There are two ways – '

'Isn't there a holy cave one way? An important power place? Can we see that?'

'Ranbyung, yes. The chorten that build itself. We see it, you like?'

'If you think we can get everyone there. One of our books says it's a difficult trail.'

'Is okay.'

'And we can still get to Geling for lunch?'

Tsering pulled a wry face. 'Long time lunch, maybe,' he said.

Mr Basnyet could detect the possibility of a rift appearing between tired trekkers, who would resent any unnecessary time-wasting that separated them from their lunch, and the Buddhist scholars who didn't give a jot if they ate late, or missed a meal altogether. What was food, after all, against a miraculous 'self-produced cave'? By now, our liaison officer must have twigged that this was a very peculiar mountaineering

188

party. No one showed the slightest interest in getting to the mountain. Some seemed hell-bent on taking every detour offered on the way.

The cave that had so captured our imagination arose, so the story goes, out of bare rock many centuries ago. A large round natural pillar in its centre gives a suggestion of vaulting, thus reinforcing a sense of holiness. The walls bear age-old religious carvings attributable to both Red and Yellow Sects, but with especial emphasis on the great tantric saint Padmasambhava – the Guru Rinpoche, who brought Buddhism from the Swat Valley into Tibet in the middle of the eighth century. Today, 'Ranbyung chorten' is a popular site for pilgrims, who commemorate their visit by leaving clay models of gods, and most especially of Padmasambhava. According to Professor Tucci, these stand stacked in every corner. We have to rely on his word since such wonders were not for our eyes. Mr Basnyet decided the time had come to assert his control. We would all travel, he declared, by the 'swifter', higher route to Geling.

'Can't those that want to see the cave go round the other way?' Sean persisted. More than any of us, he could not bear having his wings clipped in this way.

'No. Party must stay together.' The decision was final.

It wasn't as if 'staying together' was something we ever did. Always several miles separated the first and last on the trail, particularly when you took account of our porters and ponies who rarely travelled with the sahibs. Since the path we now followed led in and out of ravines and over three high passes before bringing us within sight of Geling, it is doubtful if the other way could really have taken longer.

Samar, where we had spent the night, stood a little over 11,000 feet. From there we climbed juniper-covered slopes, patchy with snow, to the first pass at 12,500 feet. The path was a tangle of roots and rocks. I trudged behind Sue, the focal point of my vision her bloomers hanging out to dry on the back of her rucksack. We made a brief stop on a sunny terrace to admire the ocean of snowpeaks stretching away to the south-east, allowing our cognoscenti to identify one deep notch as the Thorang La above Muktinath, then, climbing on, we eventually made it to the top of a higher pass by about ten that morning. Peissel's pass, we called it, and re-reading his narrative I am still sure it is the one from the top of which he describes his first sight of the Land of Lo, the hidden kingdom we had come so far to see, even though we were not to cross the actual border until that afternoon. In the distance ranged the mauve hills of Tibet, while to left and right a rim of snow-capped peaks defined the borders of the wedge-shaped realm. The Kali Gandaki river, though only a couple of miles distant, was completely hidden, tucked in its deep gorge.

No villages were visible, no terraced plots. The empty, sun-warm landscape bore no trace of man at all, the flawless sapphire sky that enfolded it no scar of any aeroplane. I was reminded of looking down into the Grand Canyon. There were the same pinks and chromes, the same shifting patterns of shadow on fluted buttes. It was a naked land, flayed by wind and sun, parched and bleached, ribs showing through its skin of sand. But it was beautiful. I felt nothing of the terror that had so affected Peissel when he stood there. A 'gullied expanse of desolation', he had written, seeing little to beguile in the 'flaming glare of this sun-scorched land'. Only later did Mustang's weird beauty begin to speak to his soul. It shouted to mine! And Reiko, too, I could see, was jigging happily. It was like coming home. Home to Tibet. Sue and I hugged one another in jubilation.

'How's this then?' I asked.

'Bliss, it's bliss,' she laughed. 'I'm blissed out!'

Everybody seems glad to be going down, the porters are singing. We have been told it's an hour to lunch. If only we *could* get in a whole hour downhill − what a treat that would be! There are huge cave-like entrances in the bluffs to our left, and the golden hillsides below are polka-dotted with juniper, sweetly scented. Behind me Colin is whooping and yodelling, making echoes in the rocks. Vultures wheel in a blue, blue sky and jackdaws or choughs . . . or they might even be ravens . . . it's hard to get a sense of scale. Looking back I see somebody still filming from the pass, a lonely figure against the sky. Every so often the carved path burrows into rock, bringing us out to a vista slightly different from the one we left. It's the way of skirting this series of dry gullies − there is a directional thrust to the land here, ribs and fins sticking through the topsoil, and on this little bit of path, where a stream crosses, tiny sastrugi, also all pointing the same way . . .

No! I was wrong. There *is* one cloud in the sky, floating high over Tibet. It is exactly the same shape as the stylized clouds with their trailing tails that you see in the tanka paintings. The *chu-chu-chu*ing noise I hear must be the choughs, and there are the most silly little mouse-like squeaks coming from the lammergeier . . . ridiculous for a bird of that size . . .

The long downhill to lunch, as we might have guessed, proved an illusion. There was yet another pass to toil over before a scattering of houses and two square red gompas appeared on a barren hillside ahead. Even then it was a scramble through gullies and dried-up water channels before we straggled into the village.

Geling is not one of those fortress settlements with tightly interlocking buildings and a warren of passages. Its square whitewashed houses stand well apart with paddocks and common land between. The hummocky ground supports a few prickly bushes and a thin coating of grass – still fawn and flattened after the winter's snow. The whole village gives an impression of fawn-ness. Apart from the red-ochre decoration on gompas and chortens, it is a blond, bleak, open place, occupying the shallow scoop between mountains still sugared in snow. Walking to where our tarpaulin was spread on the central patch of fawn was like stepping into a faded sepia print. Painted doorways were a bleached brown, and the few dusty pollarded trees were bare of any green. Dried blond hay was piled on to flat roofs. A mud-caked girl led a mud-caked pony across our path. Dark, ruminating yaks eyed us passively. The chorten, which was decorated with curious elephant-medallions, wore a spiky, blond crown.

It did not take long for word to get around that we were here. Soon – as in the other villages – every available man, woman and child had turned out for the show. They took up positions along the mani wall to watch us eat, men one end, women the other and the braver children in front. We kept to our tarpaulin, they to their wall, and across the few feet of no-man's land that separated us, scrutinized each other with mutual interest. It always surprised me how few people we saw in these places – here there were about fifty altogether. Of course this is a sparsely populated area, I knew that, and the season, too, must have had something to do with it. The Mustangis' year is divided between farming and trading, and winter is the traditional time for making the journey into Tibet. From here the passes are quite low, and rarely snowed in. In summer goods are transported down to Thak and beyond, to store and to sell.

Though the land is barren, the climate is not as harsh as in neighbouring Dolpo, immediately to the west. There, almost everyone has to decamp for the winter, spending five months or more each year in the warmer, lower valleys of Nepal. It is possible for the Mustangis to grow just about enough for people's needs, but even so, a few mouths less in the leanest months must be a saving. From the dress of the villagers it was easy to see who did most of the travelling. Without exception, the women wore traditional home-made garments of Tibetan-style – long black or maroon dress, bound several times round the middle with a length of striped cloth which doubles as girdle and apron. The precise manner in which this is tied, and whether the apron is worn to the front or behind, is particular to a village or group of villages. Coloured woollen headscarves sometimes completed the rigout, although here a little black puritan bonnet was more readily adopted. All the clothes were shiny with soot.

A good many of the menfolk were also traditionally clad – knee-length, cross-over *chubas* and baggy woollen trousers gathered into colourful felt boots – but this was usually well augmented with cardigans and jerseys of Western style, and jaunty hats or baseball caps that they had picked up in Pokhara or Kathmandu. The sharper blades sported jeans and track-shoes; and highly prized were denim or leather bomber jackets. Children, as everywhere, wore an assortment of hand-me-downs – Tibetan trousers and tunics, and the most incredibly well worn, terminally grubby tracksuit tops or bottoms. Little scraps wore trousers with the crotch seam left open – separate legs, really, joined only by bib or belt – to give quick access whenever they were taken short. There was a fresh wind coming off the snowy hilltops, and everyone was well muffled.

None of the children would have seen visitors here before. No doubt, if Mustang remains closed, they will remember the day the foreigners came, and entertain their own children with stories of our pasty faces and peculiar clothes. The only items of ours that any of the villagers really coveted were our boots.

You feel very rude intruding a camera into their lives – and rightly so, for we would not tolerate it. Yet at the same time, you know these people, this way of life, is extraordinarily fragile. Soon it will be lost for ever. Desperately you hope to cling to something of it, preserve it, if only in photographs. Without great fuss, we all stole one or two pictures, asking Lhakpa if the people minded. Only one man – the village joker, who capered foolishly and mimicked us to raise a laugh – stepped forward demanding money.

★

For centuries the people of Lo (the Lo-pa) have maintained their precarious balance with nature. Their hard life, a high infant mortality rate, and a system of polyandrous marriages have conspired to keep the

The village of Gemi – 'Fountain of Fortune' – almost camouflaged at sunset among dry hills. Here the Guru Rinpoche slew a wicked demoness – Trangmar's cliffs are streaked with her blood, the long mani wall holds down the creature's entrails.

The chorten arch that forms the gateway to Tsarang, where a fine mediaeval castle is seen in a dreamy afternoon light

Tsarang. Distant chortens at sunset, and a private prayer room in the home of the King's sister

The pleated cliffs of Yara form a curtain across the landscape. Carved caves pockmark the rock. These ancient troglodite settlements are found all over Mustang, but how did people get to them?

Left: This ravine offers a quick way from Tsarang's plateau to the Kali Gandaki river

Young female porters carried the trekkers' supply of vegetables; men found spinning in the sunshine; and a Mustangi family engaged in conversation

Colin on his rented pony climbs the gorge above Yara

Colin approaching the high camp, with Mustang stretching away behind him

The hermitage of Lori Gompa, a Khampa stronghold during the guerrilla campaign against the Chinese in Tibet

Desolate desert landscape in the vicinity of Lori Gompa, not far from the Tibetan border

Lower Ghara, a typical Tibetan-style fortified village

population more or less stable – and even in recent years there has not been the great increase found in other areas of Nepal. It has been possible for them to satisfy their modest needs by their own efforts, and they have had no use for a world outside their area of trade. To them isolation was of no consequence. Indeed, it probably held the secret of their preservation. Though the Lo-pa, in common with the other Bhotia peoples of Nepal's north-west border regions, were to remain almost unknown to the rest of the world before the middle of this century, in a few short years these age-old traditions have changed utterly.

The Chinese invasion of Tibet has disrupted trading patterns, all but obliterating the salt-trade on which the economy depended. It caused a massive exodus of Tibetans over the mountains into Nepal. Gemi, the village for which we were now bound, was one of those swamped by refugees after the attempted uprising of 1959. The Tibetans brought with them their sheep and yaks, goats, mules and donkeys, which were then forced to compete with local livestock for the meagre pasture-land. It is recorded that, in Gemi alone, a settlement of no more than a hundred houses, six hundred yaks were lost from starvation and disease, as well as several hundred other animals. The people fared little better.

★

The steep hill out of Geling soon staggered the party. As was my custom, I dropped back through the ranks to adopt a position almost at the rear, often well separated from those on either side of me. Above the village terraces I clambered towards the first col, only to find when I got there that it was merely the lead-in to another, longer, but more gentle pull up a high dry valley. The fine weather we had enjoyed that morning seemed to be breaking up. Clouds built over the mountains behind us and there was a keen breeze. Although snow lay on the rounded hills to three sides, the valley itself remained almost clear, its slopes speckled with purplish wind-carved thorn bushes. These gave the impression of heather-tufts, making you think you had suddenly been transported to the north of Scotland. In all probability they were bushes of the spiny honeysuckle, *Lonicera spinosa*, which botanists describe as one of the dominating species to be found in 'the Arid Zone' north of Dhaulagiri. We would have needed to come a few months later to appreciate fully the sparse plantlife found up here.

Taking a breather, I am passed by one of our cookboys with an enormous basket of bowls and kettles. His jingling challenges that of a herd of goats and sheep – black and white – that have just swept across the path and enveloped us. The herdsman is standing at the bottom of the valley, gaping at me in absolute astonishment as I gabble into this instrument

Over the col (Nyi La, 12,965 ft), it was a new world. Ravaged hills in red ochre and a bright blue – some sort of lias, it must have been – defied belief, fantastic colours together, and etched with typical dry-valley erosion patterns. Behind, range upon pastel range blurred into the distance, the hills in shadow appearing blue, those in sunshine, pink, mauve or yellow. On top of the col grew clumps of tight-set saxifrage, white and round, not yet open, like huddles of mothballs in a forgotten closet.

Snow on this side of the pass lay in thick textured shields, supporting the Scottish illusion. A whaleback ridge between two gullies gleaming with melting snow led down to a transverse valley, along which I could make out a donkey track. The snow was deep towards the bottom, but I followed the tracks of the porter with the tin pots. With his awkward load he had taken the descent gingerly, leaving me good big holes in which to plant my feet. Once off the snow and contouring round the donkey road, I lost sight of everyone ahead, but coming to a junction where one fork continued downhill and the other climbed to a further pass, it was easy enough to guess that ours must be the upper road. It always was. I was relieved after a while to pass the tin-pot man again and know that I really was going in the right direction. The path hugged the curve of the hill, with the little notch of the col visible ahead, and through it now the brilliant red cliffs that had caught my attention earlier.

Well, this is the col – very windy – and still no sign of anybody ahead. There's not a lot to see at all . . . Oh, yes – yes, yes! There *is* a village down there, almost camouflaged. Gemi, it must be, Fountain of Fortune, spectacularly situated on a terrace among these dry rumpled hills, and with still some evening sun on it. I'm in the shade here on this side of the pass. I really have to try for a picture, despite this wind.

I hurried steeply downhill through patches of snow, rubbly boulders, and along a broad sweep of track. Unfortunately I was just too late to reach the village before shadow had seeped across it, but the last light caught the cloven hills behind and melted them into silk.

★

From Gemi we made directly for the red hills, crossing the Trangmar Chu by a new bridge and zigzagging up the opposite, northern bank to a wide stony plateau.

There, a *mani* wall of enormous length guided the eye to the reddest splash of ochre in the garish cliffs. The wall was striped in the Sakya-pa colours of red, white and grey, and every stone carved with *Om mani padme Hum* or other religious device. It marks the spot, so the story goes, where Padmasambhava, the Guru Rinpoche, slew and dis-embowelled a fierce demoness who blocked the way to Tibet. The quarter-mile wall holds down the wicked victim's intestines, and the bloody streaks in the Trangmar cliffs are where the saint flung her liver and lights after the battle. Her heart travelled further, coming down on the other side of the mountain at a spot now marked by the monastery of Lo Gekar. A rose-red gompa under the cliffs here also commemo-rates the yogi's glorious victory, but before reaching it, we bore off to the right, up a steep golden hill.

Many years ago, the village of Gemi extended on to this plateau, but no-one lives here now. All that remains of earlier settlement are mounds of rubble and dry ruined terraces. Water must always have been a problem here. With no natural source, a supply had to be conducted from the river by way of a leat, and it was when this channel eroded beyond repair that old Gemi was abandoned. So often in this desert, the best sites for villages – from the point of view of space and land, or shelter, or defensibility – do not tally with where water can be found. A thin horizontal line of green sketched across a bare hill will indicate a man-made channel, which will sometimes bring in water from many miles away.

Climbing steeply to the top of a pass, we caught up with those of the group who had set off from Gemi ahead of us. Last night at the local chang house Sean let it be known he wanted to buy a Tibetan bridle, and this morning Reiko, Elaine and I went with him to one of the grander houses in the village, where a young man, Lobsang Chofel, had promised him something to look at. We were invited upstairs for salt tea while their transactions were conducted, and afterwards were shown into the gompa courtyard, but the gompa itself remained firmly closed to us. This was something we encountered in many places. It was not just a religious prohibition, but reflected the wariness people feel these days after so many of the country's treasures have been looted. On the voracious international art market religious arte-facts fetch high prices, and too few questions are asked about where these items come from. Many of Mustang's gompa statues were sold off by the Khampas in the 60s and early 70s to finance their campaign against the Chinese. Understandably, the few that are still left are kept strictly under lock and key. Even the villagers are not allowed inside. Only the lamas go in to make the puja.

We were making good progress. It was still only nine in the morning when we breasted the pass and we could afford a few moments to enjoy the splendid view.

'There's Bhrikuti!' Eagerly people pointed out a fine ribbed snowy dome ahead, almost due north of us.

Mr Basnyet was excited. 'What do you think? Will we be able to climb it?' He dearly wished to go home a fully-proven mountaineer. Such a feather in his cap that would be.

'If that's Bhrikuti,' muttered Sue, 'then I'm a Dutchman.'

She had a point. It certainly wasn't where it ought to be. By any of our sketch maps, Bhrikuti should by now have been lying behind us, to the south-east. We were expecting to reach it by tracking back up a valley on the opposite side of the Kali Gandaki, and the river was still away somewhere to our right.

'I'll bet you anything Bhrikuti was one of those snowpeaks we saw from the campsite in Samar, two days ago,' Sue said. 'I thought so at the time.'

Well, that made monkeys of all of us who trooped along so unques-tioningly! Even if we accepted that this one in front of us was not our peak, how could we tell with any certainty which of so many was the one we were looking for? Bhrikuti was not supposed to be the highest in its range. And, sacrilege even to say it, how disappointed would we be if we did not find it? Almost without exception we had come on this trek more for the privilege of seeing forbidden villages than any prospect of climbing a mountain. For Elaine and Lhakpa it was an exploratory expedition, a reconnaissance. Failure to reach the moun-tain this time was no great disaster. It meant they could apply to come again.

Also it was becoming clear that in the unlikely event of ever locating the sacred triple lake that would identify our Base Camp, in such a tight itinerary as ours only two or three days could be spared for an ascent. It would not be enough unless Bhrikuti proved unexpectedly easy.

Sheepishly we realigned our mental map to the landscape, accepting that the mountain ahead could not be the one we sought, then pushed the whole issue from our minds and strode down the long dusty, yellow path towards Tsarang.

Seekers of Enlightenment

IN MARCH 1899 a babyfaced young Zen monk set off from Pokhara for Mustang, hoping from there to slip unnoticed into Tibet. Kawaguchi Ekai, from Tokyo, had bought himself a tent and hired two porters to assist him on his journey: one an impatient rascally fellow from Kham and the other, less rumbustious but irritatingly opinionated, a man who stretched a little education a long way. They travelled in the company of an old woman pilgrim, 'a good honest soul, and that was all there was about her', Kawaguchi somewhat uncharitably recalled.

A few days along the road she confided to the priest that the men were plotting to kill him as soon as they reached Tibet, adding that the Khampa was well known in his own country as a robber and murderer. Even the quieter fellow had once slain another in a quarrel. Luckily for Kawaguchi, the matter unexpectedly resolved itself in Tukuche when, loaded with local beer 'even to boisterousness', the two rogues fell out, each accusing the other of murderous intent and refusing to go further unless he was fired. Kawaguchi was able to dismiss them both – and the old dame into the bargain – and continued his journey with a Mongolian scholar whom he had met in the house of the local Governor. This Serab Gyaltsan was bound for Tsarang, where he had a house. Thence too went Kawaguchi.

For eight months, the Japanese monk stayed with his new friend, taking instruction from him in Tibetan Buddhism, and all the time gaining fame and popularity among the villagers (as he saw it) for his ascetic conduct and generosity with medicines. To celebrate the new century, Kawaguchi entertained the people of Tsarang to a party, laying before them 'a full and liberal store of such viands and delicacies as were considered to be most rare and sumptious'. He had reached, he felt, a pinnacle of glory.

Yet his satisfaction quickly faded. As the days passed, the monk felt traps were being set to hold him in Tsarang for ever:

> The arch-spirit of this conspiracy was my own instructor Serab, who insisted that I should marry the youngest of my host's daughters, or rather who brought all his ingenuity to bear upon assisting her to make a captive of my heart and person. Fortunately my faith proved stronger than temptations, and enabled me to remain true to the teachings of the Blessed One. Had I yielded then, Tsarang would have had today one more dirt-covered and grease-shining priest among its apathetic inhabitants, and that would have been all.

Tearing himself away, Kawaguchi escaped to Marpha and from there, later that year, was at last able to realize his dream and enter Tibet through Dolpo. He made his way to Mt Kailas, then on to Lhasa.

I ordered Kawaguchi's book, *Three Years in Tibet*, from the public library. Months passed and nothing came, and it was not until I had completely forgotten the matter, long after my return from Mustang, that a copy arrived on a short loan from St Andrews University in Scotland. A hefty volume and well-used, it had scuffed boards and tropical worm holes. The many pencil notes in its margins were presumably the work of Hugh E. Richardson, whose name appeared under the library sticker. One of only three Britons in Lhasa in 1951 when the Chinese reached there, this popular Scot was Head of the Indian mission and the last Briton in India's Foreign Service; it gave me enormous pleasure to know I had been lent a book that probably came out of Tibet with him. Eagerly I turned to the chapter *Beautiful Tsarang and Dirty Tsarangese*, in which Kawaguchi described his Mustang sojourn.

> The days I spent in Tsarang were, in a sense, the days of my tutelage in the art of living amidst filth and filthy habits. In point of uncleanliness, Tibetans stand very high among the inhabitants of the earth, but I think the natives of Tsarang go still higher in this respect ... To say that they think nothing of making a cup of tea for you with the same fingers with which they have just blown their nose, is to give only a very mild instance of their filthiness; and I have no courage to dwell here on their many other doings, which are altogether beyond imagination for those who have not seen them done, and are too loathsome, even unto sickening, to recall to mind.

As it was, my life among these slovenly people did one good thing for me, in that it thoroughly prepared me for what I had to endure in Tibet.

Kawaguchi passed his time in study, seven hours in preparation and six in regular daily lessons with his friend Serab. This included exercises in Tibetan rhetoric, which often ended in heated argument or even blows, for the chaste and finickity Japanese found it hard to accept what to his mind were the 'lewd and detestable' teachings of the Guru Rinpoche. He regarded them as 'a sort of parody on Buddhism proper, and an attempt to sanctify the sexual relations of humankind, explaining and interpreting all the important passages and tenets in the sacred Text from a sensual standpoint'.

Who could place credence in a saint who 'lived with eight women whom he called his wives, drank intoxicants to his heart's content, and fed freely on animal food'.

Animal food? Animals, I suppose he meant.

In all his spiritual preparations for Tibet, Kawaguchi did not neglect the importance of physical training. Every day he would take a short walk, and on Sundays spend the whole day in what he called 'mountaineering', making ascents with all possible speed and a heavy load of stones on his back, to improve his lung capacity for the high altitudes ahead.

Kawaguchi pitied his friend Serab for having once succumbed to carnal weakness, which shamed and defiled him as a priest. The villagers too earned his pity for thinking of little else than eating, drinking and sensual love. Yet Kawaguchi's stay in Mustang remained afterwards an idyll in his mind:

In summer, simple as is the contrast between the verdant fields of luxuriant wheat, interspersed with patches of white and pink buckwheat, and the majestic peaks that keep guard over the plain and look ever grand in their pure white robes of perennial snow, the combination makes a striking picture. Throw into the picture a buoyant army of butterflies, that flutter up and down, keeping time, as it were, to the stirring melody of sky-larks, which is now and then softened by the clear notes of a cuckoo, while the fields below are resonant with the rustic melodies of joyous damsels, and the *tout ensemble* becomes at once as enchanting as it is archaic; and this is the picture of Tsarang in summer, when the day is bright and warm.

His soul was stirred to even greater lyricism at the memory of a winter's sunset when the snow-covered mountains glowed a luminous coral-red, or of the scene on a moonlit night after a blizzard:

> The sky is filled with clouds of dusty particles of snow, moving ever onward like phantom armies, now thickening into ominous darkness and then thinning into vapoury transparency, through which one sees struggling, the lustre of the grey steely moon. No scene so weirdly harrowing can be seen anywhere else.

You can see Tsarang's remarkable gateway chorten from a long way off. Commanding a bend in the road, it stands on the brink of the broad basin in which the small township and its many fields lie. It has been so positioned that, approaching it, the fine mediaeval castle is framed evenly through the gateway arch. Even in the all-absorbing glare of the midday sun, the chorten's colours were brilliant. Later, when Sue and I came back in the slanting light of sundown, they glowed with russet warmth.

In shape, the monument follows traditional design: a square base, pierced by the gateway, supporting a tiered plinth on which sits the globular dome. This, in turn, is surmounted by a steeple-construction incorporating thirteen concentric rings of diminishing size. A curious brushwood canopy protects the dome, resting upon nine slender poles, but the chorten's uniqueness lies in its vigorous decoration. Brick-red, gold, white and grey pigments have been used to emblazon the whole structure with bold stripes and motifs. The ceiling inside the doorway is also richly decorated, but with frescos of precise and intricate geometry, contrasting strongly with the free expression of the outer design. These inner paintings are clearly of great age and have suffered some deterioration.

Originally put up as shrines, or cenotaphs, chortens have come to symbolize the stages to buddhahood and are to be found throughout the Buddhist world. To erect them earns religious merit for a community, and Tsarang, a settlement of some importance, could boast at least three outstanding examples, all freshly painted and well cared for. This came as a pleasant surprise since earlier travellers – Tucci and Snellgrove – had remarked gloomily upon the waning of interest in religion here. Both men attributed much of this decline to the then-abbot or lama of Tsarang, a son of the Mustang Raja, who having taken a wife was seen to be falling behind in his duties. A pathetic figure, Snellgrove described him, no longer enjoying the confidence of his flock.

'There are few unhappier beings', observed the professor, 'than a man of religion who has lost faith both in his religion and in himself.'

Tucci was astonished at the rich proliferation of statues and other fine pieces collected in the monastery, and horrified to see how carelessly such sacred objects were treated. Priceless *tankas*, finer than those in any museum, hung in tatters, decomposing gently under layers of dust, and in the abbot's house dozens more were thrown higgeldy-piggeldy into a hamper with fowls nesting among them and soiling them. He wrote:

> I untangle some and my heart weeps to see the miserable fate of these works of art. As I make a brief catalogue of the most important statues and paintings, I notice that the abbot is taking a great interest in Guttaso's watch and my boots, and I take him aside and try a little bartering. We reach an agreement, and I am thus able to rescue a few relics. I would probably have got more too, if it had not been for his wife who was constantly at his elbow, grumbling, haughty and forbidding, supervising him, spying on him, following him like his own shadow.

This was before Tucci married his 'Signorina Bonardi of 1952', and from the way he has it in for the lama's poor wife, you would be forgiven for thinking him a crabbed old misogynist. He was firmly convinced that the abbot lived in constant terror of this lady, and remarked unkindly – 'Exorcism can get rid of evil spirits, but has no power against women.'

By the time Peissel arrived in 1964 Tsarang's young lama had lost his 'shadow', his wife having died suddenly the year before, leaving him with a four-year-old son. Such misfortune must be in retribution for his 'profane life', the grieving priest believed, and took a public vow to devote himself to three years of solitary meditation and study. With his small son, he withdrew into the royal apartments of the monastery, where the boy shared his prayers and isolation. The harsh regime was relaxed for the week of Peissel's stay to allow the two men to enjoy each other's company.

'It was a touching sight', wrote Peissel, 'to see the straggly-haired monk reciting endless prayers with his little boy fast asleep at his side.'

The child was of a sweet and happy disposition and must have been a great consolation to his father. A photograph of the boy playing with one of the monastery statues illustrated Peissel's *National Geographic* article, and later, came to have special significance for me.

★

From the chorten gate a wide, walled lane led into Tsarang. Besides the castle, the town is also dominated by a red gompa, both built on prominent outcrops of rock. It is the second town of importance in Mustang and traditionally the winter residence of the Raja.

The Kutak – or Bista – are the noblemen and women of Mustang, members of the Raja's immediate family. Education and their position of privilege has guaranteed that, even with the continuing democratization of Nepal, they have maintained their high status within the community. The Raja holds land and large houses in almost every village, and his relatives act as his stewards. Tsering Tamden, our Mustangi guide, was a friend of the royal family, which gave us influential contacts in all the villages we visited. Without exception the head-men and women we met belonged to the Raja's family.

At the time of Peissel's visit, the Mustang Raja (who received him in his summer palace of Trenkar, near Lo Mantang) was Angun Tenzing Trandul, a man in his mid-sixties. Fourteen years earlier this king had abdicated in favour of his eldest son, Angdu Nyingpo, but the young man then died and Angun Tenzing was obliged to reassume the throne. The Tsarang abbot was the Raja's second son – it is customary in Lo and other Tibetan cultures for the second son to go into the priesthood – but as a priest he could not succeed to the throne. Not long after Peissel left, the third son, Jigme Senge Parwar Bista, was made king and remains so still. King Jigme has three sisters, and a series of nieces and nephews, many of whom we encountered as we travelled around Mustang. His heir apparent is the Tsarang lama's son, the little boy who had so endeared himself to Peissel, now a man in his early thirties.

★

Tsering Tamden found us a roomy paddock with a supported roof at one end, which gave Chotare the shelter he needed for his kitchen. All the tents were accommodated comfortably and the pack-mules tethered on an adjoining piece of rough ground.

The young nobleman whose family owned the paddock was Tsewang Jhonden. He was in his mid-twenties and cousin to the youth

203

with the bridle whom we had visited in Gemi that morning. Tsewang was hoping to go to university in Kathmandu and glad of the opportunity our visit gave him to exercise his excellent English. He took us home to visit his mother, a sister of the king. They no longer lived in the old castle, or fort (which despite being one of the most spectacular buildlings in Nepal had been in a dangerous condition for many years), but occupied a newer, strong house close by. This had a large elaborate shrine room, with richly painted pillars and ceiling and a fine collection of religious 'books' – carved wooden blocks parcelled up in coloured cloth and stored in a system of pigeon holes. Otherwise the house was simply furnished in the custom of all the homes we visited. Seats were benches or cushions arranged around the walls and the central feature of the large living and cooking room where the family spent most of its time was an open fire with baked-mud surround and cast-iron pot-rings set into the hearth. Boiling water, roasting barley and keeping a stew going were constant requirements and the young wives of the extended household never strayed far from the blaze, tending their pans and throwing on handfuls of dried goats droppings whenever the flames looked to be burning low. The King's sister, a gentle faced woman of middle years, was spinning quietly in the shadows, while her daughter (Tsewang's sister) worked at the carpet loom. I wondered at first if the plump old gentleman in the corner, mumbling prayers throughout our visit, could possibly have been the Tsarang lama who befriended Peissel, for I fancied I could see a resemblance to photographs taken of him by Tucci and Peissel, but we were told he was now in Dolpo.

★

Tsewang took us on a tour of the town – but not alas inside either gompa or castle. Both were buildings of three or four hundred years old, the castle predating the gompa, and have been described by the earlier travellers. We were shown a meditation room, tucked like a crypt below the temple, with some particularly fine wall paintings in need of restoration. Tsewang hoped we could find some benevolent sponsor to help preserve the town's rare heritage. Before 1952, all the inhabitants of Mustang were in the retinue of the Raja. The monarch could call upon villagers to devote a number of days of labour each year to the upkeep of religious buildings. That has all changed, and with a waning interest in the initiation of new monks, many monasteries, like this one, are now almost deserted and falling into dis-

204

repair. The influx of Tibetan refugees after 1959 checked the decline to an extent, but that is unlikely to be permanent.

Eight years ago a Japanese mountaineer came to Tsarang, where he struck up a friendship with Tsewang's uncle. The man had been on an expedition, and when it returned to Kathmandu, disguised himself as a Nepalese and made his way into Mustang from Muktinath. The villagers allowed him to see inside the temple, where he took a number of photographs, but shortly afterwards, while still in Tsarang, the young man died. We were not told why – but it was felt that he must in some way have angered local deities.

'Now, no one go in gompa,' Tsewang told us. 'No more pictures. Is for own protection.'

Outside the curtained main door of the gompa were three round pits in the cobbles. These were paint pots. Ochres and lime from the hills would be crushed here and mixed with water to provide the Sakya-pa pigments – red, grey and white washes – for decorating gompa and chortens.

On the side facing away from the village, the monastery buildings on their rocky bluff gave on to a deep ravaged gully. Small children – a ragged gang of three or four year olds – were larking about on the edge, hurling stones into the abyss with squeals of delight. It was a game of chicken: they would run to the brink and just check themselves in the nick of time. I found it almost unbearable to watch, for I could not believe one would not misjudge the distance or forget to let go. Some had smaller children tied to their backs, which made the required feat of balance even trickier. What, I wondered, was the attrition rate among children in these villages? As their brothers and sisters charged down the narrow streets, babies' heads would bounce wildly from side to side at their backs. Cornerstones and gateposts were missed by inches only.

A gaggle of grubby children accompanied us wherever we went. Sue and I, off on a photographic spree, were led by them to all the chortens and places of interest in the little town. That evening we were invited back to the princess's house for chang, and were surprised to see there was electricity in the house, even more surprised that a solitary street lamp burned outside – a naked bulb on the corner of one of the buildings.

Sometime in the night, not long after I'd fallen asleep, I was awakened by a fearful, bloodcurdling bellow, followed by the sound of running feet.

205

Someone's got belly ache, I thought. All went quiet for a while, and then, just as I was dozing off, there came another yell.

My goodness, they really were sick! The groaning was coming from the doorway of a tent. Whoever it was must be throwing up where he lay, unable to make it to the loo tent. Is it a trekker or one of the Sherpas?

By the third outcry, I was sure it must be ptomaine poisoning. There were agitated voices now. I could hear Elaine and Susan among them, and Margaret, our nurse. So it was one of us. If it was food poisoning, I thought, then we'll all go down with it, one after the other. We'd eaten exactly the same meals.

What could have so disagreed with him? We had bought some fresh meat that morning; all day it had hung in the hot sun. And we'd drunk the chang and some rakshi in the princess's house. You hear of whole villages being wiped out with potent homebrews in places like this.

I was holding my breath, trying to hear what was going on. There were plenty of people out there; they didn't need any one else cluttering up the place. But I wished I knew what was happening. Who it was. Reiko was awake beside me. She was holding her breath as well. I could hear her eyes widen.

'What is it?' she breathed. 'You know who?'

'I don't. I think it might be Colin.'

I didn't tell her I thought we were all about to die. Mr Basnyet's urgent whisper had now joined the rest.

All night long the roars violated the still air. We were up before it was light. 'Who is it? What is it?' Reiko and I grabbed the first Sherpa we saw.

'Is Geoffrey.'

It was not something he'd eaten, but his old rib injury playing up. An odd movement, the stiff exercise, hard ground, thinner air as we got higher – some combination of factors had suddenly reduced him to agony. A broken rib could puncture a lung. We couldn't take any chances. From somewhere, we had to get help.

There was no telephone in Tsarang, no doctors, no healthposts anywhere in Mustang. This is how life is for Mustangis – fragile. Fine, until there's an emergency.

There was an army post in Lo Mantang, we knew. They would have a telephone. That was still half a day's ride away and only Nepalese could go there. Mr Basnyet agreed Lhakpa should gallop off to raise the alarm, see if he could call up a rescue helicopter from there.

'We can't leave you here,' Elaine told Geoffrey. 'We ought to try and get you to the next village. Could you ride if I found you a pony?'

'I would be better on my feet. I'll just take my time.'

He was a lot better now he was up, and shuffled along slowly all morning, trying not to subject himself to any twisted movement.

★

A long, steep carved gully funnelled us down from the Tsarang plateau back to the Kali Gandaki riverbed. It was an exciting descent of more than a thousand feet through primrose conglomerate, pebbles rolling under our feet as we zig-zagged down. Young Pemba was waiting at the bottom to carry anyone who needed help across the river. From there it was a gentle stroll along the sand bars to the twin villages of Zurkhang and Dri, either side of the water.

This was where a helicopter could land. Indeed the King of Nepal had landed here only two weeks before, to pay his five-yearly visit to Mustang when all the inhabitants turn out to see him, and the children are given badges.

We balanced across a log bridge and scrambled up a steep slope into Dri, where the blue tarp was already spread and Chotare busily creating at his primuses under the eyes of the entire village. Geoffrey's predicament had earned us a half-day off. We would rest up here for the afternoon, catch up on our washing, and await Lhakpa's return. Tomorrow, when we left, Geoffrey and Susan would stay behind under the care of Chotare's young son, Gombu. If a helicopter did not come, we could pick them up on our way back in a few days' time. At least the rest would have done Geoffrey good.

A room had been found for the invalid at the top of the Pradham Panch's house – a simple rooftop chamber with a bench bed on which he could prop himself fairly comfortably with kitbags as a backrest. There was no glass in the small window, but a flask of old whisky would help keep out the cold. Luxury lay in proximity to the household 'toilet'. A hole in the flat roof outside gave on to an outhouse at ground level, two floors down, in which animal dung was stored before being taken to the fields. Skill lay in aiming neatly for the hole; craft in not being the poor sod shovelling dung when the toilet was in use.

Weird Curtains of Rock

Sunday morning, my birthday, and a blissful, sunny day. I am walking at high level now, having climbed steeply up the left bank of the gorge opposite Dri, with the puckered cliffs of Yara to my right across the valley.

They are honey-gold, these Yara cliffs, fluted like a stalactite fringe and pockmarked with old cave entrances. Since the gorge is narrow at this point, rising, we are afforded one of the closest views of such 'organ-pipe' scenery as we are ever likely to encounter. Nothing could be more fantastic. Sculpted over centuries by wind-blown grit, the formations seem far removed from all mineral origin. They are fluid, alive, changing with each shift of light. The steady fall of detritus has piled up ample screes, to buttress the cliffs at what is now, I suppose, their true mid-height.

The caves are not natural: their semi-circular openings can only have been fashioned by man. We were told in Dri that clusters of caves like these, which occur all over Mustang, were not so much permanent dwellings as refuges in times of feudal strife; but we hear all manner of stories as we travel around – they are prehistoric, they were sites of ambush, places of meditation, Khampa strongholds – all or none of which explanations may be true. One book claimed they were yeti holes. What is indisputable is that they are generations old, and open out of sheer cliff. Often the caves occur several hundred feet above the ground. Ropes or staging must have been employed to get to them, or there may have been ramps which have since crumbled away. If people used them for sanctuary, the means of access would have been pulled up behind them, and some brave soul lowered each day to fetch water and supplies, neither of which are yielded readily by this barren land.

We turn a corner, and the village of Yara exudes from the crumpled hills and terraces ahead of us. It has grown from the ground, and lies perhaps ten or fifteen minutes distant. An undulating path skirts mudstone cliffs to our left, not a bad path – almost a foot wide for the most part – though airy and broken where it loops around flutings of cliff. I am carefully negotiating one such loop where a chemical seepage from rocks above has left a wet patch across the path and a white residue of salts. They have no real stability these cliffs; they have flowed and set, eroded and been replenished, then crumbled and flowed some more. Now, in this dry season, they are as compact and hard as cement.

A pile of beautifully carved mani-stones and a couple of chortens mark the entrance to Yara. It has the air of a fortified village with, as its front line of defence, the walls bounding and supporting the field terraces. The houses themselves are closely entangled on a hilltop, their windowless outer walls presenting an almost entire barrier against wind or marauder. It is a typical village pattern: white-washed buildings, with small, square wooden window frames, firewood stacked neatly on flat roofs. House-corners are painted with red ochre. There is a sense that village growth is governed by some crystallographic principle, that buildings and courtyards have a determined form and structure, and grow – erupt – like cuboid crystals one from another. House walls are not quite perpendicular, they flare at the bottoms. There are a few planted trees, prayer flags on every building, and behind the village another protective fold of hill, which looks to have once held a fort. From a distance it is hard to tell if these are ruins or rock formations. They are so alike here.

Level now with the outer terrace-wall, I see a path leading through barley fields, between two walls into the first compound, where John and Margaret are waiting for me. We pass straight through the village with a few cheery *Tashi deleks* and climb the hill on the other side, down which plashes a little man-made watercourse to supply houses and fields. From the furrowed nature of the fields, they appear – many of them – to be planted with potatoes. Every field has a pile of yellow quartz stones in its centre which must have fertility significance. Lhakpa says the first fruits of the harvest are placed on these stones for the local gods.

Looking back across the village and valley, we see that the pleated Yara cliffs continue for some distance in a perfectly straight line. With their level tops, they give the impression of a gigantic cinema curtain pulled across the landscape. 'Like an advert for Rufflette tape,' I crack weakly. There are not so many caves in the section just revealed: we have noticed before that the heaviest peppering of cave mouths is always close to traditional settlement sites.

We continue climbing. How far does this hill go? Every time I think we are coming over the crest of it, another upward sweep confounds me. Certainly, it is not as steep now, and we may even be approaching a levellish section, but I am not raising any hopes. The sky is still almost cloudless, except over the snow mountains far behind us. We are in line with the top of the curtain-cliffs and the highest terraces of Yara. A woman working in the fields shouts to me, and I am desolate that I cannot understand or return her greeting. It is such a handicap not to be able to communicate – and so rude! Perhaps Lhakpa, who is close behind me, will stop and talk with her.

At last I reach the brow of the steep hill, and the way now undulates forward comfortably: I should be able to cope with this all right, but it is stony ankle-turning ground, the surface strewn with lumps of rock the size of house bricks. A shrubby, gorsey-bush is growing sparsely . . . nothing much else. Earlier this morning, coming into Zurkhang – across the river from Dri – we saw a man taking out about a hundred goats on to a hillside completely devoid of vegetation. It is impossible to imagine what they find to subsist on. We are a good deal higher now than we were in Dri. There, barley was already sprouting; here, they are only just getting the fields ready.

Our course follows an almost dry river bed. All the water has been diverted into a rippling leat, which must feed the small reservoir we saw above the terraced fields, then bubble on down to supply Yara and the lower plots. It has been ingeniously constructed, and is maintained in very good condition, but then it is, of course, no less than the life line of the people here.

From lower down it looked as if we were heading for a great cleft, or *brèche*, in the hills, but we see as we get closer that it must be a staggering of the valley sides, which are growing higher around us all the time. Closer still, the notch defines itself as a sheer cliff on the right-hand side with a series of jagged smaller crags to the left. Those ahead, walking underneath the cliff, come such a little way up it, it must be several hundred feet high – a pyramidal bulk of golden conglomerate, its surface typically fluted, and with one or two flying buttresses anchoring it like guylines. It even looks to have small eyelets (rather like the one on the East Rongbuk) piercing one of the flutes, but when I draw closer, I see these are more weathered caves on the left-hand side of the valley. From one a dog barks, clearly unused to people tramping up his valley, and the bark echoes back and forth between the walls. At least the beast has not come hurtling out to devour us. Perhaps he belongs to a wandering herdsman or hermit and is tethered there. They are quite small, the caves here, barely big enough for people, but they cannot have been made as dog kennels.

From below, we had expected this to be the head of the valley, but no such luck. Slowly, we continue rising, travelling in single line through a narrow defile. Yu-Lha waits for me. He is always the back marker, and I have somehow dropped behind even him! Only Colin on his horse lags further back. Colin joined the trek with a broken foot – the result of a skiing accident a few weeks before – and has rented a pony on many of the longer days. He is a big man, and the ponies are all very small, man and mount often so seriously mismatched as to look ridiculous. It is probably less funny from the horse's point of view.

Usually the price is 200 rupees a day. Today, as we are going high, it is costing Colin 300. 'I hope', says Sue, 'that the extra hundred is going to the pony.'

Without a drop of water anywhere around Chotare produces another regal spread – salad, tuna, *pouris*, and tinned fruit to soften our parched throats. There is no shade, and the blue tarpaulin scorches our legs and bottoms, but my only complaint is that we have too short a rest. Coming in last always has the disadvantage that everyone else is ready to move on by the time you sit down, yet you are the one who could most use a break.

Eyes scanning the rumpled landscape, I am able to make out in the distance two villages, Kangra and Kuto, or Upper and Lower Ghara. Almost perfectly camouflaged, their existence is only given away by the presence of a few juniper trees. Less far away, but still across the valley, I see a building I first take to be the Lori Gompa, but as we climb higher after lunch, the main monastery building comes into view below it. We had met a Mustangi girl earlier, laden with supplies for Lori Gompa, who told us that it wasn't always occupied. With no good fresh water nearby, it is difficult to sustain.

No one is sure of the best way to cross the broken ravine country that still separates us from the high valley we are hoping will lead us to our mountain. The tail-enders – in this case Margaret, Pat and I, shepherded by Yu-Lha – choose the worst possible line, for in an hour we do little more than scramble in and out of steep gulleys, down, up, down and up, with Yu-Lha hauling us over the steeper sections and gradually transferring more and more of our luggage on to his own stout back. This is the sort of energy I find it difficult to summon up at a moment's notice. The steady plod I can just about muster, but I have no deep reserves for sudden bursts of effort. After the seventh ravine, I simply haven't the breath for any more. My only consolation is that we are in ammonite beds, and every so often perfect specimens will be lying at our feet like secret treasures. Too bad they weigh us down even more.

We traipse, at length, up a long, almost dry valley with old snow along its shady side . . . a terrible slog. I talk into my pocket recorder. This had seemed the ideal way to take notes as I travel, but too often, when I come to play back the tapes afterwards, all I have preserved is desperately heavy breathing.

Scrambling (*gasp*) in and out of the gulleys (*gasp, gasp*) was extra-ordinarily wearing. (*Gasp, wheeze*) I could hardly drag myself up this valley when we finally found ourselves in it. (*Long pause to draw rasping breath, then something unintelligible*) . . . nothing much growing here except . . . dry thyme . . . very aromatic . . . and a tiny saxifrage. (*Hoarse, despairing whisper*) If *only* we could have a rest . . .

Over the brow of a hill to our right, we suddenly see the others clambering up and shouting for us to join them.

We too take to the steep hillside . . . a pig of a climb. With every few steps I double over, fighting for breath. In an effort to divert my mind, I concentrate on what lies at my feet . . . a few marmots' holes, but no marmots . . . any self-respecting marmot would have taken cover long since with all the noise we're making . . .

I catch up with Elaine on the top of the ridge, a fine sharply chiselled ridge with splendid views on both sides. Ravens and eagles soar on air currents. She looks despondent.

'What's up? Were we in the wrong valley?'

'Heaven knows. Tsering Tamden hasn't been this way in a long time.'

'But doesn't he have some idea where we are?'

'Don't know. He's gone.'

'Gone?'

'No-one knows where he is. He shot off some while ago. Lhakpa will give him hell when he catches up with him.'

'So, where are we going now?'

'Without water, I can't see we can camp anywhere here. We'll probably have to go back.'

Good God! Back to *Dri*? That would take hours, even if it is downhill all the way. What a shambles! People and ponies strung out all over the mountains, and nobody, so far as I can see, with the slightest idea where we are. If we are going to have to go back, why in hell's name are folk still heading on up the ridge? I follow, thinking to catch up with them on the next rise, but find, when I get to it, that the ridge extends even higher and everybody has moved on again. After all that floundering about in ravines, then scrambling up this steep mountain, it is the final straw. My chest is bursting. I find it extraordinarily difficult to drag myself higher. I puff. I blow. But for a few overburdened kitchen boys, I am the last to trudge over the next brow of the hill.

There, to my sheer amazement, I see we have reached a marvellous plateau. The Sherpas are putting up camp. Gratefully, I collapse on to the ground.

Our tent – Reiko's and mine – is one of the first up. I grab my duffel and drag it towards the welcome blue shelter. Then I flop again. I know I ought to be out helping, but think if I can just have a few minutes sitting here, catching my breath, I will be fine and can go out and do my bit then.

Elaine comes over. 'Zoe's crying in her tent!' she announces.

'Why, what's the matter?'

'She's overtired.'

'I'm not surprised.'

'She says someone's been rude to her – I can't work out the rights and wrongs of it. Reiko, you know how well you two get on? I wonder whether you'd mind sharing with her tonight? I don't like to leave her on her own.'

All right to leave me, I think uncharitably. It is my turn to feel emotional. Elaine swings in to comfort-mode, at once to the rescue.

'Here, get in this sleeping bag,' she orders, 'and just you stay there! There's a cup of tea on the way.'

Ever since we set out on this trek, Zoe has gone through terrible trials with her tent zip. She has never yet managed a night without either being unable to close the tent entrance, or finding herself imprisoned inside. We have never learned what it was she is doing wrong, but without fail at every campsite a plaintive cry goes up and Yu-Lha comes rushing with his pliers. Anxious to avoid any such trouble up here, Elaine cedes her own tent to Zoe and Reiko.

'Lhakpa and I can squeeze in with you tonight,' she says to me. 'With three in a tent, we should keep snug!'

'Fine,' I mumble absently.

Already I am feeling better and no longer so weepy. I rummage in my bag for my pile trousers, then go out to join the others. Everyone is mooching about, dreaming of dinner, trying to keep warm. It is bitterly cold now that the sun has dropped, and there's no mess tent to huddle in. Chotare needs that for a kitchen; there's no other shelter up here.

'I suppose the order of the day', announces Margaret cheerfully, 'is down trousers, everyone!'

'Too cold to down trousers here,' we rib her.

All have dug deep into their duffles: Margaret wears not one down jacket, but also, I notice, the one she brought as emergency for Laureen. Pat's Michelin trousers bulge under a long skirt. Mufflers and balaclavas make it hard to see who's who. We are quite high here – 15,000 feet, at a guess. It means we must have made almost four thousand feet today. No wonder it has knocked the stuffing out of me.

I feel ashamed at having been so sorry for myself, for telling poor Elaine, in my tiredness, not to be so bossy – especially as it now turns out a birthday celebration has been laid on for me. We hunch round a burning bush, where I am given a card and a bundle of fossils tied up in a white ceremonial *khata* for good luck.

'The Sherpas have been scampering around all day, collecting them for you,' Elaine grins.

Ang Pasang, our Sirdar, shyly offers a little bunch of grasses, and Sean a juniper twig. It is an affecting little ceremony with night falling and storm-clouds building over the mountains. Zoe and Reiko, and David who is poorly, are the only ones missing from the group.

Just then a series of urgent whistle blasts rent the air.

'Oh my God – Zoe!'

Everyone runs to Zoe's tent, fearing to find her a victim of altitude sickness. But it is a false alarm. To be sure, Reiko is blowing the whistle to summon help, but it is because Zoe has unerringly jammed the zip once more. She and Reiko are prisoners inside their tent and bursting to relieve themselves.

In the absence of the mess tent it is 'Room Service' tonight. I sit alone, huddled under my shawl in the open doorway of my tent, looking out over Dhaulagiri and the gleaming summits of Tibet under a full moon, eating my goat, lentil and ginger stew, and reminding myself 'You won't get many birthdays like this, old girl.'

To my surprise, Chotare pops out of the darkness with Elaine and Lhakpa. He is bearing an enormous chocolate cake with a candle. I don't know how he has managed to produce such a confection up here. Solemnly, he hands me his long kitchen knife, and I cut a slice, make a wish, then embarrass him with a big kiss.

'Elaine,' I say, 'tell him what a wizard he is.'

And I sit on, dreamily drinking tea, munching cake, trying to etch every last detail into my memory. I twist round to rummage for my recorder. When I turn back the mountains have completely misted over and the moon is a luminous bubble. Clouds have rolled all around the tents, and it is time to shut the door to keep out the dew.

★

A white and wonderful world. Silently, snow has wrapped around us in the night. Elaine and I stay in our bags with our bed-tea and tent flaps open to watch the pale ball of moon float behind the mountains and the summits suffuse with a new dawn. Puffy clouds roll in – pearly at first, later with rainbows – but the rose-gilded peaks hang clear above them. We dare not blink lest we miss a scene in this evanescent pageant.

When breakfast at last forces us out, we spoon up fast-cooling porridge in a luminous mist. Ice crystals twinkle like mica in its billowing swirls. Our horses lick the morning snow from low bushes, but it is a race against time. As the sun breaks through it vanishes, taking all dampness with it.

Our camp sits on a rolling terrace facing west. Beyond the cliffs of the Kali Gandaki gorge lie the border mountains of the Mustang Himal. We find ourselves in line with the valley beyond Tsarang, looking straight up it towards Marang and Lo Gekar.

To the right (north) I can see over the dry valley we scrambled out of yesterday into a sheltered hollow, which was where Tsering Tamden had been trying to lead us when he found the way blocked by landslide. It looks a nice enough campsite, but shows no more sign of water than here. We are actually nearer Bhrikuti where we are. While we, the punters, spend an easy day lolling round camp, kitchen porters set off in search of drinking water and a group of Sherpas to scout out a way to Bhrikuti.

Over the roar of the paraffin cookers comes the throb of an aircraft. Is this the helicopter going up for Geoffrey and Sue? We try to spot it, but it seems to be flying below the rim of the Gandaki gorge, leaving its sound behind to bounce and echo off the canyon walls. Only occasionally do we pick up a glint of white through a gap in the cliffs, far ahead of its clangorous wake. Three or four flights go up and down to Lo Mantang that day. Could they be looking for us?

In the afternoon Colin and I trudge slowly up the hill behind camp to a loose pinnacled ridge from where we are supposed to gain a view of our mountain. But which? Across what we take to be the Teha Chang valley, in and out of torn cloud, flirts a row of unattractive peaks, ragged and broken, bearing snow on almost all ground that is not vertical. (This still leaves more black than white.) There will be no easy walk up any of these! I cannot see right into the valley, nor tell if the sacred lakes are indeed down there.

Afterwards, poring over a number of sketchy maps, I doubt very much that Bhrikuti was the peak right in front of us – more likely Ganjiri, with ours still some distance further south. In fact, I wonder now if Bhrikuti can be reached this way at all.

An Austrian party which went into the region in 1982, the first year the peak was 'opened', followed high paths from Muktinath to the head of the Teha Chang valley. So remote was it up there that they passed no village in four days. They set up base 'on a flowery meadow beside a small lake at 15,000 feet', and only then discovered they were in quite the wrong valley for an attempt on Bhrikuti's main summit. After placing two higher camps, Wolfgang Axt solo-climbed the north peak, but he would have needed to descend into another valley – within Tibet – to get on to Bhrikuti proper. He suspected that a Japanese expedition which preceded them there in the spring of that year must have experienced the same problem. Although in both cases, once back in Kathmandu, liaison officers claimed ascents of Bhrikuti for their teams, neither had actually made it to the main summit. A French team, which came in 1985, met with no greater success: one of its members fell into a crevasse on the summit day. He was pulled to safety, but it left insufficient time for another attempt.

So far as can be made out from the mountaineering record, Bhrikuti remained unclimbed when we arrived.

And it was to remain unclimbed after we had gone.

Our porters return to camp that evening with aching feet and backs. They'd had to walk for five hours to find water. Five hours there, five hours back. This is bad news. After losing half a day in Dri getting help for Geoffrey, and another day here, the most we can now allow ourselves before heading out is two more nights. That will mean forced marches all the way out of Mustang. It does not sound enough time to get to grips with the mountain. (And certainly isn't once you know of Wolfgang Axt's testimony.) Our climbers are still eager to try. Ang Pasang and Mingma have been pacing themselves just for this, and Sean has fished out his high altitude boots. It is why they have come, after all. They will feel cheated to give up now, before even reaching the mountain. That will be hard to live down in Kathmandu.

The rest of us are a sorry lot. David and Zoe have barely stirred all day, and none of us is skipping about with much zest. Mr Basnyet – recognizing the folornness of any success now – puts his foot down once more.

'The party stays together. All to the mountain, or all stop here.'

We cannot stop here, though. Not if it takes ten hours to fetch water. It isn't a viable position. We will have to go down tomorrow.

Guerrilla Stronghold

Though there was no more snow in the night, it became very much colder. Our Tsum-girls had no tent. They slept in the open, wrapped in their shawls. Yesterday they had gone round gathering twigs and animal droppings for little fires to curl up by, but last night they succumbed to burning dry bushes. Soon there were several such fires around camp, with people hugging themselves and stamping round the roaring flames. A bush would burn for about half an hour. Probably travellers have always kept themselves warm like this. It was a good thing so few came this way, or the scant vegetation would be devastated in no time at all.

We took to our sleeping bags as the temperature plummeted. A fierce wind blew up. In the middle of the night the cook tent ripped from its moorings and, billowing wildly, proved too heavy to hold down for the cookboys who had been sleeping inside. It and they were blown into Mr Basnyet's tent, demolishing that as well. For Zoe and Reiko, the temperature inside their tent remained the same as that outside. Their zip would now not close at all.

After his disturbed night Mr Basnyet was first away next morning, back down to Yara. We had no wish to hurry breakfast, and sat on, muffled, at our high table, letting the sun gather strength and warm us through before we made a move. Lazy as we were, we left the Sherpas to finish packing and the pony boys to scour the barren hillsides for their charges. It's a tough life being a pony up here. We had been saving them all our washing-up water to drink, but they had to roam widely for the meagre grazing.

Gleefully taking advantage of Mr B's absence, we plotted a detour to take in Lori Gompa, the remote desert temple I had seen in the distance on our way up here. After retreating down our airy ridge, it meant tracking northwards across the ravine country until we came to

218

the deep chasm in which the gompa lay. At least a thousand feet of ravaged conglomerate separated us from the valley floor, with no obvious gully to lead us down, as there had been outside Tsarang. We picked our way first along goat tracks, then down buttresses and stone shoots, slithering, sliding with always a sickening drop beneath our feet. By the time we decided it was too dangerous to go on, it was already too dangerous to go back. Tsering Tamden and Pemba handed us over the worst sections, leaning towards each other to lessen the distance we had to make on our own, but it was illusory support. They could not have held us if the stones had rolled away with our feet, and would have fallen with us if we'd had a dead-man's clutch on their outstretched hands.

Sean was first past the steepest stretch and bounded to the bottom, where one by one we joined him, adding little white stones to the pile there beside a chorten in thanks for our deliverance. John felt it easier not to look back to see how his wife, Pat, was faring. We could hear her squeaks of alarm. Vertigo had always been a problem for her, but had become markedly worse since she injured an ankle on one trek and had to be carried down on the backs of a relay of porters. Whenever they met friends on the narrow trail that led along the sheer mountain-sides and stopped for a chat, she (in her wicker basket) was left dangling over the abyss.

The gompa was only a short distance from the dry river bed. Peissel tells us it is one of the most unusual monasteries in all Mustang, and not Sakya like others in the area but Kagyu, the dominant sect of Bhutan. One of the old kings of Lo – so the story goes – married a Bhutanese princess, whom he loved so dearly he built Lori Gompa as a gift to ensure she should not feel lonely in a strange land. Only one person was in residence when we arrived, a cheeky young lad in a well-faded baseball cap. He was caretaker while the abbot – a roly, friendly old lama who we met in Dri – was away ministering around the country-side. In all, the boy told us, about forty monks would come here in a year, but it was rare for as many as half a dozen to be in the monastery at any one time.

He was happy for us to be in the gompa, and led us through a ragged curtain into the main chamber, a small square room whose only light came from a tiny window in the ceiling. There were beautiful paintings of Buddhas and deities on the walls, but what surprised us more was that it still possessed a number of fine statues. Lori had clearly been a very much more important lamasery and hermitage in its time, which made you wonder if the water shortage had always been so acute as now.

The monastery buildings were set amid a cluster of golden pinnacles, many of them honeycombed with caves. There must have been as many as fifty entrances. One slender tower was topped with a large flat stone, which geologists might try to persuade you had acted as protection to the softer rock underneath, shielding it against the ravages of weathering. The custodian knew better. The first lama of Lori was so holy, he said, that he was able to fly. The top of this pinnacle was his most favoured spot for meditation. One day, floating off in a hurry, he left his flat Bhutanese hat behind. It has remained up there over the centuries ever since.

We were hustled away after a picnic lunch in the monastery courtyard with too little time to explore properly. Peissel tells of a network of subterranean chapels, access to which is gained by wooden ladders. When he was here, he was shown into one vaulted, circular cavern which contained a polished stucco chorten that filled the entire space almost to the roof, save for a small walkway round the outside. Both chorten and the dome of the cave were decorated with exquisite miniature frescos of as fine craftsmanship – Peissel said – as anywhere in Lo. In another book, his history of the Tibetan resistance – *Cavaliers of Kham* – he published a picture of the Lori cave dwellings as one of the strongholds of the Khampa rebel army during its time in Mustang.

*

The Lhasa nobility and settled villagers of central Tibet had never seen eye to eye with the quick-tempered warrior tribesmen of Kham, the country's south-easternmost province, whom they regarded as little more than bandits, forever squabbling among themselves. Thus it happened that even when the Lhasans finally understood the appalling extent of Chinese atrocities within Kham and neighbouring Amdo after the invasion of 1950, they were slow to join their eastern countrymen in active insurrection. As devout Buddhists they were in any case committed to first seeking a peaceful resolution to Tibet's problem. It was left to the Khampas to defy the invaders, and this with little more than diehard bravery to pit against the weaponry and expertise of modern warfare.

By 1959 there was no doubt anywhere in Tibet that the Chinese were bent on complete annihilation of the Tibetan way of life, and resistance groups had sprung up all over the country. Thousands of

Khampas flooded into Lhasa to beseech the Dalai Lama to unite these factions and lead a popular revolt against the oppressors. All was turmoil within the capital and, fearful for the safety of their leader who had been invited by the Chinese general to a stage show inside the Chinese army camp, and especially requested to come without his bodyguards, several thousand Tibetans formed a human shield around the Dalai Lama's summer palace, declaring they would prevent him from accepting the invitation. For days tension mounted until, finally, mortar shells were fired at the summer palace. Using the ensuing chaos to their advantage, the Khampas assisted the Dalai Lama to make his celebrated flight to India, but days of vicious fighting followed. Many thousands of Tibetans died before the rebellion was finally crushed by Chinese tanks and heavy mortar.

Thereafter began a reign of terror more frightful even than had gone before. Inexorably, dissidents were killed or transported to labour camps; thousands of Tibetan children were removed for indoctrination. A report by the International Commission of Jurists published in August 1960 found that the Chinese had violated human rights in Tibet in no less than sixteen different ways, which included murder, rape, torture, destruction of family life and deportation. It utterly rejected Chinese counter-allegations that the Tibetans had enjoyed no human rights before their 'liberation'. Yet despite concluding that no obstacle existed to the question of Tibet's independence being discussed and decided upon by the United Nations, nothing was done – nothing official, that is.

The rebels did not give up their struggle. For another fifteen years the Chusi Gangdruk – which means 'Four Rivers, Six Ranges' and comprised mainly Khampas – continued their desperate fight for freedom. They moved their headquarters out of Tibet and into Mustang. Bases sprang up all round the tiny kingdom – like the one here at Lori Gompa, or on the hill outside Gemi, which locals still call 'Soldier Mountain'. From these, guerrillas could easily slip across the border on raids of ambush and disruption. The organizational centre was kept well back from the border on Mustang's southern rim, an hour and a half north of Jomoson, accounts say, which would put it in the vicinity of Kagbeni.

Situating themselves outside Tibet like this put them in position to receive gifts of arms and ammunition from abroad – for they were no longer completely on their own. America's Central Intelligence Agency was secretly supplying weapons and finance, and for a few years actually trained guerrilla groups in all aspects of covert operation techniques, including espionage. Volunteers were not supposed to know where they were being taken for this training, which (after a pilot scheme on Guam or Saipan) was to Camp Hale, a remote military installation in the Colorado mountains. Local people – few that there were – were put off from discovering what was going on by rumours of atomic testing in the area. It was many years before the secret leaked out, and even now details are few and hard to verify.

The rebels' first year in Mustang was a difficult one. To have several thousand men flood into an area so arid posed enormous victualling problems. The Red Cross, which had been charged to assess the Tibetan refugee problem (and saw no reason to distinguish between civilians and soldiers), reported famine on a wide scale. For a while workers were allowed to fly in emergency rations and medical supplies via the newly constructed runway for light aircraft just south of Jomoson, but when that was stopped (for fear of offending China!), it was down to the old military standby of boiling boots. Many men died before, late in 1961, two aircraft dropped guns, money and Camp Hale graduates into the area.

After his visit to Mustang at the height of the guerrilla activity in the mid-sixties, Michel Peissel alerted the world to the Khampas' struggle, and told how when preparing for his trip he was approached by a variety of foreign intelligence officers, all wanting to know how the rebel attacks were being organized. It seems that even those agencies supporting the Khampa cause remained to some extent in the dark about the complexities of the operations. The Khampas themselves weren't telling. They trusted no-one, not even their sponsors.

Jeff Long is an American mountaineer who, in 1977, after his second Himalayan expedition found himself arrested and thrown into a Nepalese jail on a false smuggling charge. 'Twenty-five years old and with all the political poise of an Irish setter flushing butterflies', Long had stayed on in Kathmandu after the failure of his climb to investigate rumours he'd been picking up of gun-running, Khampa effrontery, and the Colorado connection. His imagination was caught by tales of a near-mythic Khampa leader, a warrior called Wangdu, who although popularly supposed to have been gunned to death in the last shoot-out of the rebellion, was said by some to be still up there somewhere in the dry hills of Mustang or Dolpo, carrying on the lonely fight for his homeland.

For Jeff Long, Wangdu became 'the jewel in the lotus', his struggle epitomizing the same hopeless purity as that of Geronimo in America's own deserts and mountains. Long yearned to know more, and darted eagerly after slim leads. At the height of what he now calls his 'information frenzy', he was arrested and had to spend three months in Nepalese jails. During that time he shared cells with dozens of political prisoners, among them Mustang-hardened guerrillas who were being held without trial. Long continued to ask his questions and, when released, smuggled out 300 pages of notes.

By the turn of the 70s Washington had all but lost interest in a forlorn Tibetan cause. The training courses had long since been abandoned, but funds continued to percolate through to Khampa fighters until 1971. That was the year the Americans re-opened diplomatic dialogue with the Chinese and the political balance in Asia shifted once more. Nepal – which till then had more or less turned a blind eye to the guerrilla encampments in its remote valleys – began a propaganda offensive, denouncing the Mustang Tibetans as pillaging bandits who had to be expelled from their borders.

This came at a time when the Chushi Gangdruk was already weakened by factional infighting. And what was perhaps even more significant – the Khampas themselves were getting older. Many were now in their mid-forties or fifties. In his comprehensive history, *In Exile from the Land of Snows*, John Avedon quotes a young replacement guerrilla who was sent to Mustang:

> People did not die of bullets, but just by walking to a fight and back. Once they knew a raid was on, the Chinese would send patrols to cut off its retreat. The PLA were fresh and our men had been literally jogging night after night. So the old-timers would give out. They'd take a whole tin of coffee, mix it together with water and soup in their bowls and drink it. That kept them going. But after doing this kind of thing two or three times, their hearts would just pop.

The years-long campaign could quite easily have ended by simply running down activities, the Khampas staying put in Mustang, but resorting to their old occupations of farming, trading and livestock husbandry. After all, that's what many of them had been doing for years as a means of supporting themselves. But the Chinese wanted retribution for all the humiliation they had endured at rebel hands. With their new-found influence, they leaned on Nepal to flush out the old soldiers. 'We'll do the job for you,' they offered, 'if you haven't the heart for it.' Rather than agree to that, the Nepalese moved 10,000 troops towards the Mustang border.

First, though, they tried negotiation. But when the Khampas rejected promises of amnesty and rehabilitation aid in exchange for full surrender and the disbanding of their bases, the troops prepared to go in. Alarmed at the prospect of more spilled Tibetan blood, the Dalai Lama sent a tape-recording to his followers, urging them to lay down their arms. The tape was played over loudspeakers from camp to camp throughout Mustang to devastating effect.

With great bitterness, Wangdu told his men they should obey His Holiness's instructions.

For some, like senior officer Pachen, it was too much to ask. 'How can I surrender to the Nepalese when I have never surrendered to the Chinese?' he demanded. 'And yet I cannot disobey my lama's orders.' The dilemma was resolved for him and a number of his fellows by slitting their own throats. Others jumped from cliffs or drowned themselves in the river.

Even as columns of pack animals heavy with surrendered weapons made their way south, the Nepalese soldiery marched into Mustang. All promise of amnesty forgotten, guerrillas and their property were seized. Outraged by such duplicity, Wangdu fled over the high passes into Tibet with forty hand-picked men.

For four weeks, hounded by Chinese and Nepalese troops as well as renegade Khampas, the party leapfrogged backwards and forwards across the border, speeding west, making its way towards India where it was confident of finding sanctuary. They little suspected that half a day short of their destination, on a high pass known as Tinker, a massive ambush had been laid.

Jeff Long's exhaustive enquiries have convinced him that he now knows what happened in the early afternoon of 12 August 1974, when the party arrived to find itself hemmed in from the north by Chinese troops.

Leaving the main body to try and fend off the Chinese, six men were detailed to escort Wangdu over Tinker into Nepal. They galloped straight into the well-sprung trap. Four were killed on the spot, one escaped to warn his comrades, and one was badly wounded and captured. This man watched as Wangdu was riddled with bullets.

The larger group, still exchanging fire with the Chinese, swarmed over the pass and *en masse* pushed through the Nepalese ambush to be

Villagers invading our camp on the return through Yara

The Friendship Ceremony – Tsering Gombu, Lhakpa, Elaine and Yuma

Tangye's remarkable battery of chortens, decorated in vivid Sakya stripes. The paint is made from local sands and clays.

The Damodar and Lugula mountains. One of these, we were sure, must be Bhrikuti!

The table-porter
struggling up to the
last pass, the Mustang
Himal mountains
behind marking the
Western border with
Tibet

The author at Tayen,
the last forbidden
village

Dust devils outside
Kagbeni

Jeff Long's photograph of jubilant Nepalese waving party banners outside the King's palace in Kathmandu in April 1990, after the lifting of martial law and an end to the 30-year ban on political parties. Two days earlier, security forces had opened fire on a crowd of 200,000.

either picked up by Indian helicopters or to ride across the border into the open arms of Indian troops. 'By sunset that day,' said Long, 'the last of the guerrillas was either safe in India, property of the Nepalese king, or dead.'

Back in Kathmandu the King bestowed honours on those involved in the engagement. Those captured remained seven years in detention without trial. Wangdu's personal effects were put on display in a large tent in the city's Thundikhel field to demonstrate that the Mustang chapter was now over.

Swirling Clouds of Dust

CLAMBERING UP TO these fortified villages, it's strange how many old shoes you see on the slope – felt-boots, flip-flops, Chinese plimsolls . . . I can only imagine that when footwear gets too tattered for even these poor folk to wear, it is ritually cast from the ramparts. Blow the burning oil: watch out for the flying slipper.

Shoes apart, and the odd old bone, there's very little rubbish anywhere. Packaging simply does not exist here to be thrown away. Paper and plastic are scarce, and the villagers will find a hundred uses for the few tins or containers that come their way. Every vestige of utility has to be wrung from each item – as it must also from bodily waste. Human excrement – as we saw at Dri – is collected for the fields. Little children are sent out with baskets to gather yak dung for fuel. Many houses have moulded cakes of dung drying on sunny walls, and the droppings of sheep and goats burn well, though with acrid smoke. Although every house has its barricade of logs, brushwood and old juniper roots neatly stacked around the edges of the roof, this is burnt only sparingly. Woodpiles afford shade and shelter from the wind, converting the housetop into an extra room. In a region where, except for the occasional cosseted willow, no trees grow, wood is a scarcely renewable resource. Like the jewellery of the women, its acquisition represents insurance, confirms standing in the community.

From Lori, we passed through the honey-gold villages of Upper and Lower Ghara. Gaunt castle ruins stood against a background of snowy mountains. We were on the return leg now, walking towards the Himalaya again. Dhaulagiri was once more dominating our sights, the White Mountain, this time presenting its north-eastern aspect for our inspection.

Tsering Gombu, the headman of Dri, rode out to meet us with news that Geoffrey and Susan were picked up by helicopter yesterday – the

King's helicopter, no less, for the mountain rescue craft were out on another mission in the Everest region. The Captain consented to fly out our young Sherpa, Gombu, as well, but only at the expense of leaving behind all the luggage. A student of about nineteen years of age, Chotare's son was with the trek because the University in Kathmandu had been closed by the democracy riots and his father wanted to keep him out of trouble. Gombu enjoyed the walk in through the forests and high mountains, but Mustang baffled him.

'Sometimes, I a bit scared,' he confided at the sight of so many bare hills.

Most of the Sherpas agreed with him. 'You can't grow anything,' they would complain, comparing this chaotic wilderness with their fertile Solu Khumbu.

Peissel had travelled to Mustang with an Amdo Tibetan, ethnically not far removed from the Sherpas who also originated from eastern Tibet. One look had been enough for this man to snort in disgust, 'Mustang is as barren as a dead deer. What do the people do here – eat stones?'

For my part, I was surprised how bewitched I had become by the stark landscape. A love of plants usually coloured how I saw beauty, yet here I felt, as I had in Tibet, a purity in the sere emptiness. These fawns and ochres plucked a deep chord within me, whispered consanguinity. I came to doubt I would ever be able to shake free of them, ever stop wanting to come back.

Reiko must have felt the same. 'Is very surprising impression, this sand land,' she told me. 'White houses, red gompa, the sun and wind. People wearing dirty cloth, but smiling as the sunshine!'

Already I was dreading the time to leave, which was foolish considering we were still gloriously here. But now that our steps headed back towards 'Nepal', I could not escape a sense of impermanence.

★

We approached Yara through an intricate system of dry gorges, one of which was spanned by a wooden flume, the aqueduct bringing in drinking water. There are seasonal springs and seepages from these cliffs, marked by the white streaks of salts. Good for washing, the people told us, but not potable. Perhaps it is soda. Not that I saw any evidence of washing: clothes and faces here were perhaps the grubbiest we had come across anywhere. An audience gathered quickly as soon as we arrived in camp and our little washing bowls appeared for us to

227

sluice off the dust of travel. Ingrained modesty is hard to shed, and Reiko and I coyly pulled down the zip to perform our ablutions in private. Quite unnecessary. Each tent had little perforated air-vents at the ends, miniature net curtains positioned at just the right level for curious young eyes. Such a clustering round our shelter, such a squeaking and squabbling for turns to peep at our extraordinary performance. What strange outlanders we were and no mistake. What uncouth habits! Fancy squandering hard-won water like that. Only the even more bewildering attraction of someone shaving lured the little grubs away.

Eye infections were rampant in this village. Encrusted lids, conjunctivitis, brought about by the constant dust and firesmoke – few, it seemed, escaped. Mothers brought their babies to us, with little eyes gummed shut. But what could we do? We would know to carry plenty of eye salve another time, but we had none with us now. Even that could do no more than bring temporary relief. More water is what they need.

*

A short, easy stroll down the mud-flows back to Dri, to collect our cache of food and Geoffrey's bags, was all we had to worry about the next day. Without hurrying, we could still be there in plenty of time for lunch. All the lofty thoughts I had believed would come with walking high, solitary trails were a chimera. Visions of meals usurped the mind, dreams of sitting down, of tea and soup. Days and distances were measured by meals, places differentiated by the food taken in them.

Most of what we consumed had been brought with us, all the way from Kathmandu, as had the fuel with which to cook it. But today's dinner possessed legs of its own. Chotare had purchased a goat which walked with us, a shaggy recalcitrant brute which Pemba was endeavouring without significant success to bring to heel. Just outside Dri, leading it across the log bridge over the river, it made a forlorn break for freedom, only to be recaptured scrambling ashore. Throughout lunch the doomed creature eyed us balefully from a short tether.

'It's shameful!' Zoe spoke out in its defence. 'You can't possibly kill it!' But by mid-afternoon it was assorted hunks of meat and a plateful of spicy titbits. By virtue of his position, Mr Basnyet was accorded the skin – one of the perks of the job.

At Dri we found two policemen on the point of setting out to search for us. Calling out the King's helicopter had led to awkward questions being asked in high places. Who were these foreigners tramping around in a forbidden area? What were they after? The police had instructions to order us back to Kathmandu forthwith. Elaine, Lhakpa and Mr B were called to account, but upon being provided with a written undertaking that we would start walking out the next day, the two men retreated to Lo to report the success of their mission. Halfway there, they gave in to the temptation to see precisely what Lhakpa had written and took out the letter, whereupon a strong wind plucked it from their fingers. It floated away over the mountains, whether to Dolpo or Tibet they couldn't afterwards say, but a day later a horseman caught up with us, begging for another copy.

A grand 'friendship' party had been laid on in our honour, and once the backs of the policemen had vanished in the distance, we clambered on to the roof of the headman's house. Lhakpa and Elaine were to be adopted by our hosts, Tsering Gombu and his wife Yuma, as *tro* brother and sister, a ceremonial friendship pact that would bind them for life.

For so auspicious an occasion of course they had to be correctly attired. Dusty trekking clothes would not do. Elaine and Lhakpa were whisked off to see what the family treasure chest had to offer. They re-emerged completely transformed. Lhakpa and Tsering Gombu were clad in splendid knee-length chubas of fur-trimmed black velvet with, slung from their belts, two swinging ornaments apiece, like châtelaines or jewel-encrusted sporrans. They wore gold brocade hats with fur spaniel-ear flaps, and high black suede boots. Elaine and Yuma were in full-length chubas, silk blouses and a complicated apron arrangement in brilliant rainbow stripes. Gold charm-boxes around their necks hung from strings of turquoise beads, precious xi-stones, seed pearls and lumps of coral, some of which were as big as golf balls! A king's ransom on a single thread.

Low carved tables had been set out in the sun, at which the couples squatted on antique rugs. Gifts and *khatas* were exchanged to seal the new union, and toasts drunk from lidded silver cups. After a few sips, the cups were exchanged with their new partners and another toast drunk. We more lowly mortals – trekkers, porters – dipped tin beakers into a plastic dustbin of chang, and added our good wishes for a fruitful alliance. It was not long before the harsh afternoon light and the heady brew began sending insistent warnings to my sun-cooked brain, and I was glad to be invited into the living room of the house for some tea. Fuzzily, I scrambled down the notched log ladder, cracking my head on the low lintel as I ducked to enter.

It was an attractive cool room, lit by a small window and two holes in the roof. The walls had been freshly red-ochred and decorated with symbolic patterns to mark the Tibetan New Year. A built-in china cabinet on one wall was grand testimony that this was a very well-to-do household, particularly as it had glass in the door panels. Up in these remote villages, glass is a real luxury. One of the most poignant sights I had seen on trek was some shards of glass lying on a high pass. Somebody's dream of a windowpane shattered, and so nearly at its destination.

Two pillars supported the roof and benches surrounded the hearth on three sides. As more people came in, carpets were unrolled for them to sit on. A shelf-unit, something like a Welsh dresser, acted as a room-divider and screened off the doorway. On it stood an enormous decorated copper bowl, the household water cistern. Rows of gleaming copper and brass implements hung on the walls.

Her finery refolded and back in the trunk, Yuma – a niece of the Mustang Raja – crouched before the fire to bake some buckwheat bread, little griddlecakes, delicious when hot and eaten with chilli sauce. She made an assortment of tasty snacks all afternoon, as we drifted in and out, taking turns to enjoy her hospitality. Mr Basnyet settled himself comfortably near the fire, sipped chang and chewed *churpi* (crumbs of pungent cheese, hard as pebbles). He had visibly relaxed since the policemen left, and was only sorry there had not been enough ceremonial clothes for him to dress as a grandee too. No sooner had Lhakpa taken off his borrowed plumes than Mr B at once jumped into them, striking a heroic pose for his picture to be taken. He was a handsome man, and vain about his appearance. For the meeting with the police he had spruced himself up in a crisp official-looking khaki shirt; this afternoon he had chosen equally immaculate but more appropriately casual wear.

Chotare had been busy with the goat. Tempting strips of prime meat in a spiced sauce were sent round for the village dignitaries. Unfortunately, the platter was delivered in error to the roof, where Sean and David devoured it absently before any VIPs got the merest whiff. Luckily, the kitchen was able, in time, to produce another.

In the evening, the compound where we ate was cleared and swept clean in preparation for further celebrations. The whole village was expected and a good many people from neighbouring settlements, too.

A raised byre served as a dais, on which the little decorated tables were again set up, and out, too, came the special silver bowls. Elaine and Lhakpa joined their new kinsmen behind this high table. Ceremonial scarves were once again exchanged, and chang and rakshi flowed freely.

Night wrapped round us, drawing the group together. We squatted in the dust in a horseshoe, leaving room in the centre for dancing. Though Mustangi men and women tended to sit in groups apart from one another, quite as many fathers as mothers cuddled wide-eyed toddlers on their knees. There was certainly no question of children being sent to bed: they belonged here with everyone else. The village's schoolchildren, smartened up for the occasion, put on an impromptu show of singing and dancing – graceful set pieces by solemn, lovely children, but of Hindu rather than Tibetan character. This is because they had a Hindu schoolteacher, part of an overall policy to unify Nepal.

One little girl in a red wrap-round skirt danced a sinuous, arm wafting soliloquy to the moon; a boy and girl, each with a ring of bells round one ankle, performed in near-perfect synchronization, but the stars of the evening were two jolly little clowns in apricot suits, who executed a burlesque number about the evils of smoking and drinking. The children were accompanied by a drum and a few bells. Later, all the dancing was to singing alone, and quite definitely Tibetan. To a lilting rhythm, a group of villagers began swaying, men and women together following each other slowly round in a circle. I ran to fetch Reiko who I could see was absent from the gathering; she would not like to miss this. Our Sherpas next performed one of their traditional arm-linked dances, led, I was surprised to see, by Chotare. Usually he was very retiring, but obviously not when it came to keeping Sherpa custom and identity alive.

Mr Basnyet grew ever more expansive as the evening wore on. Emotion almost overwhelmed him. Since early afternoon, he had become increasingly genial, moister of eye, glorying in the richness and variety of Nepal. His head nodded, his hands described generous, eloquent patterns. Now he was circling the group, greeting us affectionately in turn, assuring himself we were appreciating this wonderful entertainment.

Sean, who like the rest of us had put in some serious supping that day, clapped the liaison officer on the shoulder, winked and said thickly, 'Have another drink, Mr Basnyet!'

In an instant the mood changed. The world hung fire. Singing faltered and the Sherpas' legs froze in mid-air as all eyes fastened on the pair. The echo of Sean's words shivered in the sudden silence, reverberated, distorted, came back as, 'You've drunk too much already!'

Mr B's eyes blazed, bulged like a demon's, fixed Sean with a menace equal to any we had seen in the wall-paintings. The tension was unbearable. Those basilisk eyes never blinked. Sean floundered, vainly trying to retrieve the situation, but the eyes burned on, boring into him. None of us was in any doubt that Mr Basnyet would destroy him. Their uneasy, lurching truce was at an end. The authority which Sean had challenged with such abandon was being reasserted.

And then, just as suddenly, it was all over.

The two wrapped arms round one another and swayed off for a drink together. We let out held breath. The Sherpas feet came down to earth. The world ground on.

*

'Who gets to be Meryl Streep this morning?' I yelled at Elaine and Lhakpa's tent.

Yesterday, at Elaine's request, I had dug in my kitbag and found her a skirt for the dancing. 'Very *Out of Africa*!' we teased, but she looked extremely graceful twirling around. Today it was my turn. I intended striding along the riverbed in its voluminous folds, regretting only that I hadn't the riding boots to match. Still, I was lucky to have boots at all. Elaine hadn't any more. When she went to put hers on this morning she discovered Lhakpa had traded them for a carpet. Everybody had been in a frenzy of bartering since we arrived here. All the Dri cupboards had been turned out and we were offered saddle blankets, bowls, beads, kukris, tinder pouches . . . Even the children joined in. I bought an ammonite and a brass ring with the stone missing from one diminutive pedlar who was learning this very necessary life skill.

Heavy-hearted, we tramped out of the village just as the sun rose over the hills opposite, backlighting the green barley. The crop had grown several inches since we first came up here. The mountains and cliffs had that fluid look, with blue shadows, they get in the early sunshine. It was another of those brilliant mornings, the sky a clear virgin-blue shading to deepest sapphire and the rocks glowing honey blond, streaked with gold and grey and the occasional raw splash of red. Last night at sundown, from all over these bare hills, flocks of goats had come pouring, tumbling down, thousands upon thousands of them, trickling through the gullies like sand through an egg-timer. Black confetti, Sean had said. Their shepherds leapt lightly behind them, whooping to announce their arrival. From every direction, the goats came, some being driven off to Zurkhang on the other side of the river; some to be penned in our village. We left before they were driven back up in to the hills this morning.

Yuma came running down the slope to say goodbye at the river. She had taken quite a shine to Laureen and brought her a little package of spicy patties to keep up her strength on the journey. I left Yuma the *National Geographic* that had caused such a stir everywhere we went. She particularly wanted it for Peissel's picture of her grandfather, the old Mustang Raja.

We crunched along the silver sand of the main highway of Lo, the Great North Road, every so often to be passed by a Mustangi horseman off to do business, as they say, 'in Nepal'. The long-maned little horses jingle with bells and have fine bright saddle carpets emblazoned with roses, but the traders themselves tend to dress in Western clothes, not wanting, I suppose, to appear country hicks when they get down to Pokhara or Kathmandu.

This river was here before the Himalayas started rising. We would follow it all day, just occasionally scrambling over a side spur to save our feet a drenching. Even so, there was talk of having to cross the water a dozen or more times before we were through, which was why I had elected to wear the skirt – so much easier to hoik up than trousers. The girls from Tsum had very wide loads today, which gave them plenty to giggle about as they manoeuvred awkwardly around obstacles on dizzy cliff paths. They walked in Chinese gumshoes, each day hitching their long skirts a little higher. Even in this heat they still wore an amazing amount of clothing – goodness knows how many layers in all – cardigans, shawls and, under thick serge chubas and aprons, track-suit trousers. Their loads were carried on tump lines, cushioned only by a small folded towel. I never ceased to marvel at their hardiness. They could not have been more than seventeen or eighteen, yet here they were miles from home, and completely independent. They didn't even get catered for in the trekking arrangements like the kitchen staff, although I am sure Chotare saw to it they did not starve.

We stopped for a quick picnic not far from where nomads had set up camp on the river gravel. A merciless spot on hot, sharp stones, with no shade and no blade of green for their animals. Clearly the proximity to water overruled all disadvantages. As for us, the heat radiating off the boulders and cliffsides must have addled our brains for we spent the entire lunchstop fantasizing that we were in the South of France and would soon come upon a shady bar with ice-cold beer – inter-*Stella* travel. Instead we sipped tepid, smoky water from our drinking flasks.

The going had been getting gradually tougher – rougher shingle, more ups and down and streams to ford or jump across. By this time I was carrying my boots in a plastic shopping bag and wearing trainers so that I could splash through all the little rivulets. At a golden dog-leg corner, we left the main Gandaki valley and headed up a channel on the left-hand side. Now the skein of streams was flowing towards us, rather than away, but again it was ridiculously mismatched to the capacious river-bed. Before long the valley walls became like canyons, their clifftops exhibiting the pleated patterning with which by now we were so familiar, some so intricately eroded as to appear almost like lace. It was hard to imagine that this had not been fashioned deliberately.

I had been walking most of the day with Laureen, but it was one of my good days and I kept pulling ahead. Then I would stop and wait while she caught up, an ideal kind of progress lending plenty of time to contemplation. The vertical cliff to our left was sliced as clean and abruptly as a slab of madeira cake, except that when you got in close you could see the diagonal pebble-lines of bedding planes. The cliff on the other side of the valley was more boot-shaped in profile.

I turned a corner and spotted, first, more of the semi-circular cave openings in high fluted cliffs to the left. They were not as inaccessible as some we had seen, for scree slopes beneath the cliffs reached almost to their level. Next emerged a line of chortens on a slumped terrace ledge directly under the cliff.

This, then, was Tengye, the village for which we were heading, completely contained on its terrace and overshadowed by the encroaching screes, which would one day swallow it up. Stepped fields, already green, led down to the river bed. I could see our mules just ahead, beginning the gentle pull-up towards the introductory chortens with their red steeples. Laureen and I followed the same path, entering the little village past a mani wall and a shallow pond. Already a reception committee of women and children were squatted in the centre of town to look us over. I sat gratefully and chattered away to one mother and her cheeky brood. She chattered back, neither of us with the slightest inkling of what the other was saying, but hoping by the utterance to establish goodwill between us.

H. W. Tilman came to Tangye almost exactly forty years before us. He arrived from the opposite direction, after a journey of some five or six days beyond all habitation, having found with difficulty – and crossed – the 18,000-foot Mustang La in filthy weather. 'This little green patch betokening human activity shone like a good deed in a naughty world,' he said at the end of his journey, 'a world of shocking sterility, harsh colour and violent shapes.'

It is a small village, tightly packed to protect it from the afternoon valley winds, which blew up soon after we arrived, swirling grit and dust into our eyes and mouths. The Sherpas were struggling to put up a tarpaulin roof in an endeavour to keep some of the dust from the cooking. The tents, pegged out on an exposed yard, filled with blown dust the minute we unzipped the doors. Everything quickly acquired a film of grime. Like the villagers, we could see little use in washing.

Tangye's most remarkable feature is a composite of chortens at the eastern end of town, the largest and I dare say finest such structure anywhere in Mustang. It looked like a ship, like the old multi-funnelled *Mauretania*, with extra bits added on. Clustered on either side of a large central chorten, which stood some fifty feet high, were batteries of smaller ones, one tidy group of eight with a shared flat roof looking just like bottles in a crate. All were gaudily painted in red, white and blue-grey. Though I took photographs from every angle, I am sure that, without scrambling up into the surrounding hills, there is nowhere from which the complete group can be assembled into one frame, as it extends around a corner and is partially screened by trees.

Our journey today was made with a different Mustangi guide. Tsering Tamden had been given two days off to visit his wife in Lo Mantang. He had not seen her or his two children for the six years he has been working in Kathmandu. Of course, from time to time, he has sent home gifts of money and jewellery. When Lhakpa was in Lo to raise the helicopter, he called on Mrs Tsering Tamden, thinking it best to prepare her for the shock of a sudden visit from her spouse.

'What do I want with jewellery and clothes?' the poor wife had railed at him. All I want is a husband!'

Perhaps the same went for the lady on whose sheltered balcony our meal-tables were set that night, for she wasted no time in making a play for Colin, offering him a pinch of snuff. He raised it with polite flourish to his nose. The first sniff made his eyes start from his head and triggered such a paroxysm of sneezing it could be heard all over the village. The woman was beside herself with delight, and begged him take another snort. Thereafter, these two clowned in elaborate mime for the rest of our stay, and when it came time to leave in the morning, with more hooting laughter, she made to offer him her baby. The poor child shrieked in terror, believing he really was to be handed over to the big-nosed pink bogeyman.

★

Fifty steps and then a breather . . . Fifty steps, another breather . . . Important not to look up until all fifty are taken; that way the top might creep just a little closer. I see David and Sean ahead, giving Sue a pull up. Fifty steps . . . uh, steeper here . . . make it forty steps . . . and then a breather . . .

We had toiled up this mountainside for two hours already, quite steeply but without too much difficulty at first, enjoying the frequent stops to look back at the stupendous view. Tangye on its terrace, with prayer flags limp in the still air, became so small as to be no longer recognizable for good deed or bad in a naughty world, just a tight scattering like spilt demerara until distance took it altogether from view. This was a molten landscape, heaving, forming, on the move. There was no air of permanence to it at all. Wild, contorted, weird. Streaked and striated. Deckled at the edges. To our left as we climbed, a snow dome peeped over brown mountains, bright with sunfall. That, I professed (but without conviction), was Bhrikuti. The pass for which we were heading still lay way, way above . . . Important to keep going. It would be a long morning. Come on then, another forty steps . . . It was getting harder now.

Two hours on, and still climbing. Surely, we couldn't have been higher than this anywhere in Mustang – not even at our high camp? I could see the value of mantras in easing repetitive effort. *Om mani padme hum, forty steps and then you stop, om mani padme hum . . . only thirty-eight to go . . .* They set a heartbeat rhythm, mop up the mind. You make your own chants. *This is the hill that Tilman climbed, this is the hill . . .* Did he count his steps up, I wonder? *This is . . .* In his book, *Nepal Himalaya*, there is a muddy monochrome picture of a prow of rock rising from a wide, unsettled surface. That same long wedge reared now from beyond the Kali Gandaki. 'Fascinatingly ugly country' Tilman called it. I guess he too was feeling tired. 'The more fascinating for being so little known. No snowy peaks broke like white waves upon the horizon of this tumbled multi-coloured sea.'

At any rate, not looking northwards to Tibet they didn't, although we could see clear across the enclosure that was Mustang to the Mustang Himal on the western side, and these carried snow. Tilman was making the point that the Ladakh range, which defined the border further west, had here dwindled into insignificance. Only bleached hills separated us from Tibet now.

★

Four and a half hours it took to reach the pass, from which I cast a long last look back over the inchoate landscape. The depression that marks Lo was once a lake, geologists tell us, filling a rift valley formed when the Indian sub-continent crashed into the underbelly of Asia and rucked up the Great Himalayas. The impetus that led to this titanic collision forty million years ago is far from dead. The youngest mountain system in the world continues to rise fractionally year by year.

We were sorry to turn our backs on the scene, our last view of Mustang, but a gentler, undulating path beckoned us on, skirting ridges and valleys without much loss of height. We were travelling almost due south through the remnants of what had once been a forest but was now sandy, limey scrubland. The snowy Himalaya formed a neat *broderie* trimming to the horizon. We stopped for a quick dry lunch in a bare dry valley – chapatis, pease pudding and potatoes, all gobbled down in haste. It had taken nearly five hours to reach a spot the locals told us was only two hours into a six-hour day. Clearly there was still a lot of ground to cover, beginning with a dreadful pull uphill on a full stomach.

We straggled, fighting to regain our wind, clinging to the romance of travel – a sorry bunch of autumn croakers – and then, there we were, on a broad trail looping a moor of gorsey pink bushes with the wind in our faces and a fresher step. This really was a high road, three thousand feet above the Kali Gandaki, one of the old drove roads from Tibet, nudging against the sky. We had it to ourselves, but scorched hearth-stones on either side attested to the campfires of earlier travellers. When Tilman came this way he met many flocks of sheep and goats, several hundred to a flock, either carrying rice or grain up to Mustang, or bringing salt down from the dried saline lakes of Inner

Tibet. Sheep and goats may not be everyone's first idea of pack animals, but each could wear a couple of fat little pouches, and multiplied over a large flock that represented considerable carrying capacity. The Buddhist traders ate little meat themselves, but some of the animals, fattened on Tibet's Changtang prairie, were destined for Brahman and Chettri tables down in the Nepalese midlands. The drovers would have to scoot them through this arid region if they were not to arrive at their destination with a skinny, stringy, near-worthless stock.

Our path hugged a line just below the top of a ridge, with the ground falling away to the right in the direction of the Kali. Before us reared Annapurna, Nilgiri and Dhaulagiri with a tumult of clouds boiling around them in an otherwise clear sky. Every so often the ridge would narrow to a waist where the head of a ravine on one side met the head of a canyon on the other. Then an airy notch in the crest would open up to the east a dry vista of yellow and pink columns. Badlands. At the third of these exposed notches, where the path became more in the nature of a bridge over a chasm, a clutch of conical snow peaks appeared. These would be the Damodar and Lugula Himals, and one of their number really *had* to be Bhrikuti, probably the one set back to the left. I'd settle for that: it was important to be able to say I'd seen it. On and on, the path looped. However unsung, this was truly one of the great walks of the world, a switchback in the sky.

Beyond the next notch folk were scrambling up a murderously steep pinnacle, some already quite high. I hoped they had climbed it just for the view. Surely the path would not take us up there? Yet it looked dangerously like it.

Here I am, halfway up this godawful pyramid, gasping into my recorder once more and looking out at a fantastic patchwork of shapes – erosion sculpture – to the east. Sandstone weathers into such delicate, flimsy organ pipes, conglomerate to much bolder sharkfins and flukes. In between is almost every range and colour of mud and marl, etched, incised ... and it goes on as far as the eye can see, except that the rim to south and east – and I suspect to the west, too, if I turn to look, but I don't want to topple over – is bounded by snowy peaks ...

It proved to be a scenic diversion, for from the top you could see the main path contouring round. Yet it was not one I could possibly regret

– except out of sympathy for our laden porters. This was the pinnacle in the wilderness from which in a moment of time all the wonders of creation could be observed – or rather, it was more like occupying an opera-box at the Creation itself.

From here we began the long descent down to the Kali Gandaki.

'Gravity is winning!' sang Elaine as she fell into easy step at my side.

In bright afternoon sunshine, with waist-high wind-sculpted bushes to either side of us, we swung swiftly on. I had high hopes that it could not be long before we reached our village, Tsuk, but there was a lot of height to lose and the hours continued to tick by while we were granted occasional glimpses into the valley. Presently the path wound round to the eastern side of the ridge – no place for those suffering from vertigo – to a breezy cliff ledge overlooking another pinnacle nursery, or what Elaine called a sword forest. By this time we were into the slanting sunlight of evening, and when we rounded the ridge again the Kali was lost in dark shadow. Picking our way awkwardly down interminable boulder slopes in the gathering darkness, we eventually reached the four settlements that make up Tsuk just as the sun went down. Sue came out to greet us. She had been suffering bronchitis and had ridden a horse for most of the afternoon, arriving well ahead of the main party. As she dropped down the final screes the river was a blaze of silver light. We had been on our feet for eleven hours, from sun-up to sun-down, our longest day so far. Never was Chotare's teapot more welcome. Since leaving the river at Tangye there had been only one dribble of a muddy stream to be seen all day.

We ate in the courtyard of the health post, balancing plates on our knees for the man who always struggled buckle-kneed in our wake under the burden of metal tables had failed to arrive. He had been terribly on our conscience throughout the trip: how could we not feel uncomfortable that for our ease Mohti Ram had to endure long days with a tump band sawing through the crown of his head? Did the sahibs really need to sit at tables in the wilderness at such cost? It wasn't as if these were lightweight aluminium camping tables, such as we might use at home – they were heavy-duty iron ones. Out on the dark hills was no place to be with a load like that, and as the evening ticked by and still he did not appear, we grew increasingly concerned for his safety. Some of the porters went back with lanterns to look for him and guide him down the ankle-turning screes. The last time I remembered seeing him was well before lunch when we were labouring up to the high pass above Tangye; then the incongruity of us needing such sybaritic trappings here of all places struck me as so absurd that I felt obliged to take his picture.

He finally came in to a cold dinner long after we had finished. We later learned that our table man was a schoolmaster who had fallen into debt. Undertaking to carry this double-weight load was his way of earning himself out of trouble in a land where portering paid twice as much as teaching.

★

An hour and a half outside Tsuk, Sue and I passed a ponyman returning to Lo Mantang with his daughter, having been down to Pokhara for rice.

'Too dry!' he said, indicating a dry throat, dry eyes, dry skin. May was the best time in his country, he told us. Then everybody was full-cheeked and moist.

This man had taken herbs and incense down to Marpha to trade. A little before we met him, we had spoken to a monk from a monastery north of Lo Mantang. He too had incense, which he claimed could cure colds. Rub it on your chest, he advised. For food he carried dry sausage in a sheep's intestine and offered a bite. He was dressed in Western clothes but with a fine yellow brocade jacket, and he spoke very good English. He had been to Dharamsala in North India.

Sue and I were taking the opportunity to talk to everyone we met this morning – in Tsuk and Tayen, in the fields, on the road. We were so unwilling to leave this world behind that we dallied all the way. Poor Pemba, who had been charged to hustle us along, became very concerned that his charges kept straying from the quickest route.

'No, no, ladees! This way, come!'

'No, Pemba, look! This is the way! Through the gateway chortens . . . down this lane . . . under the fruit trees . . . where those men and women are mending the path . . .'

By the time we were back on the river bed with Kagbeni in sight once more and the dust clouds beginning to blow, Pemba finally gave up, figuring that even we could not get lost now, and he streaked ahead for a *Star* beer. He couldn't wait to be back in civilization.

The last stretch was really strenuous. Kagbeni gompa, red and square, squatting on its buttress of rock, kept appearing and disappearing through the swirling clouds of dust. Head down, we battled ineffectually into the Kali Gandaki wind. When veils of stinging particles danced along the stones, whipping our faces, there was nothing to do but to turn around until they had sizzled past. Yak and pony caravans and lone traders were coming towards us, the wind at their backs butting them along, but we were the only mad dogs going into the midday dust.

★

Elaine was the first person I saw on entering again the walled camping enclosure where we had stayed on the way up.

'What happened with the old lady?' I wanted to know. 'Did she die?'

'It's amazing! You'll never believe it, but she's very much better! Never knock the powers of paracetamol!'

'Or at least, the power of faith in paracetamol.'

Still frail, the grandmother was sitting beside the smoking fire drinking tea with the other members of her family. All of them were brighter and more relaxed. It was nothing short of a miracle.

★

Sue was in her tent when a dark hand came through the tent flap waving a 100-rupee note.

'Change please! Change please! Porters gambling!' came the urgent request.

The Call to Be Free

A T FIRST THE return to Kathmandu seemed an anticlimax. To dispel the inertia Sue and I decided to pay a visit to Bodhnath, the Tibetan quarter.

'Off to look at some gompas,' we told Elaine, with Sue adding as a wistful afterthought, 'and to see the King of Mustang.'

We knew the Raja to be somewhere in the capital: people had told us that in Mustang. Everywhere we went, they used to say, 'You've only missed him by a few days.'

Almost a week had passed since we'd flown out of Jomoson, jam-packed in a Twin Otter that climbed like a moonrocket from the short take-off strip and bounced on air currents all the way down-valley to Pokhara. We had rowed on the beautiful Phewa Lake with the Anna-purnas and Machapuchhare floating filmy in a forget-me-not blue sky, and after two days of shopping and sightseeing in Kathmandu, had said goodbye to most of our friends.

Looking back, I remember that day in Bodhnath as one of desultory bursts of effort punctuated by long periods of vacant staring. We were both suffering the gastric exhaustion of being back in the capital. We circumambulated the giant stupa three times, spinning the prayer wheels, then sat on its white dome under a pair of all-seeing eyes to recover. Bodhnath had come a long way since the first tourists were here in 1949. Then the temple on its concentric terraces was sur-rounded only by a compact circle of buildings, an architectural mandala set in green fields. Now it was home to countless Sherpas and Tibetan refugees and houses were springing up on every spare plot, bits at a time as families could afford to build them. This is the centre of a lucrative rug-making industry, the raw wool for which comes in from India and Tibet – and indeed these days even from New Zealand as well. On flat roofs hanks of dyed homespun are spread to dry in the

242

sun – lilacs, pinks, soft greens, a different colour each day of the week.

Forcing ourselves to our feet once more, we walked towards the small Sakya gompa that stands to north side of the stupa platform, but its doors were closed. A cheery young monk of about fifteen was looking for a chat, and surprised us by saying he came from Tsarang. He'd been sent away at the age of four to study in Dehra Dun. It followed quite naturally to ask him about the Mustang Raja.

'You have business with King? He lives in apartment here, back of gompa. I show you.'

He led us over piles of mud and builders' debris towards a small, square block of flats. We stood uncertainly outside, wondering whether we really wanted to brazen our way in to see his majesty, when a deep-chested, round-faced, lugubrious looking man with Mongolian features walked across the waste lot. His jet hair was parted in the middle with a thin braid wound once around his head. He wore a fine lump of rough turquoise in one ear and a gold-mounted portrait of the King of Nepal on his pullover.

'Is the Raja of Mustang,' the young monk whispered, and salaamed deferentially before introducing us.

Sue and I grinned foolishly, namaste'd, then pumped the royal hand. We said how much we had enjoyed his country, how kind his family had been. He smiled stiffly, uncomprehendingly, and an awkward situation was saved only by the arrival of a younger companion who spoke impeccable English. This turned out to be the Crown Prince, none other than the sunny little boy who had so entranced Peissel when he stayed with the old lama of Tsarang. The King had no sons of his own and in time his nephew would succeed him as monarch of Lo.

The young man pointed out a small and grubby child playing in the dirt, 'That is my son.' He smiled proudly. The boy was the same size and very like the little fellow in Peissel's photograph. He was heaving a princely brick at a stray dog.

Bemused, Sue and I continued our walk. How fortunate to have met the King, the heir apparent and the heir apparent's heir apparent on neutral ground, for the more we thought of it, the more convinced we became that it would have been an extreme breach of etiquette to have arrived unannounced at the royal apartment and without gifts. Later, I did return formally with Elaine and Lhakpa, this time correctly prepared with the right grade of *khatas* and some presentation photographs of the Friendship Ceremony on Tsering Gombu's roof.

We chatted amiably with the Crown Prince, sipping tea, while the

King finished his morning meditations in the bedroom next door. At last we were ushered into the small room to sit in a line on one of twin beds, facing him. Still mumbling prayers, the King accepted the gifts vaguely. He was still unsure who we were. I had read that the royal family of Mustang owned a yeti skin, taken from a dead animal found near Lo Mantang in 1958, and to break the ice, I asked about it.

'It's true,' the prince said. 'We did have one, but I'm afraid we haven't got it now.'

He thought I wanted to buy it, and sniffing the opportunity for a future deal, added with a smile, 'We'll save the next one for you!'

★

I decided to walk to Patan. It wasn't far. Past Ratna Park, the Thundikhel Sports Field and the American supermarket, then over the Bagmati Bridge and up the hill to Patan Gate. Usually, it took me about an hour, but always depended on how crowded the streets were. Also, I wanted to call first at the Tibet Guest House to see if Jeff Long had arrived. He was to assist David Breashears in making yet another BBC film about Mallory on Everest – this time with Brian Blessed. Jeff was expected in Kathmandu a few days ahead of the others, who were off on an acclimatizing trek. I found he had checked in, but was out around the city. I continued my walk.

Pulling up the last long dusty hill, I could see crowds blocking the road ahead. There were sounds of shouting. Only then did I notice the rows of lorries, from which spilled armed and helmeted troops. Uh-uh! Another demonstration.

My first thought, returning to Kathmandu after nearly a month away, had been for how 'The Stir' – the Revolution – was going. The most visible development was an increased saturation of riot police on the streets, though many of the long marching columns were clearly raw recruits, straggling raggedly out of step. Barriers of roadstone impeded the main vehicle entrances into Thamel. The strikes had continued, and we learned that a series of 'Black Days' were held in mourning for those killed by police the last time we were here. Silent demonstrations in and outside Bir Hospital had protested against human rights abuses and the summary removal by police of slain victims from the morgue. Because the bodies always disappeared, no independent assessment of fatalities had been possible. More than a dozen newspapers had been banned and others censored or seized upon publication. Pro-democracy leaders lived a fugitive existence, and doctors, lawyers and journalists were among those singled out for detention. The whole sad city had learned to fear the midnight knock.

As I pulled closer to the mob, I saw at its hub a milling knot of student protesters outside the engineering university. They were waving fists and banners and flinging handfuls of leaflets into the air bearing the outlawed flag of the Nepali Congress. As they fluttered to the ground, the cry went up, 'Democracy – do or die!' Followed by, 'King, thief, leave the country!'

Everyone was on the street, or so it seemed: men, women, even small children ringed the agitators, passive for the most part but forming a massive shield of bodies around them. The police held to the fringes, where they grouped ominously into ranks of crouched figures. How long the stand-off would last was anybody's guess.

This was where – if I were to follow advice – I was supposed to turn round and walk back the way I had come, yet despite the obvious tension in the air, things looked quiet enough for the moment. I pushed on through. A couple of hours later, when I returned the same way, the situation showed little change except that the road was now barricaded off and police were diverting all traffic away from the area. They couldn't match the protestors in numbers, but by the very nature of the street had so far been successful in containing them. Some while later they were able to prevent a mass march on Kathmandu itself. The jittery stalemate lasted all day.

But not the next. Police finally opened fire the following morning, killing at least three people. Students quickly regrouped, declaring Patan a liberated zone, and on the other side of the city, in Bhaktipur, a traditional communist stronghold, a similar declaration was made. There were more killings in Kirtipur. Clearly, matters were brewing to a head. As their safety could no longer be guaranteed, all visitors were urged to leave Nepal as soon as possible.

★

Friday 6 April was a fine bright day that brought everyone determinedly on to the streets. Jeff Long, pushing a hired bike, joined the crowds snaking down the narrow lanes in an air almost of spontaneous festivity. Crossing a temple square littered with broken glass, his back tyre exploded, and it was only then, seeing how people froze in panic all round, that he realized how illusory the mood was. 'The crowd was one giant raw nerve,' he said.

At lunch time he returned to the Guest House for more film and took a snack up to the roof, which was set out as a garden with tables, benches and straw umbrellas. As he was dozing in the sun, he heard from not far away the sound of what he took to be cheap fireworks. It was coming from the direction of the large grassy area known as Ratna Park, and crackled on for hours.

Much later, when two of his friends reeled in off the streets, their faces grim and grey with shock, he learned what had really been happening that afternoon.

Swarming crowds from all over the city converged on Ratna Park, bringing several hundred thousand excited people together only one block away from the Royal Palace. Some hothead speeches denouncing a recent cabinet reshuffle – all that the government had offered the people so far by way of reform – were enough to encourage the throng to advance on the palace.

Police at once started hacking a bloody swathe in the crowd, at the same time lobbing tear gas cannisters deep among the protesters. The wind was blowing in the wrong direction and it was the security forces themselves who were forced to flee. Gathering new resolve, the police and soldiers turned and flayed once more with their lathis.

Then the shooting began.

After that, people were hunted down and beaten indiscriminately as they ran for their lives.

Long's friends made their way back past the city hospital. Outside its gates people had linked arms in the forlorn hope of this time keeping out the police, and they tugged at the two men.

'There are Westerners in there,' they told them. 'Wounded. Dead. Is important you see if you know them. Go inside!'

It was true. Two young men were seriously ill with gunshot wounds, and a British photographer lay dead, shot through the throat. Altogether they saw eight or nine bodies before security forces arrived outside and began spattering bullets to disperse the shielding crowd. Long's friends dodged off once more into the warren of backstreets and, helped by local residents, eventually made it safely back to the hotel.

Next morning they were disgusted to learn that official sources were reporting only one dead in the troubles. The city was under martial law and a 24-hour curfew in force. Even so, Jeff Long decided to try and get to the hospital to see for himself. One of the two who'd been the day before agreed to accompany him. Long described the journey in an article, 'Dark days in Shangri La', in the *Boulder Daily Camera*:

The streets were deserted and trashed out. Urchins haunted the deepest recesses of side alleys. Out on the main drag .60-caliber machine guns commanded every intersection, each surrounded by barbed wire. Soldiers in camouflage milled about a towering cart used in religious processions. These were Gurkha combat troops bearing Uzis, a completely different breed than the city police who we were used to seeing in their goofy khaki padding . . .

Anyone seen on the street was to be shot. But we walked slowly, and we explained to every soldier and his officers that we had to get to Bir Hospital. We were permitted past each checkpoint. We girdled Ratna Park. It looked as if a tornado had torn and twisted the iron fences and trees.

Soldiers ringing the hospital let us through. As it turned out, the hospital was under virtual siege. None of the doctors dared leave, afraid for their lives. All of them had been working non-stop since yesterday's massacre. They had a lot of work on. The wounded, several dozen in one room, lay on the tile floors. Most seemed to have head wounds from the lathis. Blood was smeared on every wall and caked the floors and sidewalks.

Weary as they were, the physicians were anxious to talk to Long. They needed to tell of their horror and disgust at what they had seen. Trying to bring in the dead and injured, their lives were threatened. Ambulance drivers had been beaten up, sirens smashed. If they wanted to carry off the dead, they were told, they could add their own bodies to the pile.

One of the Western patients, Andrew Reid, was in a serious condition. He had lost a leg below the knee. The other, a Dutch tourist, had been shot in the back. There were a good many Nepalis with gunshot wounds to the back, too. Doctors begged Long and his friend to take photos of the wounded and dead.

The bodies lay stretched on the floor, their clothes still rucked up from being dragged in off the streets. One was the young Briton, Richard Williams. He had been filming when he was shot, people said. Already there were fewer dead bodies than Long's friend had seen the night before. The security forces had been in.

All round the city people reported having seen dead civilians loaded in to jeeps and trucks; those able to pick up police channels on their radios told of overheard discussions on what should be done with them. A leading opposition spokesman later claimed that several hundred corpses were consigned to a mass grave in the military-controlled Sundarijal forest. No more than a dozen dead were formally identified, even though security forces opened fire in more than a dozen places, firing with automatic weapons at point-blank range into huge crowds.

Within a couple of days the King had announced that he would be lifting the 30-year ban on political parties. Political prisoners were to be released. The existing Panchayat would be dissolved and a new multi-party democracy installed. It sounded like victory for the people.

★

Celebrations got off to a bad start. In some areas it took time persuading soldiers of the King's peace initiative and there were yet more deaths. I had flown home by this time, but Sue Byrne, who had been away on a short visit to India, returned in the thick of it.

'The narrow street from the airport was crowded with flag-waving, cheering Nepalese,' she said. 'As our car squeezed through them, a hand came through the window to smear our foreheads with red powder. We had to be part of it as well.

'It was amazing. Trucks, cars, tractors, bikes, motorbikes, scooters were driving round and round past the palace, honking their horns and flying the red and white flags of the Communist party and the Nepali Congress party. Young men, red powder all over their faces, wore red headbands in the style of Chinese students. In every street I went down there were impromptu marches and shouts of '*Demo-crass-eee, Jai! Jai!*' Red and white flags poured from every window, appeared on the tops of statues and ancient monuments, and outside doorways on the streets were small bunches of flowers and offerings.'

Sue wandered through the jubilant crowds to the Thundikhel parade ground, where would-be politicians addressed the revellers. In the end it had all happened so quickly. Perhaps too quickly. In a year when revolutions had been overthrowing repressive regimes throughout Eastern Europe, and before anticlimax had settled in there, the future looked hopeful for Nepal's young democrats.

Of course there was no guarantee that the royal family would release its stranglehold, that corruption would be staunched or human rights abuses stopped. Almost certainly the shaky opposition coalition would not hold together.

All there was – was hope.

That is more than can reasonably be said of Tibet. Yet.

TO DREAM ON

Is it true, a journalist asked me before I left for Everest, that one in ten mountaineers who go to the Himalaya are killed?

This popularly held belief arose from Chris Bonington's big expeditions of the 'seventies, when with frightening recurrence members of his elite team failed to return. On the face of it, you could be forgiven then for thinking that almost ten percent were getting chopped.

Of course, these were climbers out on the raggety edge of what was being done in the world's highest mountains; much less was heard about the many uneventful expeditions which aspired to more modest objectives. Nor did the terrifying equation take account of the numbers of Sherpas who worked alongside Bonington's All Stars. A more realistic fatality rate on the highest mountains of the world would probably be something like 3.5 percent. Still a shockingly high figure, but far better than one in ten.

'And how many people will be on Everest when you are there?' the journalist wanted to know.

'Oh, between one and two hundred, I suppose.'

'So you can expect at least three fatalities during that time?'

I hoped she wasn't right. The words kept floating back to me throughout our expedition, and I watched anxiously every time people left Base Camp. I could not bear the thought that something might happen to any one of them. Yet in the end, the woman's prediction was not far from the mark. We lost Dawa Nuro, the Chileans Victor Hugo Trujillo, and a commercial enterprise on the southern side of Everest (on to which adventurous punters were able to buy their way) lost one Swiss and a Sherpa.

Every mountaineer will tell you that no climb is worth a life. But then no one knows in advance that a life is the price to be extracted.

We didn't even make our climb and a life had to be paid. Nothing we could do for Dawa's wife and three small sons would ever make up for his loss to them.

We made two films; Tom sustained his theory – and that apart, none of our stated objectives had been fulfilled. Was our expedition, then, a waste? A prodigal squandering of other people's money? Did we have the right to risk our own and our Sherpas' lives for so little? Should we never have gone?

It makes you wonder at the value, not only of our trip, but of all those hundreds of expeditions that in the end achieve so little. Yet in my heart I cannot wish ours had not happened. With supreme selfishness, all I can say is that my own life has been incalculably enriched by the experience.

That is not something I can square with a life lost.

Now, four and a half years after going to Everest, I am saddened to realize how many of those who were with us in Base Camp are no longer alive. Dave Cheesmond and Catherine Freer were lost on Alaska's fearsome Hummingbird Ridge, and Roger Marshall was killed when he went back for another solo attempt on Everest. The Briton, Trevor Pilling, disappeared on Pumori. Away from the mountains Steve McKinney perished in a bizarre car-breakdown accident, and Mo Anthoine died of a brain tumour. Yet it is important to remember also the happier outcomes. The British went back to the Northeast Ridge in 1988, when Harry Taylor with Russell Brice successfully crossed the Pinnacles in appalling conditions, and everyone got down safely – even Brummie, after three cerebral haemorrhages. David Breashears has been back twice to Everest, and he and Steve Shea went to Menlungtse. Mary Kay Brewster and Catherine Cullinane each revisited Everest, and Sue Giller went to accompany a women's expedition to Pumori.

Though I might never again be lucky enough to venture on to Everest, Alexandra David-Neel is inspiration enough to suggest that women of unlikely endowment can trudge the hills into extended middle-age, giving me years of hope. I know exactly why she, and Younghusband, and Eric Valli, and all the others have found themselves drawn back time and again to these mountains. Once seen, they rise unbidden on every dream horizon. They hold so much you long to see, so much to absorb of ancient faiths and earth wisdom. And even knowing there to be a communal fantasy – an occidental conspiracy almost – that romanticizes the Himalaya because we need there to be a

Select Bibliography

Fürer-Haimendorf, Christoph von, *Himalayan Traders: Life in Highland Nepal*, London, John Murray, 1975

— *Exploratory Travels in Highland Nepal*, New Delhi, Sterling, 1989

Gurung, Harka, *Vignettes of Nepal*, Kathmandu, Sajha Prakashan, 1980

Habeler, Peter, *Everest, Impossible Victory: Conquering Everest without Oxygen*, London, Arlington Books, 1979

Hagen, Toni, 'Afoot in Roadless Nepal', in *National Geographic Magazine*, Washington D.C., March 1960

— *Nepal, the Kingdom in the Himalayas*, Berne, Kummerly & Frey, 1961

Harvard, Andrew and Thompson, Todd, *Mountain of Storms: The American Expeditions to Dhaulagiri*, New York University Press, 1974

Herzog, Maurice, *Annapurna, the First 8,000 Metre Peak*, London, Jonathan Cape, 1951

Hicks, Roger, *Hidden Tibet, the Land and Its People*, Shaftesbury, Dorset, Element Books, 1988

Hillary, Edmund, *High Adventure*, London, Hodder & Stoughton, 1955

Holzel, Tom, 'The Mystery of Mallory and Irvine', in *Mountain No. 17*, London, September 1971 (Responses in *Mountain No. 21*, May 1972)

— 'The Search for Mallory and Irvine', in *Summit*, Big Bear Lake, September/October 1981

— 'Mallory and Irvine: First to the top of Everest?' in *Summit*, Big Bear Lake, September/October 1981

Holzel, Tom and Salkeld, Audrey, *The Mystery of Mallory and Irvine*, London, Jonathan Cape, 1986

Hornbein, Thomas F., *The West Ridge*, San Francisco, Sierra Club, 1965

Jackson, David P., *The Mollas of Mustang*, Dharamsala, Library of Tibetan Works and Archives, 1984

Kawaguchi, Ekai, *Three Years in Tibet* (Second edition), Kathmandu, Ratna Pustak Bhandar, 1979

Kewley, Vanya, *Tibet: Behind the Ice Curtain*, London, Collins, 1990

Long, Jeff, 'Going after Wangdu', in *Rocky Mountain Magazine*, July/August 1981

— 'Dark Days in Shangri La' in *The Boulder Daily Camera*, Boulder, July 29, 1990

Lytton, Earl of, *Antony (Viscount Knebworth), a Record of Youth* (by his father), London, Peter Davies, 1935

Messner, Reinhold, *Everest: Expedition to the Ultimate*, London, Kaye & Ward, 1979

— *The Crystal Horizon: Everest – the First Solo Ascent*, Marlborough, Crowood Press, 1989

Middleton, Ruth, *Alexandra David-Neel, Portrait of an Adventurer*, Boston and Shaftesbury, Shambhala, 1989

Morrow, Pat, *Beyond Everest: Quest for the Seven Summits*, Camden East (Ontario), Camden House, 1986

Noel, Captain J. B. L., *Through Tibet to Everest* (Second edition), London, Hodder & Stoughton, 1989

Normanton, Simon, *Tibet: the Lost Civilization*, London, Hamish Hamilton, 1988

Patterson, George N., *Tibet in Revolt*, London, Faber, 1960

Peissel, Michel, 'Mustang, Nepal's Lost Kingdom', in *National Geographic Magazine*, Washington D.C., October 1965

— *Mustang, the Forbidden Kingdom*, New York, Dutton, 1967

— *Cavaliers of Kham, the Secret War in Tibet*, London, Heinemann, 1972

Pye-Smith, Charlie, *Travels in Nepal, the Sequestered Kingdom*, London, Aurum, 1988; Penguin, 1990

Richardson, Hugh, *Tibet and Its History* (Second edition, Revised and Updated), Boston and London, Shambhala, 1984

Ridgeway, Rick, *The Boldest Dream, the Story of Twelve who Climbed Mount Everest*, New York, Harcourt Brace Jovanovich, 1979

Roberts, Dennis, *'I'll Climb Mount Everest Alone, the Story of Maurice Wilson*, London, Robert Hale, 1957

Snellgrove, David, *Himalayan Pilgrimage* (Second edition), Boston and Shaftesbury, Shambhala, 1981

Snellgrove, David and Richardson, Hugh, *A Cultural History of Tibet* (Revised edition), Boston and London, Shambhala, 1986

Tenzing, *After Everest: an Autobiography*, London, George Allen & Unwin, 1977

Tilman, H. W., *Nepal Himalaya*, Cambridge University Press, 1952, and reproduced in the anthology *H. W. Tilman, the Seven Mountain-Travel Books*, London, Diadem, 1983

Tucci, Giuseppe, *Journey to Mustang 1952*, Kathmandu, Ratna Pustak Bhandar, 1977

Ullman, James Ramsey, *Tiger of the Snows: the Autobiography of Tenzing of Everest*, New York, Putnam/London, Harrap, 1955

— *Americans on Everest*, New York, Lippincott, 1964

Valli, Eric and Summers, Diane, *Dolpo, Hidden Land of the Himalayas*, New York, Aperture, 1987

Venables, Stephen, *Everest, Kangshung Face*, London, Hodder & Stoughton, 1989

Verrier, Anthony, *Francis Younghusband and the Great Game*, London, Jonathan Cape, 1991

Waller, Derek, *The Pundits, British Exploration of Tibet and Central Asia*, Kentucky University Press, 1990

West, John B., *Everest, the Testing Place*, New York, McGraw-Hill, 1985

Young, Geoffrey Winthrop, *Wind and Hill, Poems*, London, Smith, Elder, 1909

Younghusband, Sir Francis, *Wonders of the Himalaya*, London, John Murray, 1924

Acknowledgments

M Y FIRST DEBT is to Tom Holzel, for without his preoccupying urge to discover the fate of Mallory and Irvine, and his willingness to push this to absolute limits, I might never have seen the Himalaya at all. There can be no doubt, our Everest expedition owes its inception to Tom, and by the same token so too do all the fruitful relationships that were born of it.

So many friends helped to make these adventures, and I am sure I was the recipient of encouragement and affection in far more generous measure than any support I might have been able to give. Not once did I feel anything but a full member of the team, and I should like to thank by name everyone on the 1986 Everest North Ridge Expedition. Andy Harvard and David Breashears led the Americans Ken Bailey, George Bell, Mary Kay Brewster, Catherine Cullinane, Donna de Varona, Sue Giller, Eric Green, Tom Holzel, Al Read, Steve Shea, David Swanson, Mike Weis, Jed Williamson, and Mike Yager. Dave Cheesmond and Roger Vernon joined us from Canada, and Alistair Macdonald was my only British companion. Nawang Yongden was Sirdar to our team of Sherpas and other Nepalese, who comprised Nima Temba, Temba Tsering, Nima Tenzing, Ang Phurba, Pasang Tsering, Ang Nima, Ang Tsering, Dawa Nuru, Wongchu, Temba Dorje, Ang Pasang, Arjun Tamang, Indra Bahadur Ghale, Motilal Gurung, and Tsering Tamang.

The film featuring the efforts of our three women climbers was screened in the United States as an ABC-TV sports special in February 1987. The hour-long documentary 'The Mystery of Mallory and Irvine', made jointly by Arcturus Films and BBC Northwest, was screened in Britain on BBC television in February 1988. Among those who so willingly took part in it were Captain John Noel and Professor Noel Odell from the pioneer expedition of 1924 (both, sadly, now deceased), Sir Edmund Hillary, Sir Jack Longland, Chris Bonington and the late Catalan mountaineer, Antoni Sors.

To fulfil my wish to see Mustang – a wish inspired by the writings of Michel Peissel and David Snellgrove, and in long discussions with Eric Valli and Diane Summers – I owe thanks to Elaine Brook and her husband Lhakpa Sherpa for inviting me to join their exploratory trek into this normally restricted area.

Acknowledgments

Travelling with two such sympathetic and informed guides was a delight and, through them, to be introduced to branches of the Mustang royal family a rare privilege. It is perhaps worth mentioning here to anyone interested in making a similar journey that Elaine and Lhakpa plan other tours to this remote kingdom.

I should acknowledge that my extracts from Younghusband's diary notes on approaching Lhasa were found in Simon Normanton's writings. For the description of 'Rongbuk Rosie', I thank Ronnie Faux and the *Alpine Journal*. Bruce's description of the East Rongbuk Glacier in spate is from a letter to E. L. Strutt, dated 13 June 1922, and now in the British Library. The Geoffrey Winthrop Young quotation comes from 'Knight Errantry' in his first collection of poems, *Wind and Hill*. Accounts of the finding of Maurice Wilson's body are from the personal diaries of Dr Charles Warren and the late Edwin Kempson and Eric Shipton's remarks from his foreword to Dennis Roberts' book about Wilson. Francis Nevel and Mrs Barbara Newton Dunn kindly showed me correspondence and photographs relating to George Mallory that I had not seen at the time Tom Holzel and I worked on an earlier book *The Mystery of Mallory and Irvine*; I am grateful to Mrs Newton Dunn for permission to quote from these family papers. I appreciate too, Earl C. Collins singing me what he could remember of a campfire song of his youth that was clearly inspired by the epic of Mallory and Irvine; and thank Edwin Trout of the Royal Geographical Society for information on the Pundit explorer, Hari Ram. The early Himalayan quotations I found in Harka Gurung's delightful *Vignettes of Nepal*. I am indebted to Jeff Long for allowing me to quote from his writings on the Khampa guerrillas and the recent Nepal revolution; and to my friend and fellow-trekker Sue Byrne for her notes on the Kathmandu celebrations at the end of the troubles.

For assistance with photographs I am most grateful to David Breashears, Ed Webster, and other Everest colleagues, also to Jeff Long, Elaine Brook, Sue Byrne and Sean Jones (Tibet Image Bank). The pioneer map of Everest is reproduced with the kind permission of Maggie Body at Hodder & Stoughton, and I thank my husband Peter Salkeld, for drawing the map of Mustang. Finally, I wish to place on record my deep appreciation to Tony Colwell, my editor at Jonathan Cape, for his staunch support and extraordinary stamina.

Audrey Salkeld
June 1991